# The Cross-GUI Handbook

## For Multiplatform User Interface Design

# The Cross-GUI Handbook

## For Multiplatform User Interface Design

**Aaron Marcus**
*Aaron Marcus and Associates*

**Nick Smilonich**
*Unisys Corporation*

**Lynne Thompson**
*Unisys Corporation*

**Addison-Wesley Publishing Company**

Reading, Massachusetts • Menlo Park, California • New York
Don Mills, Ontario • Wokingham, England • Amsterdam • Bonn
Sydney • Singapore • Tokyo • Madrid • San Juan • Milan • Paris

Library of Congress Cataloging-in-Publication Data

Marcus, Aaron, 1943–
    The cross-GUI handbook for multiplatform user interface design /
Aaron Marcus, Nick Smilonich, Lynne Thompson.
        p.    cm.
    Includes bibliographical references (p.    ) and index.
    ISBN 0-201-57592-2
    1. Graphical user interfaces (Computer systems)  I. Smilonich,
Nick. II. Thompson, Lynne. III. Title.
QA76.9.U83M37  1995
005.4′3—dc20                                                               93-39692
                                                                          CIP

1 2 3 4 5 6 7 8 9 10-CRW-97969594

# Dedication

To our parents, Robert and Ned Ramos, Eileen Smilonich,
and Libbie Burstein, and to our children,
BJ Thompson, Jill, Michael, and Stefani Smilonich,
and Joshua and Elisheva Marcus

# Preface

The existing graphical user interface (GUI) environments delivered on the desktop platforms continue to evolve. The human-computer interaction is advancing to a more automated and visual state. Today's users have numerous graphical user interface environments from which to choose, including Microsoft Windows, Presentation Manager (PM) from IBM, Motif from Open Software Foundation (OSF), Macintosh from Apple Computers, and NeXTSTEP from NeXT Computers. Although GUIs have common elements, each GUI vendor has established differentiating user interface philosophies, components, and its own set of style guidelines. In a truly open environment, developers and end-users must cope with several or even all of these GUIs. The *Cross-GUI Handbook For Multiplatform User Interface Design* addresses the myriad of GUI terminologies, user interface components, and interaction ramifications. It discusses considerations for designing object-oriented and multimedia user interfaces. This book serves as a single point of reference and can be used as a complement to the vendor-supplied user interface style guides.

This book examines the features, capabilities, and strengths of these GUIs based on terminology, appearance, interaction, and common actions. The *Cross-GUI Handbook For Multiplatform User Interface Design* provides portability and migration guidelines to facilitate the design of applications under multiple GUI environments, along with recommendations for handling conflicting and incomplete style guides.

## Who Should Use This Book

The *Cross-GUI Handbook For Multiplatform User Interface Design* provides a framework of comparison detail to guide application developers, user interface designers and developers, widget developers, and window manager developers in the design and implementation of applications with a consistent "look and feel" that are operable under multiple environments.

## How This Book Is Organized

This book is organized into seven chapters and two appendices.

### Chapter 1:  Design Principles

This chapter discusses the different design principles related to the user interface environment and how the various GUIs manifest these principles.

### Chapter 2:  Desktop

This chapter introduces the desktop and its environment. It describes the metaphor, appearance, and functions performed by the various GUI desktops. It discusses the object-oriented paradigm and how it will affect the "look and feel" of the desktop. Lastly, it presents design guidelines for customizing icons on the desktop.

### Chapter 3:  Windows

This chapter describes the basic elements and controls of a window. It discusses the conceptual and functional differences of windows for the different GUI environments. It discusses the comparison of window types, the hierarchy of windows, window arrangements, and window behaviors.

### Chapter 4:  Menus

This chapter provides an overview of menus, their orientation, typical components, and various types of menus. It describes in detail the appearance and behavior of these menu types. It compares the menus and menu items associated with the desktop, application and document windows, and objects.

### Chapter 5:  Controls

This chapter describes in detail the various controls used in constructing a window (application, document, or dialog box). In addition, it discusses the new controls that are specific to multimedia applications. It discusses the appearance, function, behavior, and usage of the various controls as well as the similarities and differences of the controls supported by the GUIs in the comparison.

### Chapter 6:  Dialog Boxes

This chapter discusses the fundamental elements of a dialog box, the various controls that can appear in them, the types of dialog boxes according to various characteristics or behaviors, and dialog boxes common to all applications. It also presents a summary of the various dialog box controls supported by the GUIs in the comparison. It presents guidelines for designing dialog boxes with respect to selection of the appropriate type of dialog box, selection of appropriate dialog box controls, and overall layout of the dialog box (placement, size, density, and organization). Lastly, it discusses how new metaphors and technologies such as multimedia are affecting the "look and feel" of dialog boxes.

### Chapter 7: Interaction and Feedback

This chapter describes the interaction model, which defines the communication between the user and the computer. It discusses the various interaction devices such as the keyboard, mouse, pen, touch screen, and speech recognition, along with the operations they employ. It discusses the object-action model and focus, object types and classes, and manipulation principles. It discusses the selection concept including selection highlighting, selection types, and various selection techniques for the different data objects. Lastly, it discusses the graphical, textual, and auditory feedback provided by the GUIs in the comparison as a result of the interaction.

### Appendix A: Comparison of Windowing System Component Terminology

This appendix provides a comparison of terms and definitions of the different windowing system components used by the different GUI environments.

### Appendix B: Comparison of Windowing System Components— Graphical Representations

This appendix illustrates the graphical representations for the different windowing system components used by the different GUI environments.

### Bibliography

References to published books and articles show either an author and year in parentheses, for example, (Doe 1991), or they include a style guide acronym and page in brackets, for example, [MHIG, p. 34]. The acronyms are defined in the bibliography. The bibliography includes full descriptions for all books and articles cited in the text.

## Related User Interface Style Guides

### IBM Systems Application Architecture Common User Access Guide to User Interface Design

This guide provides general knowledge of the Common User Access (CUA) user interface and the design process. It describes the basic principles, components, and techniques of user interface design.

### IBM Systems Application Architecture Common User Access Advanced Interface Design Reference

This guide provides an alphabetical list of interface components that are defined in the CUA interface and guidelines on when and how to use them.

### Macintosh Human Interface Guidelines

This book discusses the theory behind Macintosh "look and feel" and provides guidelines that all application developers should follow. It provides several examples of good design and practices for the various user interface components.

### NeXTSTEP User Interface Guidelines

This book discusses the NeXTSTEP user interface and provides guidelines that all application designers should follow.

### OSF/Motif Style Guide

This book provides a framework of behavior specifications to guide in the design and implementation of new products consistent with the OSF/Motif user interface.

### The Windows Interface: An Application Design Guide

This book provides the Microsoft guidelines for creating well-designed, visually and functionally consistent user interfaces for applications that run on the Microsoft Windows/Windows NT windowing environment.

# Acknowledgments

As authors, we all benefited from our combined knowledge and experiences gathered through progressive exposure to a variety of technical and management situations, which, to a large degree, are reflected in the book. The book is a result of many invisible hands helping directly or indirectly.

We would like to extend our appreciation to our families. They deserve medals for putting up with our endless hours and weekends of work. They have been a continuous source of encouragement during the development of the book. This book could never have happened without their patience, optimism, and support.

The Unisys authors acknowledge Aaron Marcus and his staff for the consulting services they provided to Unisys Corporation. We would like to thank Aaron Marcus for sharing with us his background in graphic design and book publishing. We would like to give recognition to Nikolai Gregory Galle, who was enormously helpful in coordinating the efforts of the Marcus' staff. We would also like to thank the following people for their contributions: Wolfgang Heidrich, Grant Letz, Sandra Ragan, and Eugene Schultz, Ph.D.

We are particularly grateful to Bill Thompson, who provided a thorough technical review and copyedit of innumerable drafts of the manuscript with extraordinary care and sensitivity. He gave so generously of his time to enhance existing graphics and create additional figures and screen dumps where needed. His contributions have greatly enhanced the overall quality of the book.

Many thanks to our Unisys editor, Sheila Harlow, for editing the early raw materials into readable prose. Her prowess in spotting errors was of immeasurable help.

Mike Barry gave freely of his time and knowledge on the subject of UNIX GUIs. We also thank him for supplying us with many OSF/Motif figures. Finally, we are deeply appreciative to Tom Taylor and Dan Thompson for their assistance in setting up our GUI platforms.

*Nick Smilonich*
*Lynne Thompson*

# Contents

# Figures

# Tables

# CHAPTER 1

# Design Principles

A user interface is simply the means by which an application communicates with the user, and the user with the application. The effectiveness and user acceptance of an application are determined primarily by the design of the user interface. The user interface needs to be designed with certain basic design principles in mind. These principles can be categorized into the different aspects of the user interface environment—human factors, presentation, and interaction. Table 1.1 lists the design principles according to this categorization. This chapter discusses the design principles under the aspects of the user interface environment, and how the various GUIs adhere to these principles.

**TABLE 1.1 Design Principles**

| Aspects of User Interface Environment | Design Principles |
|---|---|
| *Human Factors* | Empower the user.<br>Reduce the user's information load. |
| *Presentation* | Create aesthetic appeal.<br>Use meaningful and recognizable representations.<br>Maintain a consistent interface. |
| *Interaction* | Use direct manipulation.<br>Provide immediate feedback.<br>Make the interface forgiving. |

## 1.1   Human Factors

The most critical design principle to keep in mind is the human factor. It is essential to identify and understand the activities the user performs, as well as the user's general capabilities, experience, and limitations in the areas of perception, memory, learning, and attention. To tailor the design to the user's behavior, the application designer should be sensitive to these limitations rather than coerce the user to overcome them.

The following design principles relate to the human aspects of the user interface:

- Empower the user.

- Reduce the user's information load.

### Empower the User

One of the most important design principles is putting the user in control. The user has the ability to take the initiative and control the interactions with the application. The user interface design provides mechanisms that allow the user to control the type of information presented, the rate of presentation, and the manner in which it is presented. The more the user feels in control, the more the user will be comfortable and satisfied with the application.

This principle has several implications, and they vary from GUI to GUI. Common to all GUIs, however, is their support of a flexible user interface. Providing multiple ways to access application functions and accomplish their tasks increases the user's sense of control. The user interface design should be flexible enough to accommodate users with different needs and skill levels. The user should be able to customize user interface attributes such as color, function, structure, and content. Allowing the user to configure settings and select personal preferences enhances his or her sense of control and encourages the user to take an active role in understanding the application and how it works.

Other implications of this principle that are specific to each of the GUIs follow.

The *Macintosh Human Interface Guidelines* emphasizes the importance of the user's ability to perform actions by choosing from alternatives presented on the screen, as opposed to having to "remember any particular command or name" [MHIG, p. 7]. Developers should seek a balance between "providing users with the capabilities they need . . . and preventing them from destroying data" [MHIG, p. 9].

The *NeXTSTEP User Interface Guidelines* states that the "user should always be free to choose which applications and which windows they will work in, and to rearrange windows in the workspace to suit their own taste and needs. When working in an application, the user should be afforded the widest possible freedom of action. It is inappropriate for an application to arbitrarily restrict what the user can do. If an action makes sense, it should be allowed" [NeXTSTEP, p. 14].

OSF/Motif also supports the use of progressive disclosure. The necessary and common functions are presented first and in a logical manner. The use of progressive disclosure strikes a balance between overwhelming the novice and frustrating the expert user.

The IBM CUA guide supports several implementation techniques that put the user in control. "The designer should approach application design with a 'no user errors' philosophy. The user should feel that any shortcomings are in the application, not in himself or herself" [IBM CUA, p. 19]. The guide encourages the application designer to hide the underlying implementation details of the application. A good user interface frees the user from focusing on the mechanics of the application.

Microsoft Windows advocates the following:

- "Application should always be as interactive as possible. The user should not have to wait a long time for processing to be completed."

- "Designers should provide good defaults and should not depend on the user customizing these settings."

- "The interface should facilitate the user's tasks rather than calling attention to itself. The best interface is often the one that is hardly noticed" [MICROSOFT, p. 3].

### Design Tips

Implementation techniques such as the "no user errors" philosophy, along with a flexible and configurable user interface and designing to the user's expectations, provide an effective model for putting the user in control. Empowering the user leads to higher productivity and satisfaction.

## Reduce the User's Information Load

People are better at recognizing information than recalling information. For example, a person can recall from memory approximately 2,000 to 3,000 words. However, the number of words that a person recognizes can exceed 100,000. A good user interface avoids overloading the user's memory. For example, the user should not be expected to recall a set of complex commands or options. A list of commands, options, or data should be presented on the appropriate application display, allowing the user to select from the list rather than recalling the commands, options, or data from memory. A person's ability to process information deteriorates as the upper and lower thresholds in human information processing are exceeded.

The GUIs in the comparison reduce the user's information load in the following ways:

- Present commands, options, or data to the user on the appropriate application display.

- Display information appropriate to completing a task on the screen, so the user can be selective in attending to information relevant to his or her needs.

- Organize information in a meaningful way to help the user focus on essential task information. This makes the decision-making process easier as well as reducing the potential for errors.

The *Macintosh Human Interface Guidelines* recommends that the user interface provide a "clear, finite set of objects and a clear, finite set of actions to perform on those objects" [MHIG, p. 11]. Even when a particular action is unavailable, it is not eliminated from the display, merely dimmed.

The *NeXTSTEP User Interface Guidelines* promotes intuitiveness. The screen becomes a visual metaphor for the real world. Objects displayed on the screen can be manipulated in ways familiar objects in the real world are manipulated. The user interface behaves as the user expects based on his or her experience with objects in the real world.

The IBM CUA guide further promotes the use of different models that represent the perspective of three audiences instrumental in the product development. These models are the *user's conceptual model, designer's model,* and *programmer's model.* Because the IBM CUA user interface is object-oriented, the application designer is urged to spend considerable time in defining meaningful objects that the user needs, the relationships among the objects, and the properties and behaviors the objects should have.

### Design Tips

The use of different models described in the IBM CUA guide should be considered. The pervasive focus on objects, and the principles applied to those objects, provide the opportunity to simplify, and thus reduce the user's information load.

## 1.2  Presentation

Presentation refers to the visual aspects of the user interface—the overall layout, arrangement, color, font, shape, and size of the object. The following design principles address the presentation aspect of the user interface environment:

- Create aesthetic appeal.

- Use meaningful and recognizable representations.

- Maintain a consistent interface.

### Create Aesthetic Appeal

In designing the user interface, the aesthetic aspect of the visual representation is very important in achieving user acceptance and satisfaction with the application. The representation should be visually pleasing. Color, font, shape, size, arrangement, space, and other components of visual communications affect the aesthetic appeal of the user interface. When used skillfully, these components contribute to an effective and efficient user interface.

Although each GUI is created with similar components of visual design, each has its own unique aesthetic appeal and distinct appearance.

The *OSF/Motif Style Guide* recommends the following:

- "Each screen object needs to have a distinct appearance that the user can easily recognize and quickly understand. At the same time, the style of the interface needs to graphically unify these elements and ensure a consistent and attractive appearance at any screen resolution."

- "Appropriate use of contrast helps the user distinguish screen objects against the background of a window. Very dark screen objects on a light background, very bright objects on a dark background, and bright colors all command the user's attention" [OSF/Motif, p. 1-7].

NeXTSTEP uses a color scheme based on black, white, and gray. The user interface appears pleasantly clean, simple, and clear, without unnecessary and distracting visual clutter. NeXTSTEP allows the user to specify color using different models. The user can specify the amount of red, green, and blue (RGB), the hue, saturation, and brightness (HSB), or the amount of cyan, magenta, yellow, and black (CMYK). It also allows the user to specify color by *Pantone* number, a trademark system for specifying color by industry standard numbers.

The IBM CUA guide advises that "When designing the appearance of the user interface, a designer should adhere to generally accepted practices for information presentation" [IBM CUA, p. 28].

*The Windows Interface: An Application Design Guide* states that "Aesthetic appeal can be substantially enhanced by attention to basic graphic design principles concerning spatial grouping, contrast, and three-dimensional representation. The best interfaces combine powerful yet accessible functionality with a pleasing appearance" [MICROSOFT, p. 4].

### Design Tips

Three-dimensional representation contributes to a superior overall aesthetic appeal. The components of visual communications, such as color, font, shape, size, arrangement, and space, should be used skillfully. They promote aesthetic appeal and contribute greatly to ease of learning, communication, and understanding.

## Use Meaningful and Recognizable Representations

In using metaphors, the appearance of objects should be visually consistent with one another as well as with other objects in the operating environment. In addition, the representation of an object should be clear, meaningful, and visually distinguishable among objects. The application designer should observe aesthetic guidelines with respect to color, size, shape, texture, arrangement, and space to avoid overwhelming the user's vision.

The GUIs in the comparison emphasize the use of meaningful and recognizable representations as a means to increase the visual distinctiveness, visibility, and readability of the GUI elements.

The *Macintosh Human Interface Guidelines* prescribes the use of simple, clear, and readable graphics. Animation may be used to call the user's attention to a particular place on the screen.

A more significant emphasis than clarity in "look and feel" is defined in Presentation Manager and NeXTSTEP. The object-oriented design of these GUIs demands the careful analysis of the object—its purpose and state, as well as its relationship with other objects.

"A designer should consider the tasks the user wants to accomplish and should ensure that the characteristics of the objects support the user's tasks. A designer should clearly define the properties of each object and should establish a hierarchy of object classes based on these properties. The objects should be designed so that the user can easily recognize members of a class from another" [IBM CUA, p. 25].

*The Windows Interface: An Application Design Guide* advises that "the visual elements should be immediately comprehensible, ideally because they relate to real-world analogies, and should be arranged so that their functions are comprehensible" [MICROSOFT, p. 4].

### Design Tips

To provide a meaningful and highly visual representation, the application designer should consider both functional and aesthetic aspects of the user interface elements or objects. A representation of an object that is meaningful helps the user both to transfer knowledge about the real-world object to the computing environment and to remember the relationship of the object to other objects.

## Maintain a Consistent Interface

A consistent interface refers to the similarity in appearance and layout of the components. A more critical aspect of a consistent interface is functional consistency. Functional consistency means that the same action should have the same result regardless of the mode the application is in. For example, command buttons in dialog boxes within an application should be represented as a rectangular shape with a label that specifies an action. The user initiates the action associated with the command button by clicking the mouse while the pointer is over the button. Using the keyboard to access these buttons through the use of short-cut keys or accelerator keys should yield the same result.

Consistency should be maintained within and among applications. A consistent design produces an application that is predictable in appearance and behavior throughout its display of information, its manner of manipulating information, and its methods of navigation. To the user interface designer or developer, the significant benefit of consistency is reusability. The standard elements of an application can be reapplied to another application, thus capturing commonality while increasing productivity and product quality. To the user, a consistent user interface design facilitates learning, which results in greater productivity and efficiency.

Although each GUI in the comparison provides and adheres to guidelines for maintaining a consistent user interface, the emphasis varies from GUI to GUI.

The *OSF/Motif Style Guide* emphasizes the transfer of familiar skills to a new situation, which contributes to the user's sense of mastery of the application by keeping the interface simple, natural, and consistent both within and among applications. Ensuring that the appearance, position, and function of components remain consistent in every context encourages user experimentation, learning, and recall.

NeXTSTEP stresses the importance of reliable conventions. For example, operations such as selecting, editing, scrolling, setting options, and making choices from the menu should be common to some degree to all applications.

The IBM CUA guide advises "designers to make interface components consistent in ways that the user would expect. A designer must remember that consistency is a means to an end—ease of learning and reduction of errors—rather than an end itself. Sometimes it is impractical or impossible to be completely consistent. In that case, a designer must make consistency compromises based on knowledge of a user's conceptual model and should be consistent in whichever way seems more natural to a user" [IBM CUA, pp. 26–27].

*The Windows Interface: An Application Design Guide* emphasizes consistency with the real world, and consistency within and among applications. "First, applications should build on the user's real-world experience by exploiting concrete metaphors and natural mapping relationships. The use of familiar concepts and metaphors reduces the amount of new material that users must learn and thereby makes applications easier to use. Second, each application should be conceptually, linguistically, visually, and functionally consistent within itself and with other applications" [MICROSOFT, p. 4].

### Design Tips

The importance of consistency cannot be overlooked or overemphasized. It is the key to usability and interoperability. Designing for consistency should deal not only with the physical appearance and layout of the components, but, more important, with the visual metaphors and interaction techniques.

## 1.3  Interaction

Interaction is the means by which the user controls the execution of an application. The concept of pointing to an object and then selecting it, often referred to as simply *point-and-select*, is an essential factor in achieving effective human-application interaction. The interaction is achieved by the use of the keyboard or pointing devices such as the mouse. Point-and-select does not preclude the touch screen and voice interaction techniques.

The following design principles address the interaction aspect of the user interface environment:

- Use direct manipulation.

- Provide immediate feedback.

- Make the interface forgiving.

Refer to Chapter 7, "Interaction and Feedback," for detailed information on how each of the GUIs implements this principle.

## Use Direct Manipulation

The most common interaction style is direct manipulation, in which the user works directly with an object (that is, an icon or a symbol) by using a pointing device. This interaction technique closely resembles the natural way the user interacts with an object in the real world. Direct manipulation affords the user visible and immediate results.

Directness in user interaction contributes to the usability of a user interface. All GUIs in the comparison support a direct manipulation method of interaction. Interaction with various objects is easily accomplished by the *drag-and-drop* method of direct manipulation. The most commonly discussed input devices are the keyboard and mouse. The direct manipulation principle also applies to devices such as the pen and touch screen input. *The Windows Interface: An Application Design Guide* considers direct manipulation as particularly useful in pen-based systems and provides a good discussion of interaction via the pen input.

The *Macintosh Human Interface Guidelines* states that objects on the screen should remain visible while the user performs physical actions on them. Furthermore, when the user performs operations on objects, the impact of the operations on the objects should be immediately visible. The guide suggests animation as one of the best ways to show the user that a requested action is being carried out.

### *Design Tips*

Though the most commonly discussed input devices are the keyboard and mouse, support of the direct manipulation method of interaction is useful in pen-based systems. Manipulating objects with a pen is more direct than manipulating objects with a mouse. In addition, dragging objects with a pen requires less coordination. In designing pen applications, the application designer should apply the guidelines for directness in user interaction.

## Provide Immediate Feedback

In performing a task or function, it is important that the user receive the result immediately. Feedback can be extrinsic (provided by the system) or intrinsic (provided by the user's internal sensing systems). Receiving immediate and tangible feedback increases the user's rate of learning. For example, a word processor application allows the user to set the tab position by dragging the tab marker with a mouse to the desired position on the visible ruler. The affected part of the document is reformatted immediately after the action taken. Extrinsic feedback is the movement of the tab marker in response to the mouse movement. Intrinsic feedback is the user's hand and arm sensations of moving the mouse in the direction of the desired relocation.

The GUIs in the comparison consider feedback essential in the human interaction. All GUIs provide considerable feedback to the user, though its manifestations vary from GUI to GUI. The following are the common manifestations of feedback among the GUIs:

- Highlighting a menu item or object to indicate selection
- Producing a sound to verify keyboard activity
- Changing the pointer to a symbol such as an hourglass as an indication that the action is in process.

### Design Tips

Because technology continually evolves, the user interface design should exploit ways to enhance user feedback. For example, the application designer should consider the use of multimedia data types such as graphics, images, sound, speech, and video to supplement today's techniques of providing immediate and tangible feedback. Feedback incorporating these multimedia elements enriches and improves communication between the user and the application.

## Make the Interface Forgiving

Making the interface forgiving means that the computing system tolerates or accepts user actions that do not conform precisely to system specifications without negative consequences to the user. When the user is in control, he or she should be able to explore without fear of causing an irreversible mistake.

The following are common techniques used by the different GUIs in implementing this principle:

- Reversal of undesirable actions via the *Undo* function

- Confirmation of destructive actions or actions that result in an unexpected loss of user information (e.g., *Cancel, OK* command buttons)

- Disabling menu items by *graying* the option

The GUIs in the comparison offer the following advice in making the interface forgiving:

The *Macintosh Human Interface Guidelines* advises that "people need to feel that they can try things without damaging the system; create safety nets for people so that they feel comfortable learning and using your product. . . . Always warn people before they initiate a task that will cause irretrievable data loss" [MHIG, p. 10].

The IBM CUA guide suggests that the user should be able to redo any action that has been undone. If an action cannot be made reversible, the application should display a message advising the user of the condition and suggest alternative actions the user might take to avoid irreversible negative consequences.

*The Windows Interface: An Application Design Guide* advises that "error messages should not imply that the user is at fault; instead they should state the problem objectively and offer possible solutions" [MICROSOFT, p. 5].

### Design Tips

Support for a learn-by-exploring environment is a primary factor in the user acceptance of an application.

## Conclusion

There is no universally accepted set of user interface design principles. There is, however, widespread agreement among the different GUIs about the philosophy of user interface design.

The user interface design should enable the user to be in control of interactions with a computing system. It should take into account the user's unavoidable limitations in perception, memory, and reasoning.

The user interface design should avoid taxing the user's memory—particularly his or her short-term recall. It should facilitate the learning process through feedback, presentation of information in small, meaningful units that can be more easily absorbed and understood, and the use of metaphors that take advantage of the user's existing knowledge. The user interface design should be highly visual so the user can see, rather than recall, how to proceed. It should be aesthetically pleasing. Consistency in appearance and behavior is very important. To design for consistency means to produce an application that is predictable in the way it looks and acts throughout its display of information, manner of manipulating information, and methods of navigation. A consistent user interface design helps the user apply the knowledge learned from one application to another.

# CHAPTER 2

# Desktop

This chapter introduces and briefly describes the desktop and its environment. It describes the metaphor, appearance, and functions performed by the various GUI desktops. The chapter discusses the object-oriented paradigm and how it will affect the "look and feel" of the desktop. Lastly, the chapter presents design guidelines for customizing icons on the desktop.

## 2.1  Desktop and Its Environment

A *desktop* is the surface or background that the user sees when a system is initiated. Visually, the desktop appears as a gray background with objects displayed on it. The desktop is also referred to as a *workplace,* or *workspace*. Table 2.1 shows the different terminology used by the various GUIs in the comparison to describe the desktop.

TABLE 2.1  Comparison of Desktop Terminology

|  | Macintosh | OSF/Motif | NeXTSTEP | Presentation Manager | Microsoft Windows |
|---|---|---|---|---|---|
| *Desktop* | Desktop | workspace (root window) | Workspace | Workplace | Desktop |

The *desktop environment* is the working environment in which various objects such as windows, applications, files, folders, printers, and icons sit directly on the desktop. It is the launching pad for all activities. It provides a stable background for the user which can be

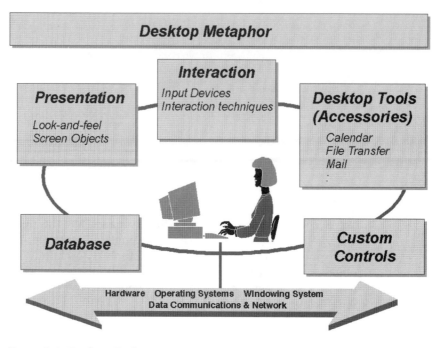

**FIGURE 2.1   Desktop Environment**

personalized. Figure 2.1 illustrates the composition of a desktop environment, namely: the *desktop platform, desktop metaphor, desktop presentation, interaction desktop, desktop tools* or *accessories*, and *customized controls*.

The user interacts with the desktop environment via the computing platform. The *desktop computing platform* minimally consists of the hardware, operating system, windowing system, data communications and network, and systems software (e.g., desktop manager). The *desktop metaphor* establishes the visual representation for the entire interface. *Presentation* defines the screen elements (objects) that constitute the "look and feel" of the desktop interface. *Interaction* refers to the collaboration between the user and the computer via a set of fundamental input elements (such as the keyboard and mouse) to perform a task. The icons and windows are used for interacting with the system and applications. The input devices provide the user with easier interactions with the objects using drag-and-drop method of direct manipulation. The *desktop tools* or *accessories* are objects represented as icons that are typically found on the user's desktop. The desktop tools are usually mini-applications, implemented as device drivers, that can operate at the same time as a full-scale application. The common desktop tools are electronic mail, file transfer, calendar, clock, and so on. The icons, files types, applications, and other data are stored within the database. The *custom controls* are the infrastructure or framework (e.g., class libraries, GUI widgets) necessary to construct a graphical user interface application.

## 2.2  Desktop Metaphor

A *metaphor* is a visual representation that denotes or depicts one object or idea but suggests a likeness or analogy with another object or idea. A metaphor provides a means through which the user can apply knowledge about interacting with concrete, real-world entities to the potentially abstract and confusing task of using computer systems. For example, a common desktop metaphor is the office environment where real-life things are used to represent objects such as a file system, electronic mail, and personal information manager.

The desktop is a metaphor itself, based on the user's working environment in which objects such as printers, letters, forms, and an address book are represented as icons. The desktop metaphor establishes the visual representation for the entire interface. It is an inviting metaphor, providing easy access to the system. The user can adapt readily to a physical environment he or she is familiar with.

There are other metaphors integrated into the desktop. For example, the most noticeable metaphor in OS/2 is the notebook metaphor implemented in the notebook control. The metaphor employs the presentation of a multipage dialog in a spiral-bound notebook with dividers.

The desktop is the primary metaphor for all GUIs in the comparison. All the GUIs in the comparison emphasize the use of meaningful metaphors to increase the visual distinctiveness, visibility, and readability of the user interface elements. The desktop is the primary metaphor for all the GUIs in the comparison, although each GUI in the comparison employs a variety of different secondary metaphors.

## 2.3  Desktop Objects

The objects on a desktop consist of applications and files that are logically organized into groups. These objects are represented as icons. The objects commonly found on the desktop are the file deletion object (trash can or file shredder), the printer object, applications (programs), and files. Representations of these common desktop objects vary from GUI to GUI.

IBM CUA Workplace Shell classifies the desktop objects into three main categories:

- *Data objects* contain the information. Examples of data objects are memos, business graphics, tables, music, recorded speech, animation, and video clips.

- *Container object*s provide a place to store and group related objects. Folders, trash cans, and in/out baskets are typical examples of container objects.

- *Device objects* are typically used in conjunction with other objects for which they provide some function. For example, a printer is a device object that is connected to a real-world physical printer.

Table 2.2 shows desktop objects for Presentation Manager.

## File Deletion Object

The file deletion object allows the user to easily delete an object from a system. The file deletion object is also known as the *trash can* (or a *file shredder*) *object*. It is usually represented on the desktop by an icon resembling a trash can (or a paper shredder). It is usually located at the lower-right corner of the desktop, but can be easily moved. Icons of objects to be deleted are dragged into the trash can. Once in the trash can, objects can be retrieved until the trash can is emptied.

Most of the GUIs in the comparison support a file deletion object. Though the appearance of the file deletion object varies from GUI to GUI, its behavior is consistent.

In NeXTSTEP, "the *Recycler* icon at the bottom of the dock represents a folder (directory) where files can be stored for deletion or restoration later. It works like the Macintosh trash can, that is, files are actually deleted only when you choose to empty it. The ball at the center of the Recycler figure indicates that there are files inside waiting to be emptied" [NeXTSTEP Programming (Garfinkel), p. 3].

IBM OS/2 Workplace Shell defines the *shredder* object as a quick and easy means to delete objects permanently. A confirmation message is displayed whenever a folder object is deleted. The user can customize the desktop by specifying when the confirmation message will be displayed. Deleted files can be recovered using the **Undelete** command.

It is expected that the next-generation Microsoft Windows desktop will support a file deletion object.

**TABLE 2.2  Presentation Manager Desktop Objects**

| Icon | Desktop Object | Function |
|---|---|---|
| Start Here | Start Here | Contains information to help the user get started with the Workplace Shell interface, including topics such as About OS/2, installing printers, sharing data, finding information, customizing the desktop, and multimedia. |
| OS/2 System | OS/2 System | Contains the objects that allow the user to tailor certain properties of the operating system, such as mouse characteristics and screen colors. |
| Information | Information | Contains on-line information, including *Tutorial, Command Reference, Glossary,* and *REXX Information.* |
| Master Help Index | Master Help Index | Provides an alphabetic list that contains most of the information the user needs to use OS/2. |
| Templates | Templates | Contains forms (templates) that help the user create new files, folders, programs, and other objects. |
| Minimized Window Viewer | Minimized Window Viewer | Provides quick access to windows that are minimized. |
| Shredder | Shredder | Used to delete an object permanently. |

Source: *Using the Operating System OS/2 2.1*, pp. 53–54

## Printer Object

The printer object allows the user to print objects by dragging and dropping the required object over the printer object. It is represented like its real-life counterpart. In some GUIs, each possible printer object accessible to the user is represented as a separate printer icon. Most GUIs provide an animated printer object as an effective means of providing feedback on the status of a print job. The printer object may be opened to display a window containing the name and status of each print job currently in the queue.

## Desktop Accessories

The user may want to place the most frequently used objects in a way that is most comfortable to him or her. Furthermore, the user may want to add or change the appearance of the desktop (for example, with respect to color, font, and language).

The *control panel* is one of the desktop accessories supported by most GUIs in the comparison. It is an application that provides the user with a visual way of modifying the desktop as well as the overall system. The control panel contains objects that help the user customize such items as icons, fonts recognized by the applications, the printer to use, keyboard and mouse settings, international settings, port and network settings, date and time, sound, and other desktop options that determine the look of the screen (e.g., object spacing, wallpaper and screen saver). *Control Panel* (Microsoft Windows) is also referred to as *System Setup* (OS/2 Workplace Shell), *General Controls* (Macintosh), or *Preferences* (NeXTSTEP and OSF/Motif).

Figure 2.2 illustrates the Microsoft Windows Control Panel.

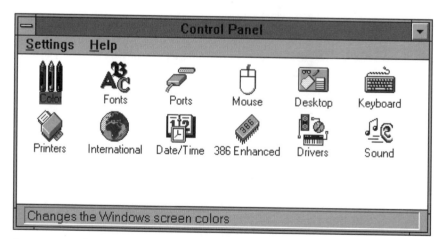

FIGURE 2.2  **Microsoft Windows Control Panel**

In NeXTSTEP, the user can personalize the workspace by selecting the Preferences icon in the Application Dock icon. The Preferences icon appears as a date and time icon in the dock.

The Preferences application not only helps the user to customize his or her workspace, but it also helps manage the hardware. It allows the user to hide application menus, set date and time, specify the language to be used within the applications, create keyboard alternatives, change fonts on the screen, display large files, and display UNIX files. Preferences also allows the user to set the screen saver, change the background color of the display, choose system beeps and warnings, change the keyboard arrangement, and change the movement and speed of the mouse. Lastly, it provides options for securing the user's computer.

Table 2.3 shows the various functions supported by the control panel for the GUIs in the comparison.

**TABLE 2.3  Control Panel Functions**

| GUI Environment | Application Name | Functions |
|---|---|---|
| *Macintosh* | Control Panel (General Controls) | Auto Remounter, Color, Date and Time, File sharing Monitor, General Controls, Keyboard, Label, Monitor Settings, Mouse, Numbers, Network, PowerBook Display, and Sound |
| *OSF/Motif* | Preferences | Color, Desktop, Icon, Keyboard, Locale, Mouse, ScreenLock, and Miscellaneous (system beep, window layering, mnemonics, accelerators) |
| *NeXTSTEP* | Preferences icon in Application Dock | Mouse, Date and Time, System Beep, Keyboard, and so on |
| *Presentation Manager* | System Setup | Color Palette, Country, Device Drivers, Font Palette, Keyboard, Migrate applications, Mouse, Scheme Palette, Selective/Install, Sound, Spooler, System, System Clock, Win-OS/2 Setup |
| *Microsoft Windows* | Control Panel | Color, Date and Time, Drivers. Fonts, International, Keyboard, MIDI settings, Mouse, Ports, Printers, and Sound |

## 2.4 Desktop Managers

The *desktop manager* controls and manages the windows and subwindows within the workplace, including displays and entry of user input. It provides a view of available applications and documents. It launches an application requested by the user, which typically opens another window. It keeps track of the files and the user's activity. The desktop manager for each GUI in the comparison differs in name but performs similar functions. Table 2.4 shows the different terminology for the desktop manager used by the various GUIs in the comparison.

TABLE 2.4  Comparison of Desktop Manager Terminology

|  | Macintosh | OSF/Motif | NeXTSTEP | Presentation Manager | Microsoft Windows |
|---|---|---|---|---|---|
| *Desktop Manager* | Finder | window manager | Workspace Manager | Presentation Manager | Program Manager |

In Macintosh, the Finder is an application that controls and manages the user's desktop interface. The Finder provides a view of available applications and documents. The Finder also launches the application requested by the user, which typically opens another window, and displays icons representing the user's application and the documents it creates. It keeps track of the files and the user's activities. The Finder provides easier, faster access to folders and documents.

In OSF/Motif, the desktop manager is called the *window manager*. The window manager is "a program that controls the size, placement, and operation of windows on the workspace." The window manager includes the functional window frames that surround each window object, and may include a separate menu for the workspace [OSF/Motif p. GL-11]. The window manager opens and manages primary windows for applications as well as each secondary window for every primary or secondary window [OSF/Motif, p. 5-3].

The NeXTSTEP desktop manager is called the *Workspace Manager* (or simply *Workspace*). The Workspace Manager is a special application that oversees the GUI environment and allows easy access to all other applications. It manages directories and files, and the launching of applications. The NeXT icon located at the top of the Application Dock represents the Workspace application. The user can activate the Workspace Manager at any time by double-clicking the icon. The Workspace Manager behaves like any other application. It has a window, main menu, submenus, and panels.

In Microsoft Windows, the desktop manager is called the *Program Manager*. By default, the Program Manager is launched whenever Microsoft Windows is initiated. The Program Manager displays available application icons. It classifies and executes the user's requests. It allows the user to organize programs into groups and to display icons accordingly [Hearst, 1990, p. 55].

In IBM CUA, the desktop manager is called the *Presentation Manager*. Presentation Manager provides windows, the selection cursor, selected emphasis, and controls for user interaction.

## 2.5   Comparison of Desktop Environments

Figures 2.3 to 2.7 compare the desktop and its environment for the different GUIs in the comparison.

### Macintosh Desktop Environment

Figure 2.3 shows the Macintosh desktop, which is the gray background area on the screen. Icons representing the user's application and the documents it creates are displayed on the desktop. The Macintosh desktop environment includes the Apple desktop interface, Apple desktop accessories, the desktop manager (Macintosh Finder) and the trash can icon. To launch an application, the user selects the corresponding icon rather than typing the name of the object it represents. When the application is launched, a window is displayed.

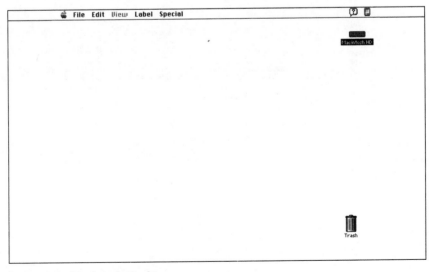

FIGURE 2.3   **Macintosh Desktop**

The desktop can be black and white or colored. Macintosh enhances its desktop by using shades of gray and subdued colors for its icons to make them look three-dimensional.

## OSF/Motif Desktop Environment

OSF/Motif describes the desktop as the area on the screen on which the windows of a user's environment are displayed [OSF/Motif, p. GL-15]. Depending on the operating system platform running on the system, the appearance of the initial screen displayed and the manner of logging on to the system will be slightly different (see Figure 2.4).

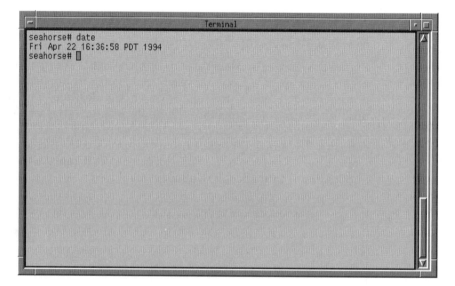

FIGURE 2.4   OSF/Motif Workspace

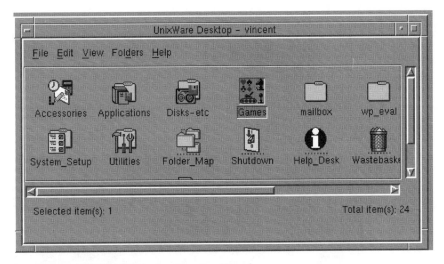

FIGURE 2.4   OSF/Motif Workspace, *Continued*

## NeXTSTEP Desktop Environment

The NeXTSTEP desktop environment includes the Workspace Manager and its main menu, and the Application Dock that contains thirteen icons—the first twelve representing applications (programs) and the last icon representing the Recycler. The NeXT icon, which represents the Workspace Manager application, is always at the top of the dock and doubles as a handle. The user can grab the NeXT icon and drag downward to create more screen real estate or drag it upward to see more of the dock. "The Recycler icon at the bottom of the dock represents a folder (directory) where files are stored for deletion or restoration later. It works like the Macintosh trash can—files can be deleted only when you choose to empty it. The ball at the center of the Recycler icon indicates that there are files inside waiting to be emptied" [NeXTSTEP Programming (Garfinkel), p. 3].

The NeXTSTEP desktop uses a monochrome scheme based on black, white, and gray. It also allows the user to specify a color scheme using different models (e.g., RGB, HSB, and CMYK). Figure 2.5 illustrates the NeXTSTEP workspace.

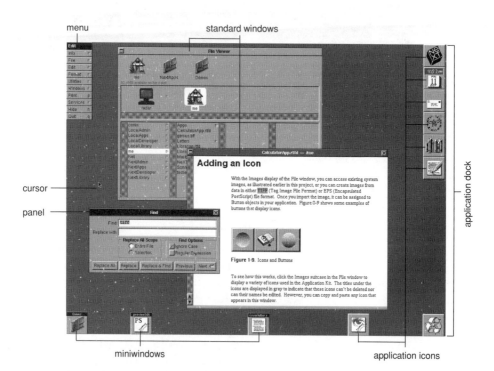

**FIGURE 2.5   NeXTSTEP Workspace**

## IBM CUA Workplace Shell

The IBM CUA Workplace Shell provides a very flexible desktop environment. It has two main components: the *desktop* and the *objects* displayed as icons. The desktop is the screen that represents the work area. The IBM CUA guide also refers to the desktop as the *Workplace*.

"The Workplace is the container that holds all objects in the CUA interface. It fills the entire screen and serves as a background for the user's work. Any object that appears directly on the background of the desktop is represented by an icon" [IBM CUA, p. 29]. The Workplace facilitates the user's productivity through the use of graphics and direct manipulation of icons on the screen. The IBM CUA Workplace Shell aims to insulate the user from the intricacies of the operating system, thereby reducing the level of knowledge and experience required for the user to successfully manipulate the system.

The Workplace Shell implements a type of interface known as an *object-oriented user interface (OOUI),* which interacts with icons representing familiar objects, such as documents, printers, and folders. Rather than interacting with applications, the user interacts with objects that represent the inputs and outputs of the user's workplace. Figure 2.6 illustrates the IBM CUA Workplace Shell.

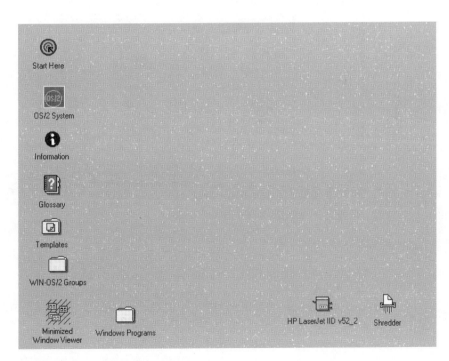

**FIGURE 2.6   IBM CUA Workplace**

## Microsoft Windows Desktop Environment

*The Windows Interface: An Application Design Guide* defines the desktop as the screen space that Microsoft Windows utilizes. When Microsoft Windows is initiated, the Program Manager window is displayed. It contains icons that represent applications and files accessible through Microsoft Windows. The Program Manager organizes the user's applications and files into logical groups to easily locate and start an application. The Control Panel application contained on the desktop provides a visual way of modifying the appearance of the desktop as well as the overall system. Microsoft Windows provides a default desktop color scheme which the user can personalize. Figure 2.7 illustrates the Microsoft Windows desktop environment.

FIGURE 2.7   **Microsoft Windows Desktop**

As Microsoft Windows moves toward an object-oriented approach, the "look and feel" of its desktop will evolve. The overall windowing design will be based on the metaphor of objects. Like their real-world counterparts, objects will have traits and behavior.

## 2.6 Icon Design

Color, font, shape, size, arrangement, space, and other aspects of visual communications affect the aesthetic appeal of the user interface. When used skillfully, these aspects contribute to an effective and efficient user interface.

"The small pictorial symbols used on computer menus, windows, and screen are icons. They represent certain capabilities of the system and can be animated to bring forth these capabilities for use by the operator" [HORTON, 1994]. The term *icon* is used in most GUIs, and generally describes any graphic representation of objects, such as documents, folders, applications, and storage media. Icons resemble their real-world counterparts. Figure 2.8 shows examples of Microsoft Windows icons.

Control Panel    Paintbrush    Write

**FIGURE 2.8 Examples of Icons**   Print Manager    Cardfile    Calendar

The desktop should be visually colorful and pleasing. Icons often give the desktop aesthetic personality and ease of use. Icon design is an essential aspect of the desktop. Well-designed icons help the user to act and respond to the system quickly and precisely. Icons provide direct access to items in the interface. Generally, it is easier to recognize an icon than it is to remember a keyboard command. For example, the user can click on a folder icon and see its contents immediately. The user can organize the desktop simply by grouping the icons, rather than having to remember several filenames. Icons also take up less space than words. The use of icons contributes to the clarity and aesthetic integrity of the interface.

Icons should be meaningful and visually distinguishable among objects. Aside from containing an image of some recognizable object, an icon can have a border around it, a background surface behind it, and a label that identifies it. The border defines the limit or extent of the icon. It tells the user where to point the cursor or finger to select the icon. If used, make sure the border is less distinctive so it does not overpower the image itself. The background emphasizes the image. The application designer should ensure that there is sufficient contrast between the image and the background. The background contributes to the visibility of the icon especially if the desktop is populated with icons. A label should be used if the symbol is not obvious or is unfamiliar to the user.

Designing the right icon that conveys a concise message can be difficult. The following are guidelines for designing icons:

- Use appropriate metaphors.

- Design two sizes of icons: 32 by 32 pixels for large icons, and 16 by 16 pixels for small icons.

- Design in black and white first. Then add color to achieve a visually aesthetic representation.

The application designer should observe aesthetic guidelines with respect to color, size, shape, texture, arrangement, and space to avoid overwhelming the user's vision.

## 2.7  Desktop Trends

### Object-Oriented User Interface

User interfaces in the future will evolve from an application-oriented to an object-oriented user interface. An *object-oriented user interface* (OOUI) is an extension of the graphical user interfaces. OOUI allows the user to focus on objects, as well as the principles applied to those objects. An object is a representation of a real-world entity that reflects the properties of the object it models. Some examples of objects are a printer, a spreadsheet, a document, and a bar chart. An object can be represented by one or more graphic images, called *icons,* that the user can interact with, much as a user can interact with objects in the real world.

OOUI is based on an object model known as a *containment model.* Objects are structured as containers such that they can hold other objects and can be held by other objects.

### Object Classes

Objects with similar behaviors and characteristics can be grouped in a *class.* A class can be thought of as a description of a set of similar objects, a template for making objects, or a mechanism for classifying objects.

OOUI includes three classes of objects as suggested by IBM CUA:

- *Container objects* provide a place to store and group related objects for easy access and retrieval. Folders, trash cans, and in/out baskets are typical examples of container objects.

- *Data objects* contain the information. Examples of data objects are memos, business graphics, tables, music, recorded speech, animation, and video clips. The purpose of these data objects is to convey information to the user.

- *Device objects* are typically used in conjunction with other objects for which they provide some function. Device objects often represents a physical object in the real world. For example, a printer is a device object that is connected to a real-world physical printer.

Through observations of real-world objects and typical user tasks, distinctive object *behaviors* can be identified. For example, a folder behaves primarily as a container. It can be used to store, group, or arrange related contents. It behaves also as a data object. Like a data object, it can be copied, archived, and mailed.

### Characteristics of Objects

Objects can be grouped according to similarities in appearance and behavior. These groups can be arranged into object *hierarchies,* which show the relationships among objects.

*Properties* represent the data or state that an object can possess. There are two kinds of properties: *attributes,* which hold values as numbers and literals, and *relationships,* which represent associations with other objects. For example, the icon used to represent an in/out basket conveys its class by resembling a typical office in/out basket. The in/out basket icon communicates its state, as in new mail being delivered to the user, by indicating a document icon being dropped into the in/out basket.

*Inheritance* is the ability to take properties from related objects that already exist. Inheritance can be single, where a derived type may inherit from a single supertype, or multiple, where a derived type may inherit from multiple supertypes. For example, a movie clip object inherits the characteristics of a motion object, but none of the characteristics unique to a clip art object. However, a movie clip object and clip art object possess common characteristics inherited from the multimedia data object.

Additional aspects of an object can be accessed by opening a window. The window provides a view of the object. Many objects can provide more than one view, showing different aspects, or the same aspects in different formats.

### Interactions with Objects

OOUI enables the user to interact easily with various objects via *direct manipulation*. Prevalent direct manipulation techniques associated with OOUI are *drag-and-drop* and *pop-up menus*. OOUI employs a direct manipulation (drag-and-drop) interaction technique that differs significantly from the object-action interaction technique of the GUI model. The OOUI interaction technique enables the user to easily invoke object-oriented processes. For example, a user requesting to print a document may do so by dragging and dropping the selected document's icon (data object) onto the printer icon (device object). Pop-up menus dynamically appear beside the object and contain only actions pertinent to the particular object in its current context. The context is affected by factors such as the type of container within which the object resides, the state of the object, and the contents of the object itself.

OOUI supports the common windowing actions of the graphical user interfaces. OOUI employs a consistent set of icons to represent common system and application actions such as printing, filing, and deleting. For example, a trash can object implies a deletion action on another object such as a document. However, the application-oriented menu bar used by the graphical user interface is insufficient to support an object-oriented environment. Thus, a new object-oriented menu bar is required to support the windows in which objects can be viewed and the objects that are selected within that view.

### Macintosh Bento Container Model

The Macintosh is modeled after the Bento container model. *Bento* is a Japanese term for "a box lunch or picnic lunch. It is a box or basket with multiple compartments, containing a collection of disparate elements arranged in an aesthetically pleasing manner" [Apple Computer, Bento Specification, 1993]. Bento provides a mechanism for storing content elements as objects. It defines a standard format for storing multiple different types of objects, allowing the interchange of application objects. The Bento Container Model specification is becoming a de facto standard.

### OSF/Motif

The alliance of major UNIX systems suppliers is driving the delivery of a common open software environment across their UNIX system platforms. This common desktop environment will provide the end-user with a consistent "look and feel" and a consistent set of application programming interfaces (APIs) for the desktop that will run across all of their systems. The common desktop environment will incorporate aspects of HP's Visual User Environment (VUE), IBM's System Object Model (SOM) and Workplace Shell, OSF/Motif toolkit and window manager, and Sun Microsystem's Open Look. The common desktop environment in discussion is predicted to be object-oriented, with graphics and multimedia capabilities integrated tightly with the environment.

### IBM CUA Workplace Model

The IBM CUA interface hides the computer-based concepts, focuses the user on his or her own objects and tasks, and increases the user's control of the human-computer interaction. The IBM CUA interface employs a workplace model. The workplace model is an object-oriented extension that specifies a standard environment for user interface objects. The workplace model allows the user to organize objects in the environment similar to the way he or she organizes objects in the real world. The user can keep the objects employed across many tasks in a common, convenient place. And they can keep objects used in specific tasks in specific places.

### Microsoft Component Object Model (COM)

Microsoft Component Object Model (COM) is a general model that describes how an object interacts on an individual platform as well as across a network supporting many platforms. It is based on the notion of a *component*. A component is a reusable piece of software that can be "plugged into" other components from other vendors with relatively little effort. COM employs many concepts of object-orientation such as abstraction, encapsulation, object identity, and messaging.

COM is the basic "wiring and plumbing" for Object Linking and Embedding (OLE). It is a set of system services that provides a powerful means for applications to interact and interoperate. OLE facilitates the creation of documents consisting of multiple sources of information from different applications. OLE is more than simple linking of one application to another. It provides the foundation for the future Microsoft object-oriented desktop.

## Virtual Desktop

Future GUI releases will support a virtual-sized desktop through both a user interface and a virtual-sized desktop protocol. A virtual desktop provides the user with the ability to pan the view over a root window that appears to be much larger than the actual size of the display screen. Client windows, not currently being used, can be moved out of the way and off the display screen. This allows many more windows to be open without cluttering the user's view. In addition, work areas can be set up where the client windows used for similar tasks can be grouped together. The implementation of the virtual desktop will allow switching from one group to another.

The virtual desktop will offer features such as panning, interactive panning, and jumping to a specific location. Panning involves a single operation that shifts the display by a specified amount. Interactive panning is linked with the mouse and causes the virtual desktop to be repositioned continuously as the mouse is moved.

Figure 2.9 illustrates a UNIX-based virtual desktop.

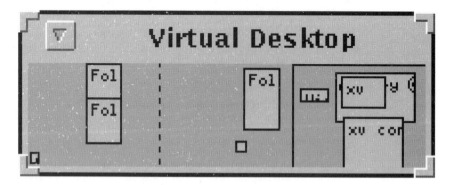

FIGURE 2.9   **Example of UNIX-based Virtual Desktop**

## New "Look and Feel"

Future GUIs will support a new desktop toolbar (menu bar) feature, often referred to as the *front panel*. The front panel resembles the dashboard of a car (see Figure 2.10). It is a horizontal window at the bottom of the desktop, which establishes a central location for frequently used controls. It is also the user's main entry point into the system. The front panel provides access to the various applications, data, and services within the desktop environment. The front panel can consist of controls (e.g., window menu, mail, text editor), workspace switch area, and subpanel access area (printer, style manager, help, trash can).

FIGURE 2.10  **Example of a Front Panel**

## Conclusion

The "look and feel" of the desktop will evolve as more and more user interfaces move toward an object-oriented approach. The desktop will be increasingly colorful and iconic. The use of the drag-and-drop manipulation technique and pop-up menus will be prevalent. The desktop will exploit multimedia capabilities such as audio, video, and graphics to enhance and enrich the desktop environment. The efforts to provide a common desktop environment will continue.

# CHAPTER 3

# Windows

**A** window is an area within the screen (or on the desktop) with which a user conducts a dialog with a computer system. Windows provide a common framework for presenting to the user the objects and various information such as actions, choices, information, and messages. A window is the fundamental component of a user interface through which a user can view and manipulate an object. The user interacts with the window using a keyboard or a pointing device such as a mouse, trackball, or pen.

The appearance of windows changes to fit their particular communication function. Windows can have title bars, window-sizing controls, scroll bars, and a menu bar. Windows can contain any combination of window controls that the user manipulates to control the appearance and behavior of the application. Windows can be opened and closed, resized, and moved. The user can have one or more windows on a desktop, often from a number of different applications. Windows can be shrunk to an icon or enlarged to fill the entire desktop.

This chapter describes the basic elements and controls of a window. It discusses the conceptual and functional differences of windows for the various GUIs in the comparison. The chapter also discusses the types of windows, window arrangements, and window behavior.

## 3.1 Elements of a Window

Every window has a *window frame, title bar,* and *content area.*

The *window frame (window border)* is the part of the window that indicates the boundaries of the window. It separates a window from other windows on the desktop. The window frame may be used in some cases to resize a window.

The *title bar* is usually located at the top of the window. It contains the name of the window, if applicable. It can also contain the close control, control (system) menu icon, and one or more window-sizing controls. The title bar is a visual cue that indicates the state of the window and can be used for moving a window to another location.

The *content area* is a region in the window that is the focus of the user's attention. It displays the contents of an object, such as a document, that the user wants to work on. The content area is also called a *client area*.

Every window has at least one window control. A *window control* is a visual user interface element that the user can manipulate with an input device. By manipulating the window controls, the user can change the characteristics of a window (i.e., size, position). The *close control* is the one control usually found in most windows.

The *close control* provides a quick and easy way to close a window. In some GUIs, a window can be closed using the *control (system) menu*. The *control menu* is an icon that is usually located at the leftmost part of the title bar. It contains choices that affect the window. **Move** and **Close** are options commonly provided by the control menu. Other options such as **Restore, Size, Minimize,** and **Maximize** may also be provided. Figure 3.1 illustrates a typical window and its components.

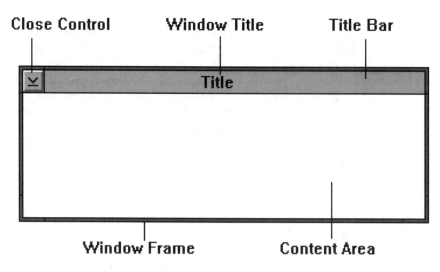

FIGURE 3.1   **Typical Window and Its Elements**

A window may also include some or all of the following elements: menu bar, message area, and status bar.

A *menu bar* is usually a horizontal bar located near the top of a window, under the window title. It contains functions that the user can choose from. (Refer to Chapter 4, "Menus," for more information on a menu bar.)

The *message area* is also known as an *information area*. It is used to provide brief help messages and explanations or descriptions of the state of an object. It is usually located at the bottom of a window. The *status bar* is a more intricate form of message bar. It displays information about the current state of the application.

Table 3.1 summarizes the different elements of a typical window for each of the GUIs in the comparison.

**TABLE 3.1  Comparison of Window Elements**

| Element | Macintosh | OSF/Motif | NeXTSTEP | Presentation Manager | Microsoft Windows |
|---------|-----------|-----------|----------|----------------------|-------------------|
| *Close Control (Control Menu)* | Close Box | window menu | Close Button | System Menu | Control Menu |
| *Content Area* | Content Area | client area | Content Area | Client Area | Content Area |
| *Message Area* | Status Bar | Message Area | — | Information Area | Message Bar |
| *Menu Bar* | Menu Bar | MenuBar | (Main Menu) (Application Menu) | Menu Bar | Menu Bar |
| *Status Bar* | Status Bar | Status Area | — | Status Area | Status Bar |
| *Title Bar* | Title Bar | Title Bar | Title Bar | Title Bar | Title Bar |
| *Window Frame* | Window Frame | Window Border | Window Border | Window Border | Window Frame |

## 3.2 Window Controls

*Window controls* are visual elements in a window that the user can manipulate with an input device. By manipulating the window controls, the user can change the characteristics of a window (i.e., window size, position). A window may include some or all of the following controls:

- Close Control (Control Menu)
- Maximize Button
- Minimize Button
- Move Control

- Restore Button
- Scroll Bar
- Size Control
- Split Box

(Refer to Chapter 5, "Controls," for detailed information on these controls.)

The windows for each of the GUIs in the comparison are highly standardized. Each GUI defines a set of standard window controls through which the user can manipulate the window. The terminology, appearance, and behavior of these elements vary from GUI to GUI.

Table 3.2 summarizes the terms and various window controls used by the GUIs in the comparison.

Figures 3.2 to 3.6 illustrate the composition of a window for each of the GUIs in the comparison.

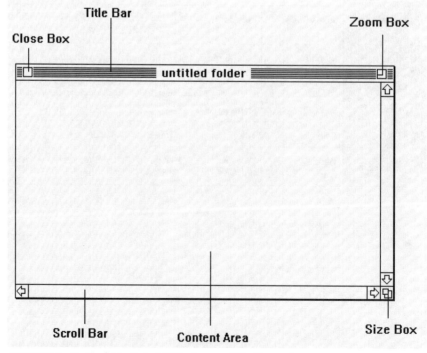

FIGURE 3.2 **Typical Macintosh Window and Its Elements**

TABLE 3.2  **Comparison of Window Controls**

| Control | Macintosh | OSF/Motif | NeXTSTEP | Presentation Manager | Microsoft Windows |
|---|---|---|---|---|---|
| *Close Control (Control Menu)* | Close Box | window menu | Close Buttons | System Menu | Control Menu |
| *Maximize Button* | (Zoom Box) | Maximize Button | — | Maximize Button | Maximize Button |
| *Minimize Button* | — | Minimize Button | Miniaturize Button | Minimize Button | Minimize Button |
| *Restore Button* | (Zoom Box) | Maximize Button | — | — | Restore Button |
| *Scroll Bar Control* | Scroll Bar | ScrollBar | Scroller | Scroll Bar | Scroll Bar |
| *Scroll Arrows* | Scroll Arrows | Arrow Buttons | Scroll Buttons | Scroll Buttons | Scroll Arrows |
| *Scroll Bar Shaft* | Gray Area | — | Scroll Bar | Scroll Bar Shaft | Scroll Bar Shaft |
| *Scroll Box* | Scroll Box | Slider | Scroll Knob | Scroll Box | Scroll Box |
| *Size Control* | Size Box | Window Frame or Resize Borders | Resize Bar | Window Borders or Resize Borders | Window Frame or Resize Borders |
| *Split Box* | Split Bar | — | — | Split Box | Split Box |
| *Split Bar* | Split Line | Separator and Sash | — | Split Bar | Split Bar |
| *Split Windows* | Window Panes | PanedWindows | — | Window Panes | Window Panes |

### Macintosh Windows

In addition to the typical window elements described previously, a Macintosh window has a *close box, zoom box, scroll bar,* and a *size box* (see Figure 3.2).

The *close box* is a visual user interface component that provides a quick means to close a window. It is located in the upper-left corner of the window as part of the title bar. Clicking on the close box control closes the window.

The *zoom box* allows the user to switch between two window sizes and positions: the window size and location established by the user (*user state*), and the window size and location defined by the application (*standard state*).

Macintosh windows can have a vertical scroll bar, horizontal scroll bar, or both. A vertical scroll bar is placed on the right of the window. A horizontal scroll bar is placed along the bottom of a window.

A *size box* is a control with which the user can change the size of the window. It is located in the lower-right corner of a window.

### OSF/Motif Windows

Figure 3.3 shows an xterm window running with the OSF/Motif window manager (*mwm*). The framed window is designed to allow the user to change the size and dimensions of the window. The frame is divided into two horizontal and vertical long borders and four corners. (Refer to Section 3.6, Window Behaviors, in this chapter for more information on resizing a window.)

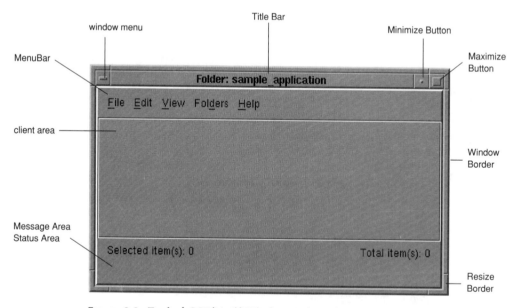

FIGURE 3.3   Typical OSF/Motif Window and Its Elements

The title bar contains four parts: *window menu button, window title, minimize button,* and the *maximize button.* The *window menu* is located on the left side of the title bar. It provides the user with choices to manipulate the window and its icon. The *minimize* and *maximize buttons* are graphical representations of the options in the window menu.

### NeXTSTEP Windows

In NeXTSTEP, every window has a title bar, content area, resize bar, and a border surrounding the overall window structure. Figure 3.4 shows a typical NeXTSTEP window and its components. The title bar contains the *miniaturize button, window title,* and the *close button.* The *miniaturize button* appears in the left corner of the title bar. Clicking on the button reduces the window to a small, icon-sized window. The *close button* appears at the far right of the title bar. It closes the window and removes it from the workspace.

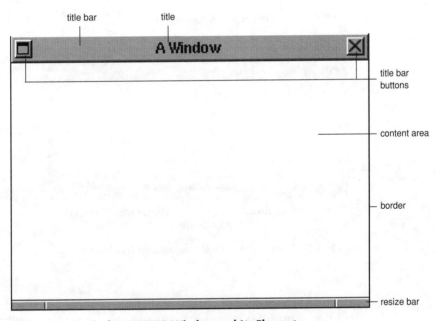

FIGURE 3.4 **Typical NeXTSTEP Window and Its Elements**

The *resize bar* runs along the bottom of a window. The window can be resized by grabbing and dragging the resize bar to the desired size or shape.

NeXTSTEP windows may have a scroll bar (scroller) depending on the type of window. If present, the scroller is placed along the left side of the window.

### IBM CUA Windows

Figure 3.5 identifies the various components of a window as defined by the IBM CUA guide. The terms used for control menu, content area, and message area are *system menu, client area,* and *information area*, respectively. The system menu, which is located at the upper-left corner of the title bar, is typically represented as a down arrow. It can appear as a picture of an object that represents the window. For example, a folder icon may be used instead of the down arrow as a system menu. The folder icon represents an application object.

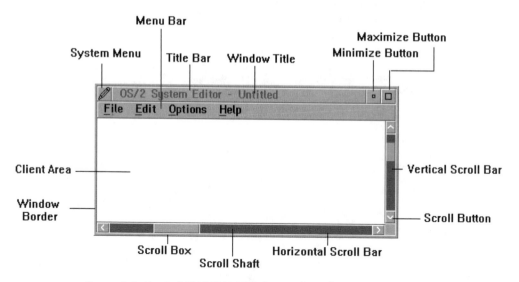

FIGURE 3.5   Typical IBM CUA Window and Its Elements

"The system menu, window border, and window-sizing buttons (minimize and maximize buttons) allow the user to change the size and position of the window. The menu bar and scroll bar allow the user to work with the content area. The system menu and window-sizing buttons are a part of the title bar. The window title indicates the name of the object being viewed as well as which kind of view is displayed" [IBM CUA, p. 34].

### Microsoft Windows

Like most GUIs, Microsoft Windows supports the standardized set of elements for a window—a frame, title bar, and control menu. Microsoft Windows can have optional components such as a menu bar, scroll bar, message bar, and status bar. Figure 3.6 shows a typical window and its components. All windows have frames except when they are maximized and fill the entire screen. Depending on the type of window, the window can be sizable (or nonsizable), and/or movable (or nonmovable). The window frame and the window-sizing controls (maximize, minimize, or restore buttons) change the size of the window. (Refer to Section 3.6, Window Behaviors, in this chapter for more information on resizing a window.) The status bar is a more intricate form of message bar. It displays information about the current state of the application.

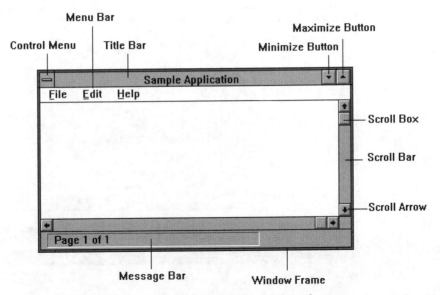

**FIGURE 3.6  Typical Microsoft Windows Window and Its Elements**

## 3.3 Types of Windows

Generally, there are three types of windows according to functionality:

- *Application window*
  An application window appears when the user opens an object. It is the main focal point for the user's activities.

- *Document window*
  A document window is associated with the application window. It usually appears within the application window.

- *Dialog box*
  A dialog box is a window through which the application presents alternatives for the user to choose from.

Figure 3.7 shows an example of an application window, document window, and dialog box in Microsoft Windows.

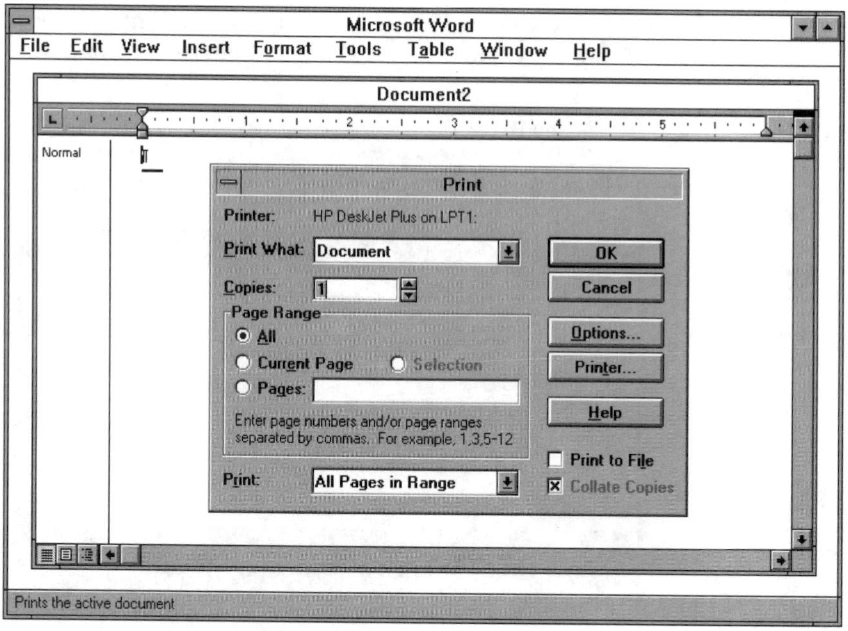

FIGURE 3.7   Types of Windows

## Application Windows

Every object has a window called the *application window*. The application window appears when the user opens an object. It is the main focal point for the user's activities. An application window should always include a sizable window frame, a title bar that contains the name of the application, a control menu, and maximize and minimize control buttons. It can have a message area, menu bar, and status bar. An application window is resizable and movable. Application windows can be maximized and minimized. Minimizing the application window causes the application window and all associated windows to be reduced to a single icon.

A typical environment has several applications running simultaneously. Therefore, there can be multiple application windows open at the same time. There can also be multiple application windows open for a given application. However, the user can interact with only one application window at a time. The application window with which the user is interacting is the active window. It appears in the foreground. Most GUIs in the comparison provide a means to switch from one application window to another.

## Document Windows

A window associated with an application window is a *document window*. A document window may include a sizable window frame, a title bar that contains the name of the document in the window, a control menu, and at least a maximize button. It may also include a scroll bar and split box. It shares the menu bar of the application window. The control menu for a document window contains the same choices as the control menu for an application window. A document window is resizable and movable. It does have a minimize button and can be reduced to an icon.

A document window cannot be larger than the application window that created it. A document window can be visually clipped (that is, partially visible) within the application window. It shares the resizable window frame and title bar of the application window. There is a restore button for reestablishing the document window to its previous size.

Multiple document windows associated with the same application window can appear simultaneously on the desktop. However, the user can interact with only one document window at a time. The document window with which the user is interacting is the active document window. It appears in the foreground. Most GUIs in the comparison provide a means to switch from one document window to another.

## Dialog Boxes

A *dialog box* is a window through which the application presents alternatives for the user to choose from. NeXTSTEP refers to dialog boxes as *panels*. Macintosh refers to a special-purpose dialog box as an *alert box,* which warns the user or reports an error.

Dialog boxes generally have a title bar and a control menu. The title bar describes the command that displayed the dialog box. It contains at least one dialog box control. Depending on the type of dialog box, a dialog box can be moved within the window, and/or resized (expanded to display additional options). (For a detailed discussion of dialog boxes, refer to Chapter 6, "Dialog Boxes.")

## Other Window Types

In addition to the aforementioned window types, Macintosh defines another type of window—a utility window. "A *utility window* is an accessory window that provides additional tools or controls to the user. Utility windows float on top of document windows" [MHIG, p. 137].

Utility windows are extremely useful for keeping information or control accessible at all times. For example, a tool palette or a set of text attributes could be implemented in a utility window. Several utility windows can be open at a time. The suitability of utility windows to other applications is largely dependent on the type of application.

Generally, a utility window has a title bar with no title and a close box. A zoom box can appear optionally in a utility window. Macintosh uses racing stripes within the title bar to indicate that it is an active window.

A utility window can be considered as a modeless dialog box that allows the user to perform operations without responding to the dialog box. Unlike modeless dialog boxes, a utility window remains available to other active applications until the user dismisses it. Though other GUIs, such as Microsoft Windows, may provide support for such a window type, they make no distinction between utility windows and dialog boxes.

## Comparison of Window Types

The GUIs in the comparison classify windows differently (see Table 3.3). The classification of windows into primary and secondary windows as in OSF/Motif and Presentation Manager is related to the hierarchy rather than functionality of windows.

TABLE 3.3 **Comparison of Window Types**

| Types of Windows | Macintosh | OSF/Motif | NeXTSTEP | Presentation Manager | Microsoft Windows |
|---|---|---|---|---|---|
| *Application* | (Virtual Window) | Primary or main application | (Virtual Window) | Primary | Application |
| *Document* | Document | Secondary Dialog Box | Standard Window or Main Window | Secondary | Document |
| *Others* | Dialog Box Alert Box | Menu Window | Panel Menu | Dialog Box | Dialog Box |

### Macintosh

Application windows do not exist in Macintosh. However, the entire screen space can be thought of as a *virtual* application window. The menu bar at the top of the screen can then be thought of as the menu bar for the virtual application window.

A Macintosh application typically creates a *document window*. A document window is a window in which the user can enter and display text, graphics, or other information. The components of a document window include the title bar, size box, close box, zoom box, and scroll bars. A document window shares the menu bar of the desktop.

Only one application can be active at a time. As the user switches from one application to another, the menu bar and all windows associated with an application change accordingly.

### OSF/Motif

OSF/Motif classifies windows based on their hierarchy rather than their functionality. Each application typically has a *main application,* or *primary, window* that displays the data and allows interaction between the user and the application. All other windows for that application are created from the primary window. Windows associated with the main application, or primary, window are called *secondary windows.* These windows are used by an application to conduct interim, context-dependent dialog with the user. OSF/Motif considers dialog boxes secondary windows. (Refer to Section 3.4, Window Hierarchy, for a detailed discussion on primary and secondary windows.)

### NeXTSTEP

The concepts of application and document windows do not exist in NeXTSTEP. However, the entire screen space can be thought of as a *virtual* application window. Each running application has its own menu (at the top-left corner of the screen) called the *main menu*. It is not constrained within a formal window. Only one application can be active at a time. Like the Macintosh, the main menu and all windows associated with an application change accordingly as the user switches from one application to another.

In NeXTSTEP, each application on a desktop has a variety of windows. There are three kinds of windows: *standard windows, panels,* and *menus.* NeXTSTEP also considers on-screen objects such as pop-up lists, pull-down lists, miniwindows, and freestanding and docked icons as windows. Figure 3.8 shows the different types of NeXTSTEP windows.

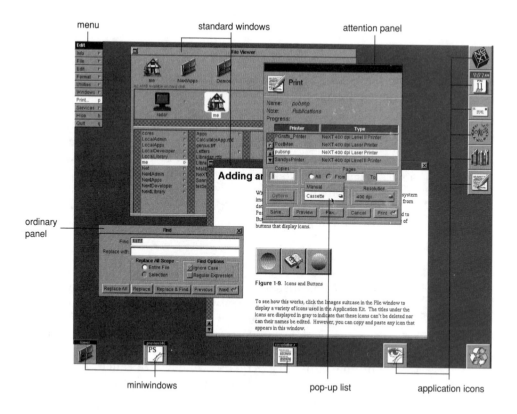

**FIGURE 3.8   Types of NeXTSTEP Windows**

A standard window is the primary window in which the user is currently working. An example of a standard window is the **File Viewer** window. It can be considered a document window. A standard window has a title bar, a window border, and a content area. It may have a resize bar, and one or two title bar buttons—either a close button or a miniaturize button. All windows are standard windows except for pop-up lists, pull-down lists, miniwindows, and freestanding and docked icons.

The status of the standard window can be a *main window* or a *key window*. NeXTSTEP refers to the standard window, which is the focus of the user's actions, as the main window. A main window cannot be opened without launching the application to which it belongs. Each application can have multiple standard windows displayed at the same time. For example, the user can open multiple documents in a word processing application, and each document appears in a separate standard window. The key window receives characters from the keyboard.

*Panels* can look like standard windows, but their role is to perform secondary functionality by supporting the work done in standard windows. Panels typically contain a set of controls and fields that allow the user to have additional input into the program. NeXTSTEP distinguishes two types of panels: *ordinary panels* and *attention panels*. (Refer to Chapter 6, "Dialog Boxes," for more information on panels.)

### Presentation Manager

There are two basic types of windows: *primary* and *secondary*. "A *primary window* is used to present a view of an object or group of objects when the information displayed about the object or group of objects is not dependent on any other object. A view of an object is typically displayed in a primary window" [IBM CUA, p. 9].

A *secondary window* is a movable and sizable window associated with a primary window for conducting a modeless, parallel dialog with the user. A secondary window can be used for help screens and to display large amounts of information that otherwise would require scrolling.

(Refer to Section 3.4, Window Hierarchy, for a detailed discussion on primary and secondary windows.)

### Microsoft Windows

Microsoft Windows classifies windows as application, document, and dialog boxes. All activities take place within the application window except for the Help window. When the user chooses the **Help** option from the menu bar, a Help application window appears.

An application window has a title bar, control menu, window border, menu bar, minimize button, maximize button, and restore button. Depending on the application, other controls may be present. For example, a word processing application may have other controls such as a toolbar and/or ribbon.

The Microsoft Windows Multiple Document Interface (MDI) allows an application to manage multiple documents, or multiple views of the same document, within the main application window (also known as the *workspace*). The views of the document are displayed in separate windows called the *document windows*.

A document window provides a view of the contents of an object though it is not limited to viewing document objects. It can be used to provide the primary view of other container objects, or other types of views of an object. A document window can be manipulated in the same way as an application window. It is composed of a window border and a title bar. The title bar includes a title bar icon located in the upper-left corner, representing the object being viewed in the window. Optionally, it can include a menu bar, toolbar, status bar, and scroll bar.

All document windows appear within the borders of the application window. They can be clipped so that they appear within the application window. All document windows share the menu bar and other controls, such as the toolbox (toolbar), ribbons, rulers, and status bar, provided by the application window. Document windows can be minimized to an icon. Double-clicking the mouse while the pointer is over the minimized icon causes the document window to be restored. The **Window** menu allows the user to switch from one document window to another.

Figure 3.9 shows an MDI application and its associated document windows.

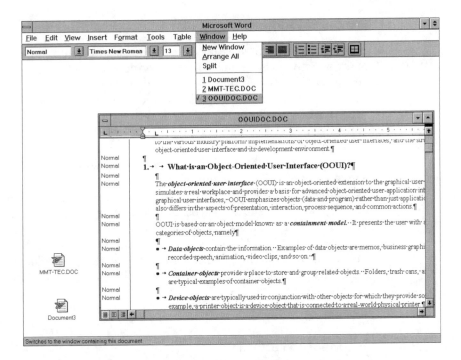

**FIGURE 3.9 Microsoft Windows Multiple Document Interface**

## 3.4 Window Hierarchy

An application has a main window known as the *parent window,* and may have one or more windows subordinate to the main window, known as the *child windows.* The child windows themselves may be the parents of other child windows. Thus, an application may have a hierarchy of windows. Windows that are of the same level in the hierarchy and have the same parent window are known as *siblings.* As a result of this hierarchy, windows that are subordinate to the parent window inherit the characteristics of the parent window. The parent and child windows share common characteristics and behaviors.

OSF/Motif and Presentation Manager offer another classification for windows. For these two GUIs, there are two types of windows: *primary* and *secondary* windows.

## Primary Windows

The *primary window*, which is considered the parent window, is the main window from which all other windows, such as secondary windows used by the application, are generated. All primary windows should always include the basic window components described earlier in this section. There can be at least one primary window for each application.

A primary window is resizable and movable. It can be maximized and minimized. Minimizing a primary window causes the primary window and all of its secondary windows to disappear and be replaced by a single icon for the primary window. To maximize a window, the primary window and all associated secondary windows are restored. The windows are displayed in the same position and order from which they were iconified. Moving a primary window in the display hierarchy causes all associated windows to move to the same location in the hierarchy. When a primary window is closed, all secondary windows are also closed.

## Secondary Windows

A *secondary window* is a window that provides secondary and transient interaction with the user. Secondary windows are considered to be child windows. They are children of primary windows or, in some cases, children of other secondary windows. Secondary windows are used by an application to allow an interim, context-dependent dialog with the user.

The primary and secondary windows share common characteristics and behaviors. The overall appearance of secondary windows is similar to primary windows with a few exceptions. Secondary windows share the same menu bar as primary windows. They can be clipped within their parent window. They must always appear on top of that parent window in the window hierarchy if they are not clipped. When the primary window associated with it is closed or minimized, the secondary window is removed.

In OSF/Motif, the appearance of secondary windows is similar to primary windows. However, secondary windows do not have a minimize button and cannot be minimized. Resize borders are not generally present in secondary windows. Dialog boxes are considered to be secondary windows in OSF/Motif.

Secondary window behavior can constrain user interaction. An OSF/Motif window manager supports four modes of interaction as listed in Table 3.4.

TABLE 3.4  OSF/Motif Modes of Interaction with Secondary Windows

| Mode of Interaction | Description |
| --- | --- |
| *Modeless* | Allows interaction with the secondary window and all other windows |
| *Primary modal* | Does not allow interaction with any ancestor of the window |
| *Application modal* | Does not allow interaction with any window created by the same application, even if the application has multiple primary windows |
| *System modal* | Does not allow interaction with any window on the screen. This includes windows from all other applications and any icon box. To indicate a system modal secondary window, the pointer should be change shape to a caution pointer whenever it leaves the system modal secondary window. |

Source:   *OSF/Motif Style Guide*, p. 7-5

## 3.5  Window Status

Since more than one application can run at the same time, there can be many application windows displayed on the desktop. There can also be multiple application windows open for a given application. For each application window, there can be multiple document windows open at the same time. However, the user can interact with only one application.

### Active and Inactive Windows

The user can choose which particular window to work with. The window the user is working with is known as the *active* window. The active window is the window that currently has the input focus. It is the window that receives input from either the keyboard or the pointing device.

There can be only one active window at a time. The user activates a window by clicking anywhere within that window. The active window appears in the foreground. All other windows are inactive. An active window is distinguishable from other windows by the emphasis displayed on its title bar and border. In Macintosh, the title bar of an active window displays racing stripes, and controls in the window frame are visible.

An *inactive* window does not have the input focus. The user can deactivate a window by closing (using the close box or control menu), minimizing (using the minimize button), hiding (using the **Hide** command in the case of NeXTSTEP), and terminating (using the **Quit** or **Exit** command). When the window that belongs to an application becomes inactive, the visual characteristics of the active state reverse. Figure 3.10 shows an example of an active Macintosh window. Note that the close box, zoom box, size box, scroll bar, and racing stripes disappear when the window is inactive. However, the outline of the scroll bar remain visible.

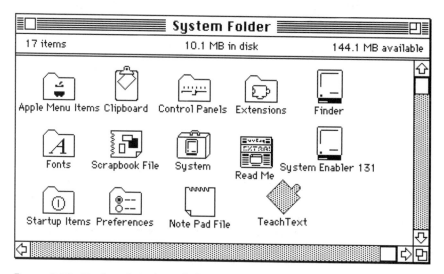

FIGURE 3.10  Macintosh Active Window

## Key Windows

A window will receive input from the keyboard, mouse, or both. The window associated with the keyboard actions is referred to as the *key window*. Only one window at a time can be the key window. The key window is highlighted in some way, usually by a change in shade or color to the window border.

## 3.6 Window Behaviors

### Opening a Window

Each of the GUIs in the comparison supports similar ways of opening windows. The user can open a window by double-clicking on the icon representing the object (e.g., file), choosing the **Open** option in the **File** menu, choosing the **New** option in the **File** menu, or choosing a file from a dialog box. When opening an existing file, the title bar displays the name of the file. However, if the file is being created using the **New** option, the window is untitled until the user saves the file. Most GUIs allow the user to open as many windows as desired.

#### Design Tips

The application should keep track of files that were previously worked on. A list should be provided at the bottom of the **File** menu for quick and convenient access. When a window is re-opened, position the window in the foreground, and retain the previous size and location attributes.

### Closing a Window

The user can close a window by using the close control or choosing the **Close** option.

In most GUIs, the close control is a visual component located at the upper-left corner of the window. Table 3.5 shows the terminology for the close control used by the various GUIs. Closing the window preserves the state of the window (i.e., size and position).

TABLE 3.5  **Controls for Closing a Window**

|  | Macintosh | OSF/Motif | NeXTSTEP | Presentation Manager | Microsoft Windows |
|---|---|---|---|---|---|
| *Close control* | Close Box | window menu | Close Button | System Menu | Control Menu |

When an application window is closed, the window and its associated document windows are also closed. If the content of a document window has not been saved, a dialog box appears to notify the user. The application window will be closed once all the document windows are closed.

In the case of OSF/Motif, Presentation Manager, and Microsoft Windows, the control menu is used to close a window. To close the window, the user positions the pointer over the control menu and double-clicks the mouse. When the information contained in the window needs to be saved, a dialog box appears as a notification to the user. Otherwise, the window is removed immediately from the desktop.

In NeXTSTEP, the close control is called a *close button*. It is located on the upper-right corner of the window. Most standard windows have a close button, unless it is unnecessary. For example, the workspace manager main window has no close button, because closing this window would terminate the application. Clicking the close button causes the window to disappear from the screen. If the information contained in the window is not saved, the close button changes its appearance to a partially drawn close button. When the information is saved, the button returns to its normal appearance. Clicking a partially drawn close button causes a panel to appear requesting the user to save the information. The window closes after responding to the panel.

All GUIs in the comparison provide a **Close** menu option as an alternative way to close a window.

### Design Tips

In designing applications, a control specific to closing a window should be implemented. A single mouse click to close the window promotes consistency with the interaction techniques for other controls. The application designer should be cognizant of the GUI's concept of application and document windows and the effect of closing these parent-child windows. The state of the window (i.e., size and position) should be preserved when closing a window.


## Positioning a Window

When the user opens an application (program), the associated application window is usually positioned in the foreground. The document window associated with the application window, when opened, is positioned below and to the right of its predecessor. Dialog boxes are displayed at the center of the screen.

*Design Tips*

To determine where to place a window, consider the type of window being opened, the type of other windows that are open, and the relationship of the window being opened to the other windows. When a window is re-opened, position the window in the foreground, and retain the previous size and location attributes.

## Moving a Window

Windows can be moved using the title bar. The user positions the pointer over the title bar and drags the window to a new location. As the user drags, a gray ghost or dotted outline of the window frame appears on top of the regular frame. The gray ghost or dotted outline of the window frame moves with the pointer until the user releases the mouse button. At the release of the mouse button, the window appears at the new location. Moving the window does not affect the appearance of the window. Moving an inactive window changes it to active mode. Figure 3.11 shows how moving a window looks to the user.

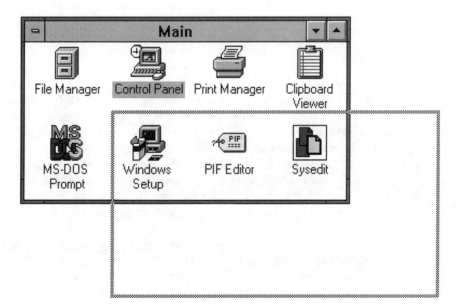

FIGURE 3.11 **Moving a Window in Microsoft Windows**

In addition to direct manipulation, some GUIs such as OSF/Motif, Presentation Manager, and Microsoft Windows provide the **Move** option to move a window. When this option is selected, a gray ghost or dotted outline frame appears on top of the regular window frame. The pointer changes in appearance (for example, a movement pointer or cross pointer) as an indication to the user that the ghost or dotted outline frame can be moved to the desired location. When the user releases the mouse button, the window appears at the new location.

### Design Tips

An application should not allow the user to move a window to a position from which it cannot be repositioned. For example, the user should not be allowed to move the window completely off the screen. The application designer should provide visual cues such as changing the appearance of the pointer, and a gray ghost or dotted outline window frame to indicate that the window is being moved.

## Changing the Size of a Window

Direct manipulation is often used in resizing windows. The following window components are used to manipulate the size of the window: the window frame, maximize button, minimize button, and restore button. Resizing the window affects the width and/or height of a window.

The window frame contains a resize border at each corner, and one at the midpoint of each side of the window. To change the height or width of the window, the user selects one of the edges of the window frame. To change both the height and width of the window, the user selects one of the corners of the window frame. The pointer changes in appearance (for example, a bi-directional arrow or a hand pointer). The user drags the edge or corner of the window frame to a desired position. As the user drags, a gray ghost or dotted outline of the window frame appears and moves with the pointer until the user releases the mouse button. At the release of the mouse button, the window assumes a new size.

The user can also resize the window by using **Size, Maximize, Minimize,** and **Restore** options from the control (system) menu, which is located on the leftmost side of the title bar. The graphical representations for these options are the maximize button, minimize button, and restore button. (Refer to Chapter 5, "Controls," for more information on these controls.)

OSF/Motif, Presentation Manager, and Microsoft Windows have similar interaction techniques for resizing a window using direct manipulation. These GUIs also provide similar menu options for resizing a window. In OSF/Motif, as the window is being resized, a digital readout appears outside the pointer showing the window size in pixels.

In Macintosh, the application determines the minimum and maximum size of the window. The size of the window is based on the physical size of the display. Unlike other GUIs in the comparison, the user can only change the size of the window by using the size box. The size box is located in the lower-right corner of the window, if a window has one. "When the user drags the size box, a dotted outline of the window moves with the pointer. The upper-left corner of the window remains in the same place. It acts like an anchor on the screen; the window shrinks or grows from that point. The outline of the lower-right corner of the window follows the pointer. When the user releases the mouse button, the window is drawn in the shape of the dotted outline" [MHIG, pp. 156–157]. Figure 3.12 shows resizing of a window in Macintosh.

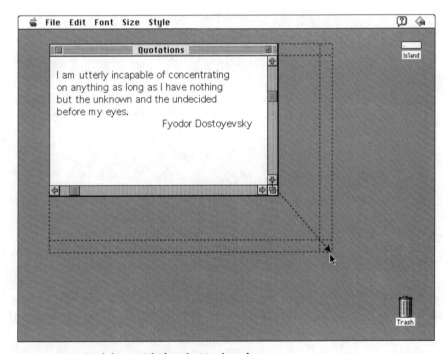

**FIGURE 3.12   Resizing a Window in Macintosh**

In NeXTSTEP, the resize bar is used to change the size of the window. It is a narrow strip located at the bottom of a window. The resize bar is divided into three regions: a large middle region and two smaller end regions. To change the height of the window, the user drags vertically from the middle region of the bar. To change the width of the window, the user drags horizontally from either end region of the bar. To change both height and width of the window, the user drags diagonally from an end region. As the resize bar is dragged, an outline of the window follows the pointer. No special pointer appears to indicate the resize mode.

### Design Tips

Direct manipulation is a preferred method for resizing a window. In resizing a window, the application designer should provide the following visual cues:

- Bi-directional arrow pointer or hand pointer to indicate that the resizing will take place

- Gray ghost or dotted outline window frame to show the new size of the window

- Digital readout appears outside the pointer showing the window size in pixels

Visual effects such as animation provide an effective feedback for resizing a window using direct manipulation. However, they should be used sparingly.

## Maximizing a Window

Maximizing a window enlarges the window to its maximum size. On many screens, the maximized window fills the entire screen. The user can maximize a window by clicking the maximize button located on the title bar of most windows. In some GUIs, such as Presentation Manager and Microsoft Windows, a restore button is provided that returns the maximized window to its previous size and position. The restore button replaces the maximize button when the user clicks the maximize button. The maximize button replaces the restore button when the user clicks on the restore button.

### *Design Tips*

In designing applications, the designer should provide a maximize button on the title bar when the size of the window can be changed and the window is not currently maximized. The designer should save the state (i.e., the size and position) of the window before maximizing the window. If a restore button is provided, the maximize button should be changed to a restore button when the window is currently maximized.


## Minimizing a Window

Minimizing a window reduces the window to a minimum size—usually to a small icon located at the bottom of the desktop. Minimizing a window allows the user to view more than one window at a time. A window can be minimized by clicking on the minimize button located on the title bar of most windows. While minimized, the window is open and continues to run. The user can move the minimized window around the desktop. Double-clicking on the minimized window or icon causes the window to be restored to its original size and location.

Typically, only application windows can be minimized. When minimized, all associated windows, including floating palettes and toolbars, are hidden. Some GUIs, such as the Microsoft Windows MDI, allow document windows to be minimized as well.

In NeXTSTEP, clicking on the *miniaturize button* of a window causes the window to be reduced to a small icon called a *miniwindow*. Even while miniaturized, the window is still active; any changes will be applied when the window is re-enlarged. Miniaturized windows will not "snap" into the Application Dock icon or into a directory window.

In Presentation Manager, the title of a minimized window is placed in the **Window List.** Depending on the window setting, the icon for the minimized window is placed in either the Minimized Window Viewer or on the desktop.

Some windows have a *hide button*, instead of a minimize button. Hiding a window is similar to minimizing a window except that objects for the hidden window are not placed in the Minimized Window Viewer or on the desktop. However, the titles of hidden windows are placed in the **Window List.**

*Design Tips*

In designing applications, the application designer should provide a minimize button on the title bar to distinguish it from a maximize button. The application designer should save the state (i.e., the size and position) of the window, along with the state of each of its associated windows, before minimizing the window. In minimizing a window that has not been previously minimized, place the minimized window visual or icon near the bottom of the desktop. In minimizing a window that has been previously minimized, place the minimized window visual where it had been before being restored.

## Splitting a Window

Splitting a window allows the user to view and change different parts of the same object simultaneously. A single window can be split into two or more viewing regions called *window panes*. A window that can be divided contains a *split bar, split box,* or a *separator.* The dividing line between panes is referred to as a *split line.* Splitting a window affects the size of the window. However, the contents within a window remain unaffected.

Windows can be divided horizontally, vertically, or both ways. To split a window horizontally, the user positions the pointer over the split box located at the top of the vertical scroll bar. To split a window vertically, the user positions the pointer over the split box located at the leftmost edge of the horizontal scroll bar. The pointer changes to a two-headed arrow pointer to indicate a change in state. The user drags the split box to the desired location. As the user drags, a dividing line appears and moves with the pointer until the user releases the mouse button. At the release of the mouse button, the split line appears to visually separate the panes. After a single split, each window pane has its own scroll bar. Each pane can usually scroll independently of the other. To remove a window pane, the user drags the split bar to its original position. Figure 3.13 shows how a window may be split in Microsoft Windows.

Except for Presentation Manager, most GUIs allow windows to be split into two regions. Presentation Manager allows the user to split a window into multiple panes—horizontally or vertically.

All GUIs in the comparison support a direct manipulation technique for splitting a window. Presentation Manager provides a **Split** menu option as an alternate way of splitting a window.

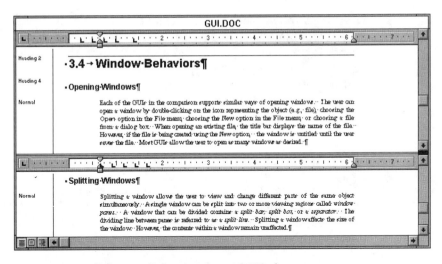

**FIGURE 3.13  Splitting a Window in Microsoft Windows**

### Design Tips

A single mouse click while the pointer is over the split bar should be implemented as a technique to split a window. It promotes consistency with the interaction techniques for other controls. The application designer should allow the user to split a window multiple times both horizontally and vertically.

## Switching from Window to Window

The user can switch from one window to another by simply clicking the desired window. The selected window becomes an active window, appearing in the frontmost position. Parts that were previously covered by other windows are now visible. Most GUIs in the comparison provide a menu option to switch from one window to another. This option is helpful and convenient especially if there are several windows opened and the desired window is obscured by other windows.

For example, Microsoft Windows provides a **"Switch To"** option in the control menu that allows the user to switch from one application window to another. The application window also provides a **Window** menu in the menu bar that allows the user to switch from one document window to another. Microsoft Windows allows the user to switch to an application window that is completely obscured by other windows by double-clicking on the screen background (typically outside any application window). A dialog box containing a list of currently running applications is presented to the user. The user can activate the desired application window by selecting the name of the application window and pressing a confirmation button in the dialog box. Double-clicking the name of the application immediately activates the application without requiring confirmation.

## 3.7 Window Arrangement

Multiple windows can be displayed on the screen at the same time. Most GUIs allow the user to arrange the windows in two typical ways: *cascaded* and *tiled*. The user can also arrange each window individually.

### Overlapping Windows

Windows are overlapping when one or more windows are fully or partially hidden behind other windows. Overlapping windows appear stacked on top of each other. The active window appears in front of all the other windows. Figure 3.14 shows overlapping windows.

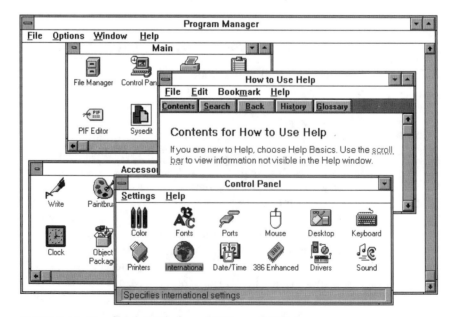

FIGURE 3.14   **Overlapping Windows in Microsoft Windows**

Windows can overlap each other for all the GUIs in the comparison. To bring a window in front of others, the user usually positions the pointer anywhere within the window to be raised and clicks the mouse button.

In OSF/Motif, the window manager can control the stacking order of the windows by lowering a particular window to the bottom of the stack or raising it to the top. Lowering a window can be accomplished by selecting the **Lower** option in the control (system) menu. Once selected, the appearance of the pointer changes (i.e., target pointer). The user moves the pointer to the appropriate window. When the user clicks any of the mouse buttons, the desired window is placed behind all windows except the root window.

Lowering a window can also be accomplished using direct manipulation. To lower a window, the pointer is positioned within the title bar of the window to be lowered, and the user clicks the appropriate mouse button (usually the middle button of a three-button mouse).

In NeXTSTEP, overlapping windows can be reordered. To bring a window forward, the user points and clicks anywhere on the window. The **Arrange in Front** option in the **Window** menu neatly stacks all standard windows that are open in the application.

## Cascading Windows

*Cascade* stacks open windows one behind the other, keeping the title bar of each window visible. The active window appears as the topmost window. Figure 3.15 shows a cascading window arrangement.

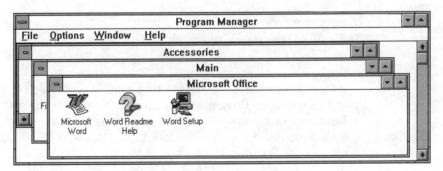

FIGURE 3.15  **Cascade Arrangement in Microsoft Windows**

Only Presentation Manager and Microsoft Windows support the cascade arrangement. Presentation Manager allows the user to cascade all or selected windows whose title appears in the **Window List,** using the pop-up menu or direct manipulation. In Microsoft Windows, the **Cascade** option in the **Window** menu allows the user to cascade all open windows. Unlike Presentation Manager, Microsoft Windows does not provide direct manipulation techniques for cascading windows.

## Tiling Windows

*Tile* arranges all open windows so that they are all visible to the user. The windows are resized and arranged like floor tiles. Most GUIs place the active window at the top left corner. Figure 3.16 shows a tiled window arrangement.

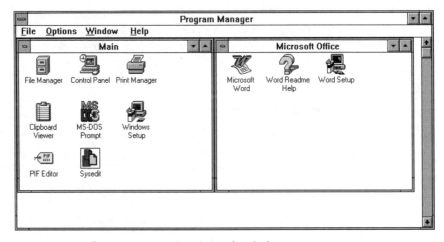

**FIGURE 3.16  Tile Arrangement in Microsoft Windows**

Only Presentation Manager and Microsoft Windows support the tile arrangement. Presentation Manager allows the user to tile all or selected windows whose titles appear in the **Window List,** using the pop-up menu or direct manipulation. In Microsoft Windows, the **Tile** option in the **Window** menu allows the user to tile all open windows. Unlike Presentation Manager, Microsoft Windows does not provide direct manipulation techniques for tiling windows.

### *Design Tips*

The application designer should provide overlapping, cascaded, and tiled arrangements via a menu option and/or direct manipulation technique. The user should be allowed to cascade or tile all or selected windows. The user should also be allowed to arrange each window individually.

## Conclusion

Windows represent views into objects and applications. Interaction with windows should allow both direct and indirect manipulations. The window controls should be consistent in appearance and behavior within an application and across applications. The application designer should anticipate situations where numerous windows are open at the same time, and should provide direct manipulation techniques for organizing the open windows. Grouping windows into a task-based or document-based hierarchical relationship can improve the user interaction. GUIs are evolving into object-oriented user interfaces which emphasize objects (data and programs) rather than just applications (programs). The different aspects of the user interface, such as presentation, interaction, process sequence, and common actions, will change to support the object-oriented paradigm.

CHAPTER **4**

# Menus

$\mathbf{M}$enus are an important component of the user interface. Menus provide an easy-to-use visual interface that allows the user to browse and select an item from a list of choices or commands that the application provides rather than having to recall the commands, options, or data from memory. This makes the decision-making process easier and reduces the user's information load.

Menus are usually presented to the user in a horizontal form like the menu bar. They may also have a vertical orientation like those in NeXTSTEP. Menus can include a list of choices in words or icons that represent the menu item. There are several types of menus—pull-down, cascading, pop-up, and tear-off.

This chapter provides an overview of menus—their orientation, typical components, and the various types of menus. The chapter describes in detail the appearance and behavior of these menu types. It compares the menus and menu items associated with the desktop, application and document windows, and objects.

## 4.1 Menu Presentation

The menu bar is usually a horizontal bar located at the top of a window, under the window title. The menu bar contains a horizontal list of words, icons, or both, referred to as *menus*. Menus usually appear in the menu bar of the application window except in Macintosh and NeXTSTEP. The Microsoft Windows menu bar (see Figure 4.1) displays menus (e.g., **File, Edit, View, Insert, Format, Tool, Table, Window,** and **Help**) horizontally.

In Macintosh, the menu bar that extends across the top of the startup screen and contains the title of each available pull-down menu is the menu bar for the application window. There is only one menu bar displayed at a time. It is the menu bar of the current active application.

The main menu (application menu) in NeXTSTEP can be considered as the menu bar, with a vertical orientation. It appears in the upper-left corner of the screen. It is a vertical list that appears when the application first starts up and is contained in a rectangle. The rectangle is shaded and can extend vertically for the length of the screen. Like Macintosh, there is only one menu bar displayed at a time. It is the menu bar of the current active application.

Menus can be presented to the user as textual, graphical, or both. The Microsoft Windows menu bar (see Figure 4.1) shows examples of textual menus. A *graphical menu* is a menu in which choices are represented as graphical icons, rather than text. Some GUIs refer to a graphical menu as an *iconic menu*. The NeXTSTEP Application Dock, as shown in Figure 4.1, is an example of a graphical menu.

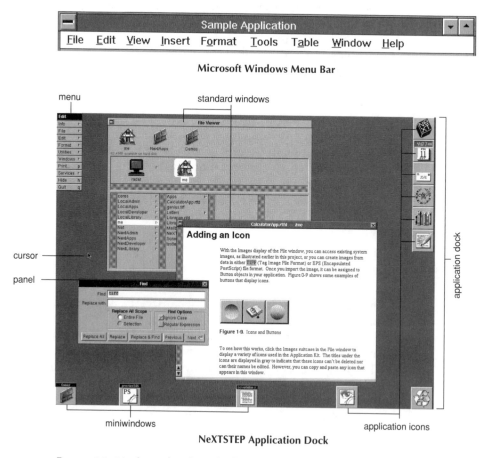

**Microsoft Windows Menu Bar**

**NeXTSTEP Application Dock**

FIGURE 4.1   **Horizontal and Vertical Menu Bars**

*Toolbars and value set controls* can be considered graphical menus. They are groups of buttons that provide quick and convenient access to many of the choices and commands from the menu bar. Toolbars and value set controls are specific to the application. For example, ribbons and rulers are toolbars used in word processing applications. Palettes are value set controls used in graphics applications. Toolbars and value set controls appear as independent movable windows. They may occupy a fixed position within the application window, or may be placed in a supplemental window or dialog box.

## 4.2 Components of a Menu

Each menu consists of a *menu name* (title) and one or more *menu items* (choices or options). The menu name indicates the purpose of the commands in the menu. Some examples of common menus are **File, Edit,** and **Help.** A menu can display a number of items or commands. The items in a menu are usually arranged vertically down the screen. The items on a menu can be presented as text, graphics, or a combination of both. A menu can include access keys, short-cut keys (accelerator keys), dividers, check marks, dashes, ellipses, and cascading menu indicators. Figure 4.2 shows the different components of a typical menu.

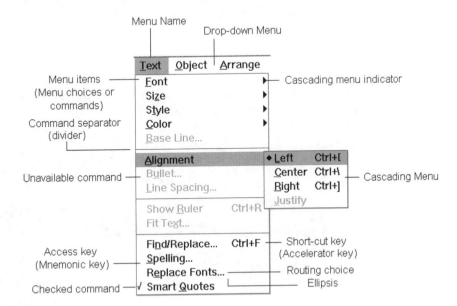

**FIGURE 4.2  Components of a Menu**

When the use selects a menu name, the selected menu name is highlighted. In most GUIs, when the menu bar is horizontal, the user opens the menu by clicking the mouse while the mouse pointer is positioned over the menu name. The menu then remains open until the user dismisses it. A subsequent mouse-click while the mouse pointer is over the menu name or anywhere outside the boundaries of the menu closes the menu. In a vertical menu bar, the user opens the menu by selecting a menu name with an arrow to the right of a choice. The arrow indicates that additional choices are available.

Most GUIs provide an access key or predefined mnemonic for each of the predefined textual menu items in a pull-down menu. Often menu items are accompanied by short-cut or accelerator keys (names or symbols) for frequently used menu items that act as alternatives for accessing these items via the keyboard.

Menu items can appear as normal, selected, unavailable or inactive, or grouped (see Figure 4.2). They are distinguishable from each other by their appearance. Most GUIs highlight a menu item to indicate that it has been selected. The dimming effect indicates that items are unavailable or inactive. Grouped items are usually separated across the menu by a horizontal line or divider. A check mark (✓) next to a menu item indicates that the menu item (or setting) is currently toggled on. The setting usually applies to the entire selection. Selecting a menu item with a cascading menu indicator causes an associated menu (submenu) to appear to the side of the item. The ellipsis character (. . .) indicates that a dialog box will appear, prompting the user for additional information.

In Macintosh, the menu divider can be a dotted line (for black and white screens), or a gray line (for color and gray-scale screens). In addition to check marks, the Macintosh also uses a dash (-) next to a menu item to indicate that the menu item (or setting) is currently toggled on and applies only to part of a selection (see Figure 4.3).

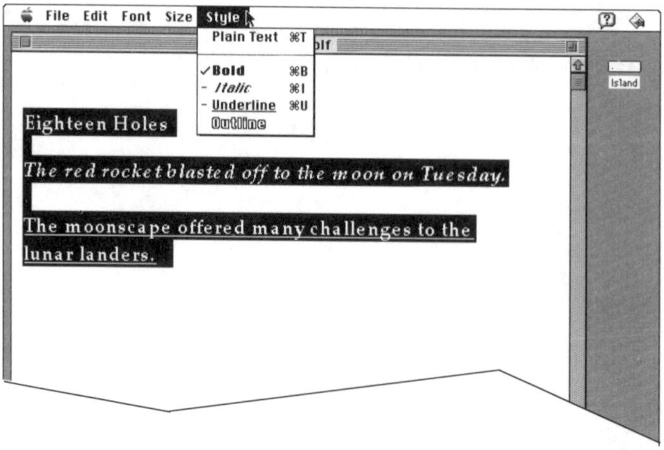

FIGURE 4.3  **Check Marks and Dashes in Macintosh Menus**

# 4.3 Types of Menus

Menus can appear in the following forms:

- *Pull-down menu* is a menu that extends from a selected menu on a menu bar or from a system-menu symbol.

- *Cascading menu* is a specialized pull-down menu in which the menu that is pulled down extends from the side of this option.

- *Pop-up menu* is a floating menu that is hidden until the user invokes it. The items contained in a pop-up menu are displayed when the user clicks the mouse button within a particular area. Pop-up menus can also be displayed when the user clicks the mouse button while the pointer is over the menu name. The menu extends upward from a selected menu on a menu bar.

- *Tear-off menu* is a menu that can be removed from its menu bar and continuously displayed until closed.

Table 4.1 shows the types of menus supported by the GUIs in the comparison.

TABLE **4.1** **Comparison of Menu Types (Terminology)**

| Types of Menus | Macintosh | OSF/Motif | NeXTSTEP | Presentation Manager | Microsoft Windows |
|---|---|---|---|---|---|
| *Pull-Down* | Pull-Down | Pulldown | — | Pull-Down or Action bar Pull-Down | Drop-Down |
| *Cascading* | Hierarchical or Submenu | Pulldown | Submenu | Cascaded or Cascading Pull-Down | Cascading or Submenu |
| *Pop-Up* | Pop-Up | Popup | — | Pop-Up | Pop-Up |
| *Tear-Off* | Tear-Off | TearOff | Submenu | — | — |
| *Other* | Scrolling | Option | — | — | — |

## Pull-Down Menus

A *pull-down menu* is a menu that extends from a selected menu name on a horizontal menu bar or from a system menu symbol. The items in the menu are hidden until the menu is opened. Pull-down menus are also called *drop-down menus.* IBM CUA also refers to a pull-down menu as an *action bar pull-down.*

In the case of a movable menu bar or front panel (dashboard), when the menu name is selected, the menu extends upward or downward depending on the location of the menu name within the menu bar or front panel.

To display a pull-down menu, the user positions the mouse over the menu name and presses the mouse button. The pointer can be moved to a desired menu item while the button is held down. If the user releases the mouse button while the pointer is still on the menu name, the menu remains open so that the user can move the pointer to a desired menu item. The user can move from one menu to another by dragging the mouse pointer across the menu bar. The menu is closed when the user selects an item, switches to another menu, or clicks the mouse anywhere outside the boundaries of the menu. Figures 4.4 and 4.5 show closed and open drop-down menus.

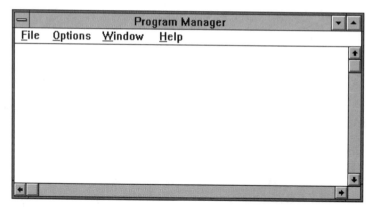

FIGURE 4.4   Microsoft Windows Closed Drop-Down Menus in Menu Bar

FIGURE 4.5   Microsoft Windows Open Drop-Down Menu in Menu Bar

OSF/Motif supports both pull-down and cascading menus, though it does not make any terminology distinction between pull-down and cascading menus. "Pulldown menus are pulled down from a Cascade-Button. A CascadeButton contains a Label that indicates the Menu displayed. A CascadeButton can also contain an arrow graphic after the Label to distinguish it from PushButtons and to indicate the direction of the cascading menu" [OSF/Motif, p. 9-8].

In NeXTSTEP, the pull-down menus are not relevant because of the vertical orientation of its menus. However, NeXTSTEP considers a pull-down list as a specialization of a menu. Pull-down lists are not as common as submenus (cascading menu).

In Microsoft Windows, pull-down menus are called *drop-down menus*. It is a menu that extends from the menu bar or the control menu symbol. Microsoft Windows provides an ellipsis (. . .) to the right of a menu item to inform the user that selecting that option will cause a dialog box to be displayed.

### Design Tips

Pull-down menus are by far the most common type of menu in current applications. The application designer should ensure that the menu is reasonable in length. Provide visual cues to the user to distinguish normal from selected, active from inactive, and the states of toggled menu items. When grouping menu items, place the most frequently used items at the top of the menu. Place the least frequently used items at the bottom of the menu. The application designer may want to consider the use of graphical menu items. Graphical menu items should provide meaningful and recognizable representation and be aesthetically pleasing to the user.

## Cascading Menus

A *cascading menu,* or *cascading pull-down, submenu,* or *hierarchical menu,* is a submenu (child menu) that is usually attached to the right of the menu item (parent menu). A cascading menu can be attached to the left of the menu item if the right side space is limited. It is a specialized pull-down menu in which the menu that is pulled down extends from the side of this option. A right-pointing arrow or solid triangle to the right of a menu item indicates that selecting that option will cause a cascading menu to be displayed. Cascading menus are used to reduce the length of a menu. All GUIs in the comparison support the concept of cascading menus or submenus. However, the term cascading menu is not emphasized. Figure 4.6 shows an example of a Microsoft Windows cascading menu.

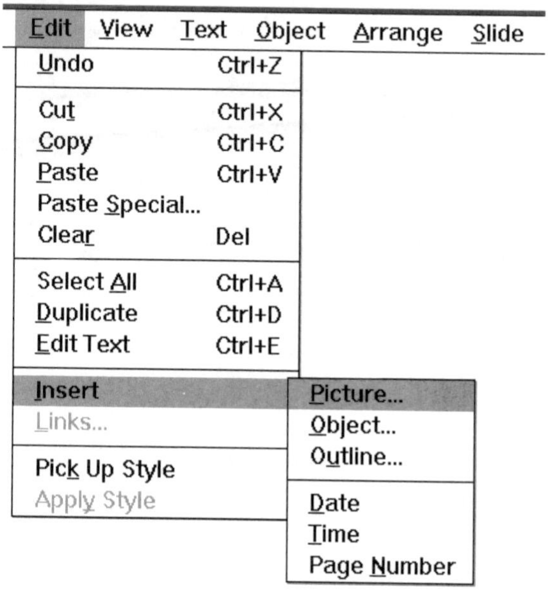

**FIGURE 4.6**
**Microsoft Windows**
**Cascading Menu**

### Design Tips

The application designer should use cascading menus sparingly. Avoid excessive menu depth, preferably limiting the levels of cascading menus to two levels. For long lists of options (more than seven options per menu), the application designer should provide dialog boxes instead of menus because menu item browsing is difficult.

## Pop-Up Menus

A *pop-up menu* is a floating menu that is hidden until the user invokes it. The items contained in a pop-up menu are displayed when the user clicks the mouse button within a particular area. The items displayed depend on where the pointer was located when the mouse button is pressed. Pop-up menus are also called *contextual menus*. Other GUIs refer to pop-up menus as *spring-loaded menus*.

Pop-up menus provide a convenient way to access commands. The user does not have to navigate the menu bar or control bar to browse through the menu items. In most GUIs, pop-up menus are displayed for the desktop, application and document windows, and objects. Figure 4.7 shows a Microsoft Windows pop-up menu associated with a document window.

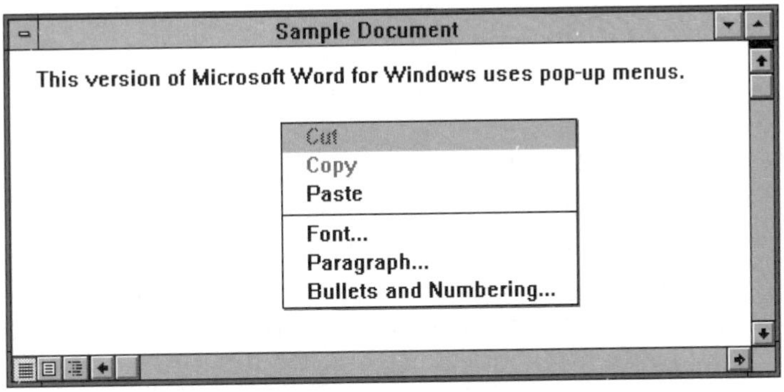

FIGURE 4.7  **Microsoft Windows Pop-Up Menu**

In Figure 4.8, the border surrounding the object indicates that the Presentation Manager pop-up menu applies to that particular object only.

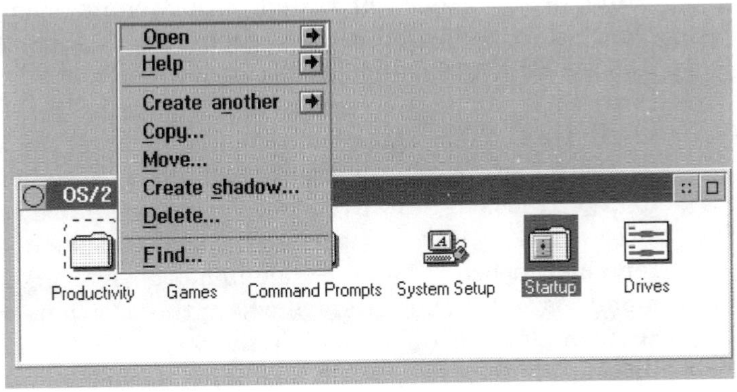

FIGURE 4.8  **Presentation Manager Pop-Up Menu**

### Design Tips

The application designer should carefully consider frequently used commands when designing applications using pop-up menus. The pop-up menu should not simply repeat the menu items on the menu bar. Pop-up menus should not include too many commands or multiple levels of submenus or cascading menus. Lastly, the symbol or region on which the user can click to bring up a pop-up menu must be designed for visual distinctiveness and to indicate clearly its relationship to a pop-up window.


## Tear-Off Menus

A *tear-off menu* can be removed from its menu bar and be displayed continuously until closed. A tear-off menu can be moved around the screen to the location the user desires (Marcus, 1992, p. 197). Tear-off menus are useful when the user does not want the menu to disappear after a menu selection. Menu entries in a tear-off menu are usually enabled or disabled when the state of the application changes (e.g., from active to inactive).

Macintosh allows the user to "detach a menu from the menu bar by pressing the mouse button while the cursor is over the menu name and dragging beyond the menu's edge" [MHIG, p. 92].

"A TearOffButton tears off a Menu in place when activated, or it is dragged to tear off and move in one action. This component is composed of a button with a graphic that indicates the tear-off action. The graphic is a dashed line representing perforations" [OSF/Motif, p. 9-126]. "After the user tears off a Menu, the Menu elements are placed in a DialogBox that is tiled with the Menu title, and the Menu is unposted. The TearOffButton should be removed from the DialogBox, but if it remains, it can be used to close the DialogBox" [OSF/Motif, p. 6-44].

In NeXTSTEP, submenus may be "torn off" and placed anywhere on the screen. When a menu is torn off, a close button appears. The items on the menu that are inactive or unavailable are grayed-out. Any submenus that were attached to the torn-off submenu move with it and remain attached. "Once a submenu has been torn away from its super-menu (parent menu), it stays where the user puts it. To reattach the submenu, the user should close the torn off submenu and then choose its controlling command" [NeXTSTEP, p. 104].

Figure 4.9 shows examples of tear-off menus for the various GUIs in the comparison.

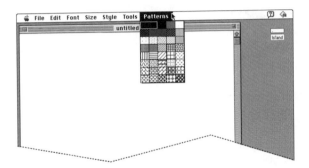

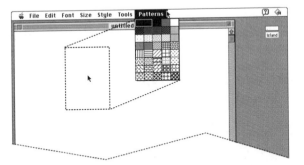

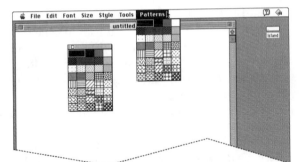

**Macintosh Tear-Off Menu**

**NeXTSTEP Tear-Off Menu**

FIGURE 4.9  **Tear-Off Menus**

*87*

### Design Tips

There are some interaction contexts in which continuously displayed menus can be advantageous, especially when the user needs to refer to information in an application before making a menu choice. In addition, the ability to move these menus allows the user to utilize screen space in a manner that is advantageous to him or her. In designing applications using tear-off menus, the application designer should take into account reattaching the torn-off menu to its menu (parent or supermenu). The NeXTSTEP implementation of tearing off and reattaching submenus should be considered.

## Additional Menu Types

OSF/Motif supports an additional type of menu called the *Option Menu*. "An Option Menu is popped up from an OptionButton" [OSF/Motif, p. 6-41]. "It allows for a one-of-many selection. An OptionButton consists of a Label that indicates the current state of the Option Menu, and a bar graphic on the right side of the button to distinguish it from a PushButton" [OSF/Motif, p. 9-8].

Macintosh supports an additional type of menu called the *scrolling menu*. A scrolling menu contains more menu items than are visible from the screen. "If a menu becomes too long to fit on the screen, an indicator appears at the bottom of the menu to show that there are more items. When the user starts to scroll, an indicator appears at the top of the menu to show that some items are no longer visible in that direction. When the user drags past the last visible item, the menu scrolls to show the additional items. When the last item is shown, the downward-pointing indicator disappears" [MHIG, p. 78]. Figure 4.10 shows this behavior.

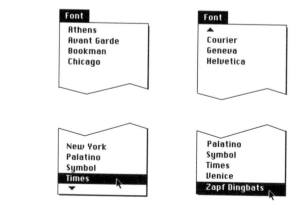

FIGURE 4.10  Macintosh
Scrolling Menu

## 4.4 Types of Menu Items

Menu items can represent an *action, routing,* or a *setting* choice. An *action menu item* immediately performs some task. For example, a menu item labeled **Save** saves an object as soon as the user selects the choice.

A *routing menu item* displays a menu or a window from which the user can specify additional information related to the task to be performed. The menu item as a routing choice is represented by a right pointing arrow or an ellipsis (. . .). A menu item with an arrow or cascading menu indicator displays another menu (submenu). A menu item with the ellipsis character opens a dialog box. For example, a menu item labeled **Find** opens a dialog box from which the user can specify the object to be located.

A *setting menu item* displays or changes the properties of an object. The setting menu item is also referred to as a *toggled menu item*. One type of setting menu item is a menu item name with a check mark next to its name to indicate that the option is in effect. For example, the menu item labeled **Underline** when set to on allows the user to display or change the emphasis of selected text to underlined. Another type of setting menu item is a menu item name that changes to reflect the current state of the item. An example is the Macintosh **Show Balloon** menu item from the **Help** menu. **Show Balloon** changes to **Hide Balloon** when the balloon help is displayed.

## 4.5 Desktop Menus

Menus available for the desktop can take different forms; namely, pop-up (contextual), and control (system) menus.

## Pop-Up Desktop Menus

The pop-up menu for the desktop contains the menu items that apply to all objects on the desktop and to the operating environment. Desktop pop-up menus are spring-loaded menus that appear when the user points to an empty area on the desktop and depresses the mouse button (usually the right button). The same activation technique may be used for displaying the pop-up menu for the objects on the desktop. Figure 4.11 illustrates the OS/2 desktop pop-up menu.

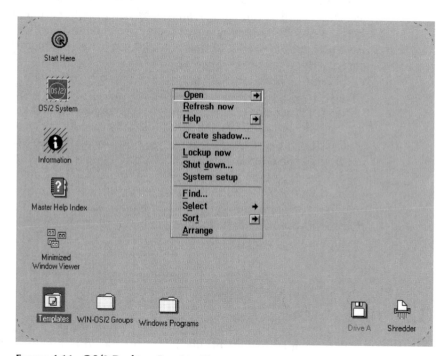

FIGURE 4.11    OS/2 Desktop Pop-Up Menu

Only Presentation Manager uses pop-up desktop menus extensively. Presentation Manager and Workplace Shell support menu names such as: **Open, Refresh now, Help, Create shadow, Lockup now, Shut down, System Setup, Find, Select, Sort**, and **Arrange.**

## Desktop Control Menu

A *desktop control menu* is a menu that contains choices that affect the desktop and other specific operating environment functions. The desktop control menu is also called a *system menu* or *window menu*. The desktop control menu is located at the left end of the title bar. It is activated by clicking the control menu icon. The OS/2 desktop pop-up menu can be considered a desktop control menu. The Microsoft Windows Program Manager and OSF/Motif *window manager* provide a desktop control menu with the following common menu items:

- **Restore** changes the window to its previous size and location.

- **Move** enables the user to change the position of a window within the workplace.

- **Size** allows the user to alter the window's height, width, or both.

- **Minimize** changes the window to an icon. The minimized window is usually placed at the bottom of the workplace.

- **Maximize** enlarges the window to fill the maximum display space (in some cases, the maximum allowable for that window).

- **Close** causes a window to be closed and removed altogether from the workplace. It halts any processes running within the window. **Close** is the same as quit or exit when invoked from a primary application window or the main window manager.

Microsoft Windows provides a **Switch To** option, which starts a program that has been minimized or inactive. This option usually brings up a task list window that presents a list of active programs and a set of options. **Switch To** provides the user with an additional, parallel interaction technique in a multitasking environment. When the Microsoft Windows architecture evolves to its eventual multitasking operating environment, this command will not be necessary.

OSF/Motif provides the **Lower** menu item that moves a window to the bottom of the window hierarchy. This command allows the user to manage window position without using direct manipulation.

## Apple-Controlling Menus

Macintosh does not provide a control menu, but it does provide two menus—the Apple and Application menus—that can be said to be similar to a control menu. The *Apple menu*, often called the *desktop accessory menu*, is always the leftmost menu (see Figure 4.12). It lists the various desktop applications installed on the system along with their iconic representations.

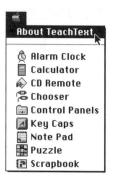

FIGURE 4.12   Apple Menu

The Application menu is the one farthest to the right in the menu bar. It contains the icons of the active applications or desktop accessories that are running. The Application menu contains, among other functions, the option to switch to another application. The user can also hide the open windows of the active application or any other open applications.

## NeXTSTEP Application Dock

Like Macintosh, NeXTSTEP provides a menu of applications (programs) through its Application Dock. The Application Dock is a collection of icons representing commonly used applications that are lined up along the right edge of the screen. They stay on the screen even when the applications they represent are not running.

## Future Desktop Menu

The evolution of user interface technology will bring a new and common desktop environment supporting the use of a *front panel* or *dashboard*. A front panel is a horizontal window at the bottom of the desktop that will be the central location for frequently used controls.

It will also be the user's main entry point into the system. The front panel will provide access to the various applications, data, and services within the desktop environment. Figure 4.13 shows an example of a front panel.

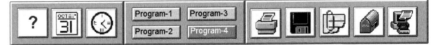

FIGURE 4.13  **Future Desktop Menu—Front Panel**

## 4.6  Application Menus

Application menus are menus available for the application. With the exception of Macintosh and NeXTSTEP, the menu for the application is within the application window. It is typically displayed on the menu bar of the application window. An application menu can include the control (system) menu and standard application menus.

### Application Control Menu

An *application control menu* is a menu that contains choices that allow the user to work with the window itself. The application control menu is also called a *system menu* or *window menu.* The application control menu is displayed from the control (system) menu symbol, which is usually located at the upper-left corner of an application window or a dialog box. The common application control menu items are: **Restore, Move, Size, Minimize, Maximize,** and **Close.** (Refer to Section 4.5, Desktop Menus, for descriptions of these common menu items.)

Table 4.2 shows the terminology for the control menu used by the GUIs in the comparison.

TABLE 4.2  **Comparison of Terminology for Control Menu**

|  | Macintosh | OSF/Motif | NeXTSTEP | Presentation Manager | Microsoft Windows |
|---|---|---|---|---|---|
| ***Control Menu*** | — | window menu | — | System menu | Control menu |

There is no application control menu for Macintosh and NeXTSTEP. Among GUIs that provide a control menu, there is considerable similarity in the menu items supported. Table 4.3 shows the menu items for the control menu.

TABLE **4.3**   **Comparison of Control Menu Items**

|  | Macintosh | OSF/Motif | NeXTSTEP | Presentation Manager | Microsoft Windows |
|---|---|---|---|---|---|
| *Control Menu* | — | Restore, Move, Size, Minimize, Maximize, Lower, Close | — | Restore, Move, Size, Minimize (Hide), Maximize, Close, Window list, Split | Restore, Move, Size, Minimize, Maximize, Close, Switch To, Run |

## Standard Application Menus

Every application provides a set of standard menus in order to maintain consistency across applications. By providing a set of standard menus, the user can apply the knowledge learned from one application to another. The standard application menus that are supported by the GUIs in the comparison are: **File, Edit, View,** and **Help. File** is generally the first menu on the menu bar. **Help** generally appears last on the menu bar. Table 4.4 shows the application menus supported by the various GUIs.

TABLE **4.4**   **Comparison of Application Menus**

| Macintosh | OSF/Motif | NeXTSTEP | Presentation Manager | Microsoft Windows |
|---|---|---|---|---|
| File | File | Document | File (Application windows) <name of object> (Object windows) | File |
| Edit | Edit | Edit | Edit | Edit |
| — | View | — | View | View |
| Application-specific | Application-specific | — | Application-specific (Options, Windows) | Application-specific |
| Help Icon | Help | Info | Help | Help |
| Application Icon | — | — | — | — |

*File Menu*

The **File** menu contains menu items for performing actions on files such as creating, opening, saving, closing, and printing. This menu generally appears as the first menu on a menu bar as illustrated in Figure 4.14.

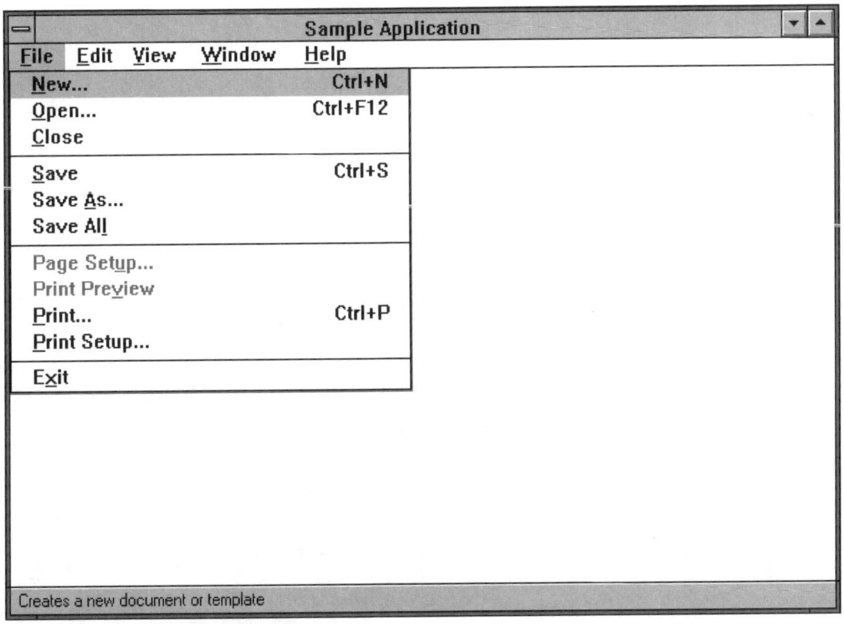

FIGURE 4.14  Sample File Menu

IBM CUA differentiates an application-oriented **File** menu from an object-oriented **File** menu. The application-oriented **File** menu contains choices that affect the object presented in that window. The object-oriented **File** menu contains a choice labeled with the class name of the object in the window. The menu items provided affect the underlying object presented in that window. For example, the menu name can be labeled **Worksheet** for a worksheet object. The menu items for the Worksheet menu can include **Open As**, **Save**, and **Print**.

Table 4.5 shows the common menu items in the **File** menu for each of the GUIs in the comparison.

TABLE **4.5**   **Comparison of File Menu Items**

|  | Macintosh | OSF/Motif | NeXTSTEP | Presentation Manager | Microsoft Windows |
|---|---|---|---|---|---|
| *File Menu* | New, Open, Close, Save, Save As, Page Setup, Print, Quit | New, Open, Save, Save As, Print, Exit | Open, New Application, New Module Save, Save As, Save All, Close | New, Open, Save, Save As, Print | New, Open, Close, Save, Save As, Print, Print Setup, Exit |

### Edit Menu

The **Edit** menu contains menu items for performing actions on the current data of the application such as copy, paste, delete, and global replacement. It also generally allows the user to undo the most recently entered command. This menu usually follows the **File** menu as illustrated in Figure 4.15.

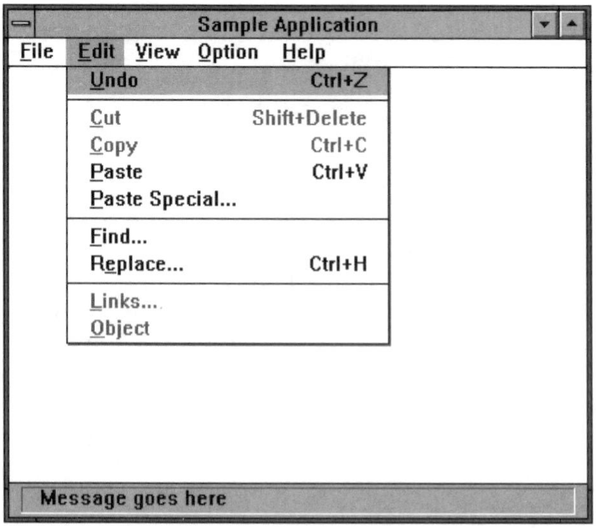

FIGURE **4.15**   Sample Edit Menu

Table 4.6 shows the common menu items in the **Edit** menu for each of the GUIs.

**TABLE 4.6 Comparison of Edit Menu Items**

| | Macintosh | OSF/Motif | NeXTSTEP | Presentation Manager | Microsoft Windows |
|---|---|---|---|---|---|
| *Edit Menu* | Undo, Cut, Copy, Paste, Clear, Select All, Create Publisher, Subscribe To, Publisher Options, Show Clipboard | Undo, Cut, Copy, Paste, Clear, Delete | Info, File, Edit, Format, Utilities, Windows, Print, Services, Hide, Quit | Undo, Redo, Cut, Copy, Create, Paste, Clear, Delete, Find, Select all, Deselect all | Undo, Cut, Copy, Paste, Paste Link, Link Paste Special, Repeat \<action\>, Find, Replace, Clear, Delete |

In Microsoft Windows, menu items such as **Paste Special, Repeat \<action\>, Find, Replace, Clear,** and **Delete** are considered optional items.

### View Menu

The **View** menu includes commands for changing the user's view of the data in the window without actually changing the data or objects themselves. It may also include commands for controlling the display of user interface elements such as the ribbon, ruler, and toolbar. The **View** menu typically follows the **Edit** menu as illustrated in Figure 4.16.

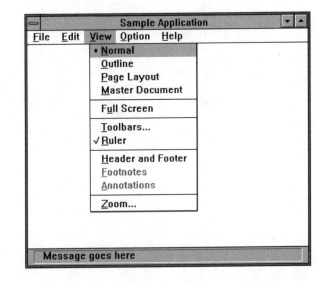

**FIGURE 4.16 Sample View Menu**

The menu items on the **View** menu are application dependent. For example, menu items on the **View** menu for a word processing application might include commands for switching from normal text to outline view. In a graphics application, menu items on the **View** menu might include **Zoom In** or **Zoom Out** commands.

### Help Menu

The **Help** menu is normally a pull-down menu that provides options to display additional information about data, objects, or actions. It is typically the last menu on the menu bar. In some GUIs, such as Macintosh and OSF/Motif, the **Help** menu is separated from the rest of the menus and is located at the right-hand side of the menu bar.

The **Help** menu provides an easy-to-find and easy-to-use method for the user to obtain help. The **Help** menu should be in a consistent location at the far right of the menu bar (as in OSF/Motif). The application designer should establish a standard set of **Help** menu items as well as application-specific items for consistency across applications and ease-of-learning. Table 4.7 lists the **Help** menu items for each of the GUIs in the comparison.

**TABLE 4.7   Comparison of Help Menu Items**

|  | Macintosh | OSF/Motif | NeXTSTEP | Presentation Manager | Microsoft Windows |
|---|---|---|---|---|---|
| *Help Menu* | About Balloon Help Show Balloon \<application> Help | On Context On Help On Window On Keys Index Tutorial On Version | Info Panel, Show Menus, Preferences, Help | Help index General help Using help Tutorial Product Information | Contents Search for Help On How to Use Help About |

Figure 4.17 illustrates the Macintosh **Help** menu which is represented by an icon located at the extreme right of the menu bar, away from the other menus.

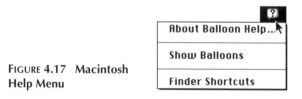

**FIGURE 4.17   Macintosh Help Menu**

Macintosh is the only GUI in the comparison that implements a help balloon. A help balloon is a rounded, rectangular window that contains explanatory information for the user. To use balloon help, the user selects the **Show Balloon** menu item from the **Help** menu. When the user points to items on the screen, a help balloon is displayed (see Figure 4.18).

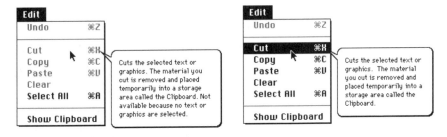

FIGURE **4.18** Macintosh Balloon Help

In NeXTSTEP, the **Info** menu contains menu items or commands that allow the user to obtain information about the application. The **Help** command brings up a panel with information on how to use the application.

In OSF/Motif, the **Help** menu is located at the extreme right of the menu bar, away from the other menus. OSF/Motif supports two acceptable models for the contents of the **Help** menu. Help is usually provided in DialogBoxes but can also appear in the message area.

In Microsoft Windows, the **Help** menu is the rightmost menu in the menu bar. It supports additional application-specific menu items such as **Commands, Procedures,** and **Keyboard.**

Most GUIs supporting toolbars and value set controls provide brief help descriptions of the various buttons within the toolbars and value set controls. When the user points to a button with the mouse, the button name or command appears in a box. Some GUIs refer to these brief help descriptions as *pop-up help* or *bubble help*. Microsoft Windows refers to it as *ToolTip*.

## 4.7 Object Menus

Each object contained on a desktop or in an application window has an associated menu, which is referred to as an *object menu*. The object menu is a pop-up menu that appears when the user clicks the mouse button (usually the right button of a two-button mouse). In Figure 4.19, the pop-up menu associated with the OS/2 System icon is displayed by pointing to the icon and clicking the right button of the mouse. The menus are **Open, Help, Create Another, Copy, Move, Create Shadow,** and **Find.**

FIGURE 4.19   Object Menu for OS/2 System Icon

## Conclusion

The human-computer interaction continues to evolve with advances in technology. The emphasis on an object-oriented development approach will create a more powerful human-computer interaction that is predictable, intuitive, and as close as possible to matching the user's conceptual model.

The focus on objects will enable the user to interact easily with various objects via direct manipulation techniques such as *drag-and-drop* and *pop-up menus.* The support for pop-up (contextual) menus by the different GUIs will be prevalent. Pop-up menus are particularly useful for objects that incorporate other objects of different types, each requiring a set of menu choices. The application designer should be aware of the factors affecting the context of a pop-up menu—such as the type of container within which the object resides, the state of the object, and the contents of the object itself.

With the evolution to direct object-oriented manipulation, the role of menus needs to be re-evaluated. The application-oriented menu bar used by today's user interface is insufficient to support an object-oriented environment. To respond to the evolutionary pressures, GUIs will need a new object-oriented menu bar that will allow the user to view the different aspects of an object.

When constructing graphical (iconic) menus, the application designer should consider the following:

- The icon representing the menu item should be designed to be easily recognizable and meaningful.

- Icons should help the user to act and respond to the menu selection quickly and precisely.

- User comprehension and subsequent retention of icons are affected by the directness of the link between what is depicted (icon) and the object represented. The more direct the link between the icon and the object, the more easily the user correctly associates the object with the icon.

(Refer to Chapter 2, "Desktop," for more information on icon design considerations.)

# CHAPTER 5

# Controls

Controls are the visual user interface components that the user can manipulate to interact with the computer. Controls can be command buttons, radio buttons, and text boxes. By manipulating the controls, the user can provide certain kinds of information for an immediate action or change to occur.

There are a number of common controls to help the user respond quickly. The application designer should give careful consideration to the appearance, placement, order, space, and fonts of the controls to be used within an application. Existing controls should be used as much as possible before using custom controls. The widespread use of custom controls could defeat the benefits of consistency.

This chapter describes in detail the various controls used in constructing an application, in terms of their appearance, function, behavior, and usage. The chapter serves as a single point of reference and it complements the vendor-supplied information on controls available in the style guides. It discusses the similarities and differences of the various controls supported by the GUIs in the comparison.

## 5.1 Check Box (Check Button)

A *check box* is a toggle-type dialog box control that may appear singly or in groups (see Figure 5.1). It is usually a square with a descriptive label next to it that represents a choice. Each box can be selected independent of other check boxes. Because the user can choose more than one option within a group of options, the options are said to be *nonexclusive.*

The user selects a check box by clicking the mouse while the pointer is over the square box or its label. When the user makes a selection, an X appears in the check box to indicate that the choice is

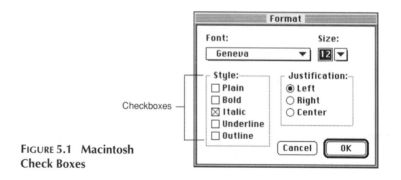

Checkboxes —

FIGURE 5.1  **Macintosh
Check Boxes**

selected. When the check box is deselected, the X symbol is removed, and the box appears empty. When a check box is inactive, its label is usually dimmed.

Any number of check boxes can be present within a dialog box. It is good practice to group sets of check boxes that are related and to separate a group from other groups of check boxes and other controls such as radio buttons.

Macintosh uses an X to indicate that the action is on. When the option is off, the box is empty.

In OSF/Motif, the check box is referred to as the *CheckButton*. The CheckButton is a special form of ToggleButton. "It is a ToggleButton in a group of ToggleButtons where any number of ToggleButtons can be on at a time. The graphic indicator for a CheckButton is usually a filled square to indicate the on state or an empty square to indicate the off state. On color systems, the on state color can be distinct from general application colors to visually distinguish the on state" [OSF/Motif, p. 9-9]. Figure 5.2 shows the use of check boxes in OSF/Motif.

FIGURE 5.2  **OSF/Motif Check Boxes**

NeXTSTEP refers to this control as *standard two-state buttons* or, simply, *buttons*. Standard two-state buttons include *switches* and *radio buttons*. When the button is clicked (or pressed), the button appears pushed in and/or highlighted. A check mark character (✓) is used instead of an X to indicate that a choice is selected. Figure 5.3 shows the different buttons used in NeXTSTEP.

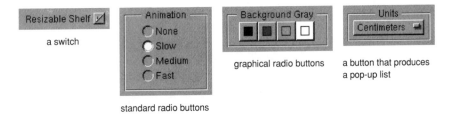

FIGURE 5.3   NeXTSTEP Check Boxes

Like NeXTSTEP, Presentation Manager also uses a check mark character (✓) to indicate that a choice is selected.

In Microsoft Windows, check boxes may also be used to set properties of a selection (see Figure 5.4). "If the selection is heterogeneous, the check box for each heterogeneous property should be filled with a gray pattern. Grayed check boxes can be cycled through three states. Clicking a grayed box once turns on the associated property for the entire selection (and places an X in the box). Clicking the check box again turns off the associated property for the entire selection (and removes the X). Clicking the check box the third time returns the selection to its original heterogeneous state (and restores the original gray pattern in the box)" [MICROSOFT, p. 107].

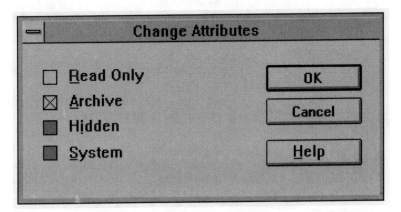

FIGURE 5.4   Microsoft Windows Check Boxes for Heterogeneous Selection

### Design Tips

Though most of the GUIs refer to this control as a *check box* or *check button,* the term *nonexclusive setting control* is more appropriate, because it best describes the functionality of the control. Filling the check box with an X or a check mark character to represent a selected choice is meaningful. Its visual representation conveys a real-world check box.

## 5.2  Close Control

The *close control* is a visual component that the user manipulates to interact with the application. It is used primarily for closing an application (primary) window, a document (secondary) window, and a dialog box.

The close control is referred to as *close box* (Macintosh) and *close button* (NeXTSTEP). Figure 5.5 shows the close control for the Macintosh, which is represented as a square box.

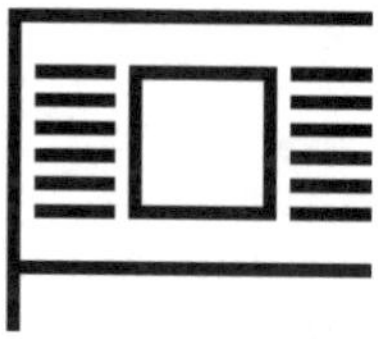

FIGURE 5.5  Macintosh Close Box

There is no close control in OSF/Motif, Presentation Manager, and Microsoft Windows. The control menu contains the **Close** menu option for closing an application (primary) window, a document (secondary) window, and a dialog box. The control menu is used for other functions related to the window such as moving the window from one position to another, enlarging or reducing the size of the window, and switching from one window to another. The control menu is referred to as *window menu* (OSF/Motif), *system menu* (Presentation Manager), and *control menu* (Microsoft Windows). It is typically located on the left side of the title bar. The appearance of this control varies from GUI to GUI. When the user clicks on the control menu icon, it displays a list of choices such as **Restore, Move, Size, Minimize, Maximize, Lower,** and **Close.** (Refer to Chapter 4, "Menus," for more information on the control menu options.) The user selects the **Close** option to close the window. In most GUIs, double-clicking the close control closes the window. If the window is a primary (parent) window, all associated secondary (child) windows are also closed.

In NeXTSTEP, the close button is on the right side of the title bar. Figure 5.6 shows the different appearances of the close button. The window in front shows the normal appearance of the close button. The window in the back shows a *broken* close button. "The application should break the close button whenever the user would lose work by closing the window" [NeXTSTEP, p. 71]. If the user attempts to close the window that has a broken close button, a **Close** or **Quit** panel will be presented to the user as confirmation of the request.

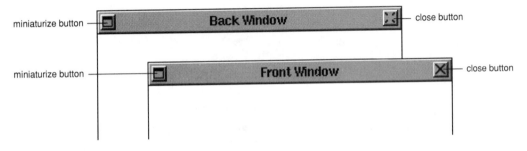

**FIGURE 5.6  NeXTSTEP Close Button**

In Presentation Manager, the system menu is represented as a spacebar. However, the system menu symbol can represent the object being viewed in the window.

### Design Tips

The use of a different close control icon for each window being viewed should be considered. The control (system) menu symbol should represent the object being viewed in the window.

## 5.3  Combination Box (Combo Box)

The *combination box* is a control that combines the capabilities of a text box and a list box. It contains a list of choices that the user can scroll through and select from, and a text box in which the user can directly enter text as an alternative to selecting from the list of choices. The typed text does not have to match one of the list of choices.

The left border of the list is indented from the text field by the width of a numeric digit in the character set. A combination box is scrollable or nonscrollable depending on the number of choices in the list. Figure 5.7 shows an example of a combination box.

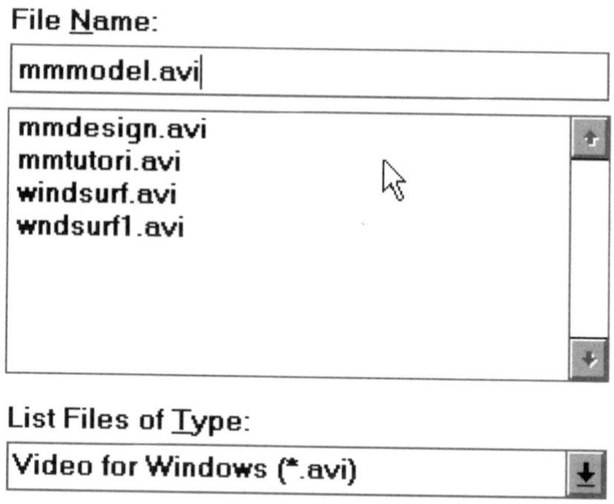

File **N**ame:

| mmmodel.avi |

mmdesign.avi
mmtutori.avi
windsurf.avi
wndsurf1.avi

FIGURE 5.7   **Microsoft Windows Combo Box**

List Files of **T**ype:

Video for Windows (*.avi)

Only Microsoft Windows and Presentation Manager support this control. This control is not supported by the Macintosh Toolbox. Hence, the appearance and behavior of this control are application-specific.

### Design Tips

The application designer should consider the use of this control when the user has to enter values that cannot be provided by the application. A set of commonly used choices should be provided to assist the user in completing the text field. The combination box should be large enough to display a minimum of six choices at a time. The designer should provide a scroll bar (vertical or horizontal) when some choices are not visible.

## 5.4  Command Button (Push Button)

A *command button* is a control that represents an action or routing choice that is initiated when the user selects it. It is usually a rectangular shape with a label that indicates the operation of the button. The label can be text, graphics, or both. Command buttons can be arranged horizontally in a row or vertically in a column. Figure 5.8 shows an example of command buttons.

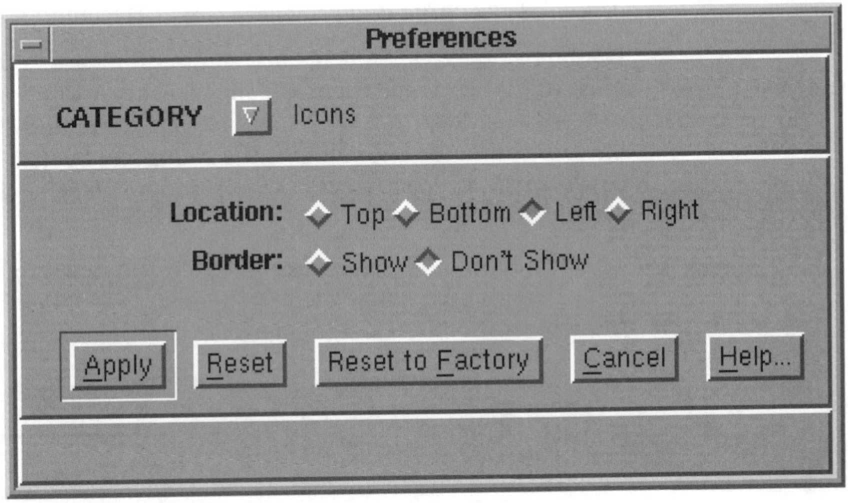

FIGURE 5.8  OSF/Motif PushButton

The user can choose a command button by clicking the mouse while the pointer is over the button. The command button changes its appearance during the click, as soon as the mouse button is pressed. The button appears pushed in. In some GUIs, a change in color may also be observed. If the pointer is dragged to another location, the command button returns to its original state. The action associated with the command button is performed only when the mouse is released while the pointer is positioned over the button.

Many of the GUIs identify specific types of command buttons. The types of command buttons correspond either to a kind of command the button represents, or to an interaction technique the button will accept. The following are examples of Microsoft Windows command buttons (see Figure 5.9):

- Command buttons that initiate the action described by the text contained in the command buttons (e.g., **Open**, **Print**, **Remove**, and **Stop**).

- Command buttons that close one dialog box and open a related one. These buttons are often referred to as *GoTo* command buttons.

- Command buttons that open a related dialog box on top of the current dialog box without closing the current dialog box. These buttons are often referred to as *GoSub* command buttons. The ellipsis character (. . .) follows the command button text. It indicates that a dialog box will appear, prompting the user for additional information.

- Unfold command buttons that expand the dialog box to include additional options. The chevron symbol (>>) following the command button text distinguishes it from other controls.

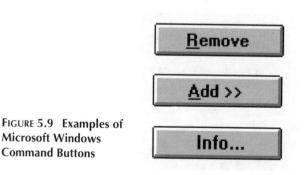

FIGURE 5.9 **Examples of Microsoft Windows Command Buttons**

Macintosh refers to the command button as a *button*. Macintosh includes a special kind of button called the *default button*. "The default button represents the action that the user is most likely to perform if that action is not potentially dangerous" [MHIG, p. 206]. The default button is distinguished from other buttons by the presence of an additional border around the button. The extra border has a line weight of three pixels and is separated from the normal border by a one-pixel white space. The default button can be activated by clicking the mouse while the pointer is over the button or pressing the Enter or Return key of the keyboard.

NeXTSTEP refers to the command button as a *button* or an *action button*. An action button is a one-state button that performs a single task such as canceling a dialog box (i.e., closing a dialog box without carrying out the associated command). It varies in size and may contain a text and/or graphics label. An example of an action button containing both a text and graphics label is the *default action button*. This button contains text with a Return (Enter) symbol beside it. The arrow indicates that pressing the Return key on the keyboard has the same effect as pushing the button. Figure 5.10 illustrates a NeXTSTEP default action button.

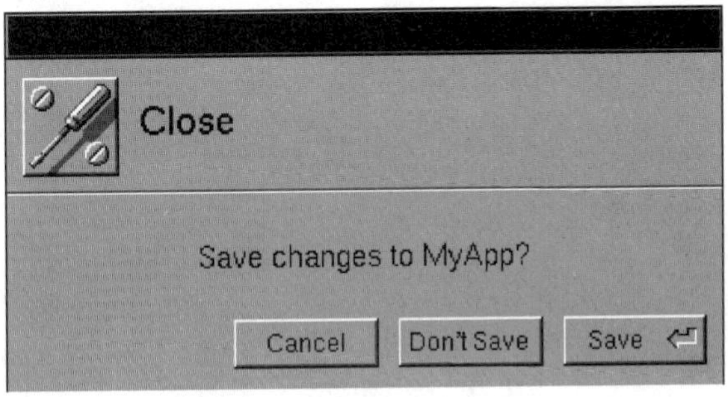

**FIGURE 5.10  NeXTSTEP Default Action Button**

### Design Tips

Although the term *push button* is commonly used, the term *command button* is preferable, because this type of control is generally used to initiate an action or routing choice. Placement of command buttons within a dialog box should be designed carefully, so that the appearance of the dialog box is visually and aesthetically pleasing. The label for the command button should indicate briefly what action it causes the application to take.

## 5.5 Container

A *container* is a control that holds other objects. "It allows the user to group and view objects in ways that are not provided by the system-provided containers" [IBM CUA, p. 51]. Figure 5.11 shows an example of a Presentation Manager container.

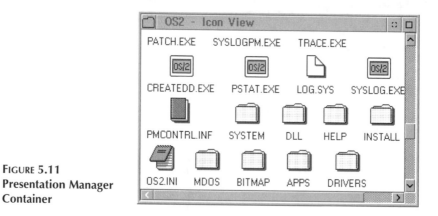

**FIGURE 5.11
Presentation Manager
Container**

As more user interfaces move toward an object-oriented approach, this control will become increasingly supported. Microsoft Windows implements a file folder container that resembles a folder for presenting a multipage dialog box. Figure 5.12 is an example of a Microsoft Windows file folder container.

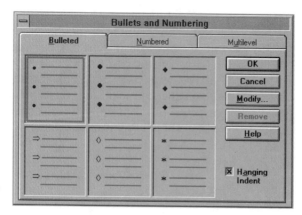

**FIGURE 5.12 Example
of a Microsoft Windows
File Folder Container**

## 5.6 Drop-Down Combination Box

A *drop-down combination box* is a control that combines the functions of a text box and a drop-down list. The list of choices is hidden until the user takes the action to make it visible. The user has the option to scroll through and select from a list of choices in the drop-down list or type the text directly into the entry field. The text does not have to match one of the choices contained in the list. Figure 5.13 shows an example of a drop-down combination box.

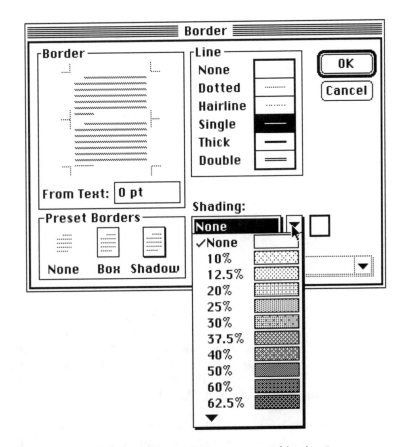

FIGURE 5.13  Example of a Macintosh Drop-Down Combination Box

The current value is displayed in the text box. When the user clicks the drop-down arrow button, the list portion of the drop-down combo box is opened. A vertical scroll bar is provided to allow the user to view the choices that are not visible.

Only Presentation Manager and Microsoft Windows support this control. The appearance and behavior of this control are similar between these GUIs. The Macintosh Toolbox does not support this control. Hence, the appearance and behavior of this control vary from application to application. Some Macintosh applications that support this control use a small arrowhead pointing downward to indicate that there are more items on the list.

### Design Tips

When presentation space is a concern, the application designer should use a drop-down combination box instead of a combination box. A drop-down combination box should be used when the user will more frequently complete an entry field by typing in the text, rather than selecting the entry field text from a list. The choices should be displayed alphabetically or in an order that is meaningful to the user. A minimum of six choices should be displayed at a time.

Because the support of the drop-down combination box is limited to a few GUIs, the application designer should carefully evaluate and design the "look and feel" of this control for his or her application.

## 5.7 Drop-Down List Box

A *drop-down list box* is a control similar to a list box (single-selection list box) in that it is used to display a list of choices or objects for the user. Unlike a list box, it displays the current choice item from the list of choices. A drop-down arrow button abuts the end of the associated drop-down list box. The list extends downward to display additional entries when the user clicks the drop-down arrow button.

When the user clicks on the drop-down arrow button, the drop-down list box displays the other choices in the list. The item initially displayed is highlighted. As the user drags the selection highlight, the selection highlight moves up or down. The item where the selection highlight is located at the time the mouse button is released is selected. If more than eight items are contained in a drop-down list box, a vertical scroll bar is used. Figure 5.14 illustrates a Microsoft Windows open and closed drop-down list box.

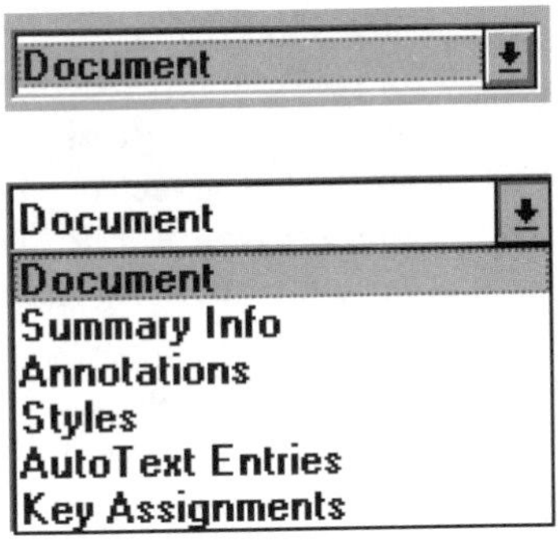

FIGURE 5.14  Microsoft
Windows Closed and
Open Drop-Down List
Boxes

A drop-down list box is sometimes called a *drop-down single-selection list box* or *drop-down list*. OSF/Motif calls this control an *OptionButton*. An OptionButton is used to display an OptionMenu, as illustrated in Figure 5.15. It is composed of a button, with either a text or graphics label. The button is represented as a three-dimensional square box with an arrow pointing downward.

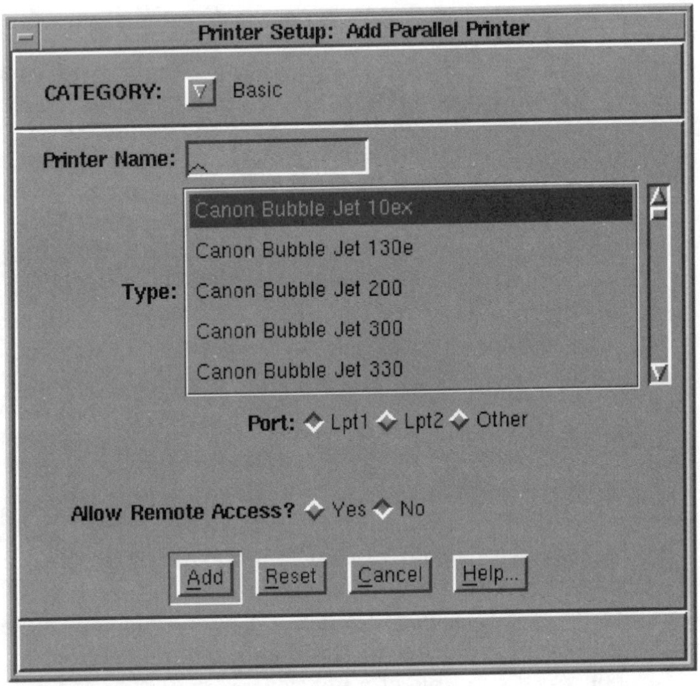

FIGURE 5.15  OSF/Motif OptionButton

The *Macintosh Human Interface Guidelines* refers to drop-down list boxes as *pop-up menus*. A pop-up menu usually has a title that appears to the left of the current selection. The current selection appears within a rectangle that has a one-pixel-wide drop shadow on the bottom and right side. When the user positions the pointer within the rectangle and then holds down the mouse button, the rectangle expands either up, down, or in both directions to reveal other options. The current selection is usually accompanied within the rectangle by a downward-pointing black triangle that helps the user recognize this component as a drop-down list box.

NeXTSTEP supports two button-list controls that can be considered drop-down list boxes—the *pop-up list* and *pull-down list*. They look similar, but have different functions. A pop-up list may be used in place of a radio button. A control button that can be recognized by the rectangular symbol (□) appears to the right of the pop-up list. When the user presses the button, items in the pop-up list are displayed.

A pull-down list is used to initiate actions rather than set a state. In this respect, it is like a menu. A downward-pointing triangle appears at the far right of the label. The label of a pull-down list never changes.

### Design Tips

A drop-down list box is a very useful control that may be used instead of a standard list box when the presentation space is limited. The application designer should create a visually distinctive appearance for this control. For example, the drop-down list box should be easily distinguished from a combination box. The application designer should consider the appearance and behavior of a drop-down list box as implemented by Microsoft Windows. Lastly, the choices displayed in the drop-down list box should be arranged alphabetically or according to the user-predicted response.

## 5.8 List Box (Selection List or Scrolling List)

A *list box* is a control that displays a list of choices or objects for the user. The list of choices or objects can be text or graphics. A list box can be scrollable or nonscrollable. A scroll bar is provided especially when all the information in the list box is not visible at once. Figure 5.16 shows an example of a list box.

**FIGURE 5.16  Microsoft Windows List Box**

With the exception of NeXTSTEP, the scroll bar appears on the right. The scroll arrow or scroll box can be used to move up or down the list. The selected item is highlighted. The selection highlight moves up or down as the user scrolls the list. Most of the GUIs disable scrolling by dimming the scroll bar when all the information is visible or the list is inactive.

The list box allows one or multiple items to be selected from the list. If only one item can be selected from the list, the items in the list are functionally similar to radio buttons or option buttons. A list box should be used when the set of choices consists of more than four or five items and space is scarce. If the list box allows multiple items to be selected at the same time, the user may add items to the current selection by holding down a control key while selecting each additional item. In most GUIs, the active list box is distinguishable by the presence of a bold, or double, outline.

Macintosh refers to a list box as a *scrolling list*. Macintosh makes no distinction between single and multiple-selection list boxes. To make multiple selections, the user holds down the SHIFT key and clicks on additional items in the list.

In OSF/Motif, a list box is simply referred to as a *List*. "The List elements can be selected using either the single selection model, the browse selection model, the multiple selection model, or the discontiguous selection model. This control can optionally have vertical and horizontal scroll bars, which show different views of the List elements" [OSF/Motif, p. 9-64].

NeXTSTEP refers to this control as a *browser* or a *selection list*. In addition to the interaction technique described earlier for selecting an item, NeXTSTEP allows an item in the list to be selected by typing the name of the item into an associated text field. This makes the selection list behave more like a combo box. Figure 5.17 illustrates the NeXTSTEP browsers and selection lists.

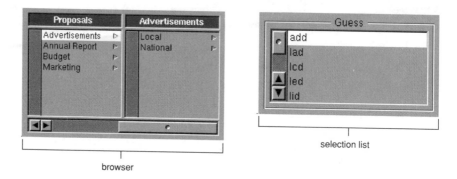

FIGURE 5.17   NeXTSTEP Browser and Selection List

Microsoft Windows distinguishes the different kinds of list boxes. A list box can either be a *standard single-selection list box, drop-down list box,* or an *extended-selection* and *multiple-selection list box.* Microsoft Windows recommends that the scroll arrows be dimmed, the scroll box be removed, and the scroll bar shaft be changed to the background color of the dialog box when scrolling is not possible. Microsoft Windows also suggests that " . . . when the list contains an item that is too wide for the list, a horizontal scroll bar may be optionally placed at the bottom of the list" [MICROSOFT, p. 109]. When space is limited, a standard list box may be replaced by a drop-down list box.

### Design Tips

The use of a list box in a dialog box should be evaluated carefully. A list box should be used when the set of choices consists of more than four or five items. If space is not at a premium, radio buttons or option buttons should be used because they provide easier access to the information. The approach used by Microsoft Windows to differentiate scrollable from nonscrollable, and active from inactive list boxes should be followed.

Although not universally implemented among GUIs, the *multiple-selection list box* should be considered as a useful component. A multiple-selection list box allows the user to select more than one noncontiguous entry at a time. It should be visually distinguishable from the standard single-selection list box.

## **5.9**  **Maximize Button**

The *maximize button* allows the user to directly manipulate a window so that it enlarges to its maximum size. In some cases, the maximize button may expand a window to fill the entire display space. The maximize button is usually located at the right side of the title bar. It is usually represented as a large, box-shaped button or an up-arrow. Figure 5.18 shows an example of a maximize button.

**FIGURE 5.18  Microsoft Windows Maximize Button**

In some GUIs, such as Presentation Manager and Microsoft Windows, a restore button is provided that returns the maximized window to its previous size and position. The restore button replaces the maximize button when the user clicks the maximize button. The maximize button replaces the restore button when the user clicks on the restore button. The user can also maximize a window by using the **Maximize** option from the control (system) menu, which is located on the leftmost side of the title bar.

OSF/Motif, Presentation Manager, and Microsoft Windows have similar interaction techniques for maximizing a window using direct manipulation. These GUIs also provide similar menu options for maximizing a window. Microsoft Windows provides another direct manipulation technique for maximizing a window; that is, double-clicking on the title bar.

In Macintosh, the *zoom box* (shown in Figure 5.19) allows the user to switch between two window sizes and positions: the window size and location established by the user (*user state*), and the window size and location defined by the application (*standard state*). "Using the zoom box, the user can quickly manipulate windows to have access to other icons or windows, or to look at a document in a larger size or different location. The user must drag or resize a window at least seven pixels to cause a change in the user state" [MHIG, p. 168].

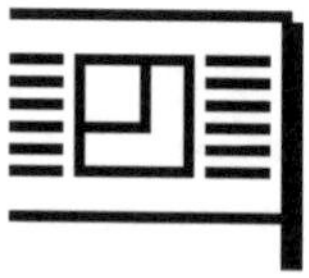

**FIGURE 5.19   Macintosh Zoom Box**

### Design Tips

In designing applications, the designer should provide a maximize button on the title bar when the size of the window can be changed and the window is not currently maximized. The designer should save the state (i.e., the size and position) of the window before maximizing the window. If a restore button is provided, the maximize button should be changed to a restore button when the window is currently maximized.

## 5.10  Minimize Button

The *minimize button* allows the user to directly manipulate a window so that it becomes as small as possible. In some cases, minimizing a windows may reduce a window to an icon located at the bottom of the desktop. The minimize button is usually located at the right side of the title bar, to the left of the maximize button. It is usually represented as a small, box-shaped button, or a down-arrow. Figure 5.20 shows an example of a minimize button.

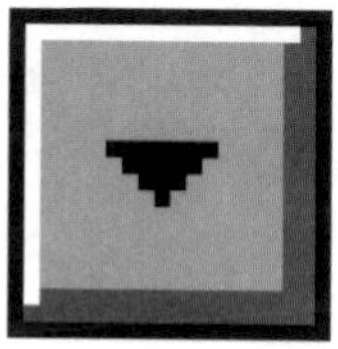

**FIGURE 5.20   Microsoft Windows Minimize Button**

Minimizing a window allows the user to view more than one window at a time. A window can be minimized by clicking on the minimize button located on the title bar of most windows. While minimized, the window is open and continues to run. The user can move the minimized window around the desktop. Double-clicking on the minimized window or icon causes the window to be restored to its original size and location.

Typically, only application windows can be minimized. When minimized, all associated windows, including floating palettes and toolbars, are hidden. Some GUIs, such as the Microsoft Windows MDI, allow document windows to be minimized as well.

In NeXTSTEP, the minimize button is referred to as a *miniaturize button*. It is located at the left side of the title bar. Clicking on the miniaturize button of a window causes the window to be reduced to a small icon called a *miniwindow*. Even while miniaturized, the window is still active; any changes will be applied when the window is restored. Miniaturized windows will not "snap" into the Application Dock icon or into a directory window.

In Presentation Manager, the title of a minimized window is placed in the **Window List**. Depending on the window setting, the icon for the minimized window is placed in either the Minimized Window Viewer or on the desktop.

Some windows have a *hide button*, instead of a minimize button. Hiding a window is similar to minimizing a window with the exception that objects for the hidden window are not placed in the Minimized Window Viewer or on the desktop. However, the titles of hidden windows are placed in the **Window List**.

### Design Tips

The designer should provide a minimize button on the title bar to distinguish it from a maximize button. The designer should save the state of the window (i.e., the size and position), along with the state of each of its associated windows, before minimizing the window. In minimizing a window that has not been previously minimized, place the minimized window visual or icon near the bottom of the desktop. In minimizing a window that has been previously minimized, place the minimized window visual where it had been before being restored previously.

## 5.11  Multimedia Controls

*Multimedia controls* allow the user to play back, record, copy, edit, and mix multimedia data types such as sound, digital video, and music. Multimedia controls make entry-level multimedia applications easy to use. Figure 5.21 shows a dialog box containing various OS/2 multimedia controls for playing back digital video.

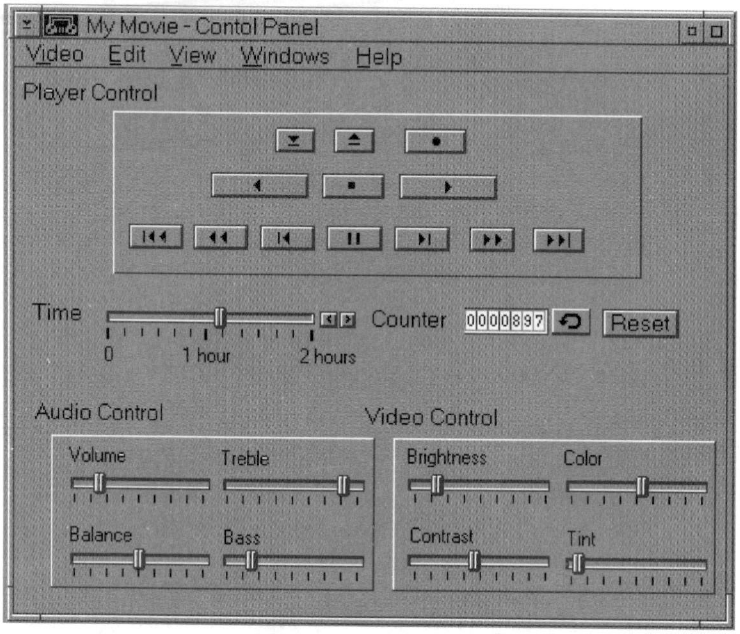

FIGURE 5.21   OS/2 Multimedia Controls

Multimedia controls vary from GUI to GUI, and from application to application. However, the controls implemented closely resemble the actual controls found in the audio/visual devices such as a tape recorder and video recorder. Table 5.1 lists the multimedia controls commonly used by the GUIs in the comparison that support multimedia capabilities.

TABLE 5.1  **Multimedia Controls**

| Icon | Multimedia Control | Description |
|------|--------------------|-------------|
| ■ | Stop | Suspends all action |
| ⏮ | Rewind | Go to the beginning of the track. Clicking and holding down this button achieves a controllable fast-reverse function. |
| ⏪ | Back Step | Step backward through the current media sequence by a specific increment (usually 10 percent increments) |
| ▶ | Play | Plays the current track. If the file is newly loaded or rewound, playing starts at the beginning. |
| ⏭ | Forward | Go to the next track. Clicking and holding down this button achieves a controllable fast-forward function. |
| ⏩ | Forward Step | Opposite of Back Step. Step forward through the current media sequence by a specific increment (usually 10 percent increments) |
| ❚❚ | Pause | Toggles between stopped and playing |
| ● | Record | Used for recording |
| ⏏ | Eject | Eject currently loaded media electronically |

## 5.12  Notebook

A *notebook* is "a control that resembles a bound notebook that contains pages separated into sections by tabbed divider-pages. It allows the user to turn the pages of the notebook and to move from one selection to another" [IBM CUA, p. 163]. Figure 5.22 shows an example of a notebook control.

FIGURE 5.22  Presentation
Manager Notebook

The notebook control presents data that can be organized logically into groups. The label for a tabbed-divider page can be text, graphics, or a combination of both. Page numbers are used within the section if a section has more than one page.

Only Presentation Manager supports this control at this time. As the various GUIs move to object-oriented user interfaces, however, the notebook control will become more prevalent.

## 5.13  Radio Button (Option Button)

A *radio button* represents a single choice in a limited set of mutually exclusive choices. It is typically used for setting states or modes. Radio buttons can be arranged in a row or column. They may be grouped, and usually contain a descriptive label. Only one option in a group can be selected.

A radio button is generally represented as a circle with text beside it. The user selects a radio button choice by clicking the mouse while the pointer is over the button or its label. The circle becomes partially filled with a smaller, concentric, solid-black circle when a choice is selected. Some GUIs allow double-clicking on a radio button for selecting the button, and choosing the default command button in the dialog box, thus closing the dialog box. Figure 5.23 shows an example of radio buttons.

**FIGURE 5.23   Radio Buttons**

In OSF/Motif, a radio button is a special ToggleButton. It is usually a filled diamond to indicate the on state, and an empty diamond to indicate the off state. Figure 5.24 shows an example of OSF/Motif radio buttons.

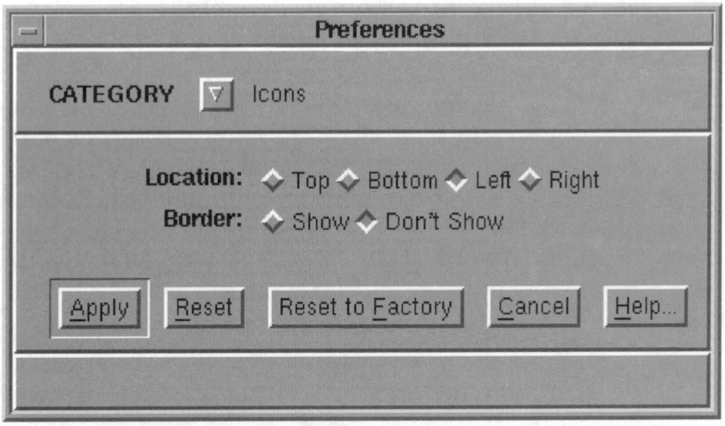

**FIGURE 5.24   OSF/Motif Radio Buttons**

Radio buttons are useful when the user needs to select only one mutually exclusive choice. If the number of radio buttons exceeds four, the buttons can be replaced by a list box or drop-down list to save space. However, if space is not at a premium, radio buttons provide easier access to choices.

NeXTSTEP also refers to this control as *standard two-state buttons* or, simply, *buttons*. Standard two-state buttons include switches and radio buttons. Figure 5.25 illustrates the types of radio buttons, standard radio buttons, and graphical radio buttons. When the button is clicked (or pressed), of the button can appear pushed in, highlighted, or both.

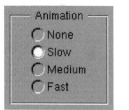

graphical radio buttons

**FIGURE 5.25   NeXTSTEP
Radio Buttons**          standard radio buttons

In Microsoft Windows, "a group of option buttons may be used to choose among a fixed set of attributes for a selection. Whenever the user makes a new selection, the option button group should indicate which attribute currently applies to the selection; that is, the option button corresponding to the current attribute should be filled, and the other option buttons should be empty. If the current option is heterogeneous with respect to the set of attributes (that is, if more than one attribute is represented in the selection), all the option buttons in the group should be empty. Choosing any button applies the associated attribute to the entire selection" [MICROSOFT, p. 105].

### Design Tips

Although the term *radio button* is commonly used, the term *exclusive setting control* best describes the function of this control. The label for the radio button should state succinctly what choices are available. Radio buttons should support both implicit and mnemonic selections.

## 5.14 Restore Button

The *restore button* is a visual component of a window that returns the window from its maximum or minimum size to its previous intermediate size. It is usually located on the right side of the title bar. Figure 5.26 shows an example of a Microsoft Windows restore button. The restore button is easily recognizable as it combines the appearance of the maximize and minimize buttons.

**FIGURE 5.26  Microsoft Windows Restore Button**

The GUIs in the comparison do not support a restore button except Microsoft Windows and Presentation Manager. Existing controls, such as a maximize button, are used to return the window to its previous size and location. In most GUIs, restoring a window to its previous size and location can be accomplished using the **Restore** option from the **File** menu of the menu bar.

In OSF/Motif, there is no actual restore button. Instead, the maximize button is a toggle control that can invoke the restore function. Clicking on the maximize button of a maximized window restores the window to its size and location before being maximized.

In Presentation Manager and Microsoft Windows, a restore button is provided that returns the window to its previous size and position before it was maximized or minimized. When a window is maximized or minimized, the restore button replaces the maximize button (if maximized) or the minimize button (if minimized). The maximize or minimize button replaces the restore button when the user clicks on the restore button.

### Design Tips

Consider changing the maximize or minimize button to a restore button in the title bar when the size of a window can be changed and the window has been maximized or minimized. Change the restore button to a maximize or minimize button after a window has been restored to a state other than maximized or minimized.

## 5.15  Scroll Bar

A *scroll bar* allows a user to view hidden parts of displays when a display is too large for all of it to be visible simultaneously in a window. A scroll bar is also known as a *scroller* (NeXTSTEP).

The scroll bar is composed of the following:

- *Scroll Arrows* are arrow-shaped icons or symbols, which usually appear at the end of the scroll bar. The arrow points in the opposite direction away from the center of the scroll bar. The scroll arrows are referred to as *scroll arrows* (Macintosh and Microsoft Windows), *scroll buttons* (NeXTSTEP and Presentation Manager), or *arrow buttons* (OSF/Motif). The arrows can appear together within a button on a scroll bar.

- *Scroll Bar Shaft* is a rectangular container that provides the range of motion for the scroll box. The scroll bar shaft is also called a *gray area* (Macintosh) or *trough* (OSF/Motif).

- *Scroll Box* is a part of the scroll bar that when dragged causes the scrolling to occur in the direction of the movement. The view of the contents of the display shifts in proportion to the relative distance the scroll box moves. The relative position of the scroll box indicates how much scrolling is available in either direction. The scroll box is referred to as *scroll box* (Macintosh, Presentation Manager, and Microsoft Windows), or *slider* (OSF/Motif).

Figure 5.27 shows an example of Macintosh scroll bar.

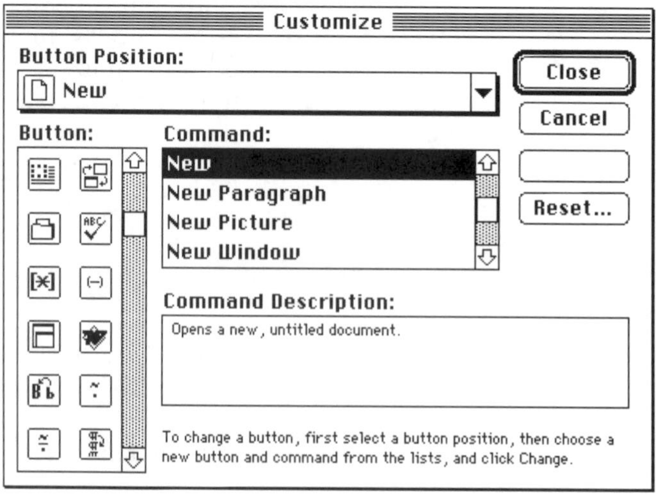

**FIGURE 5.27**
**Macintosh**
**Scroll Bar**

Figure 5.28 shows an example of an OSF/Motif scroll bar. Note that the slider indicates the proportion of the total display contents shown in the scrollable window.

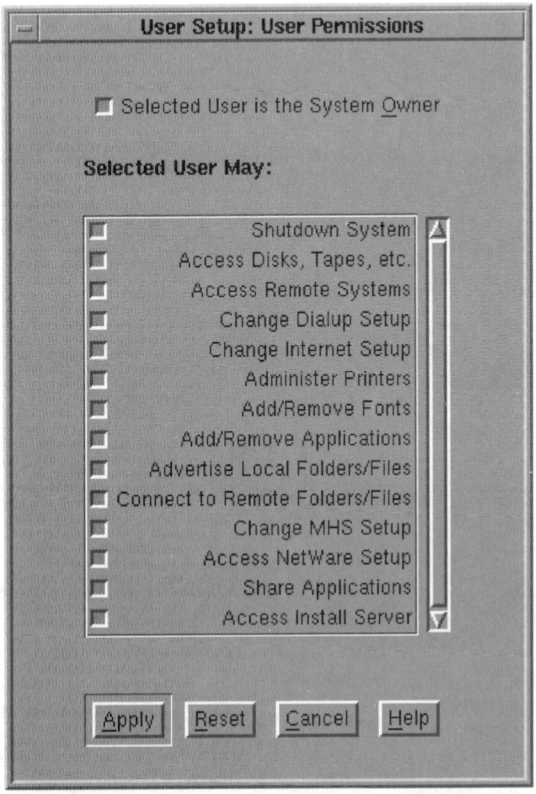

**FIGURE 5.28 OSF/Motif Scroll Bar**

A window can have a vertical scroll bar, horizontal scroll bar, or both. In most GUIs, a scroll bar is not displayed if the window is nonscrollable. In Macintosh, if the contents of a window are no larger than the window, the scroll bars are inactive. The scroll bar appears with an outline border, with no gray area, and a scroll box. The scroll arrows are hollow outlines.

A scroll bar can be displayed on both an active and inactive window. Most GUIs do not distinguish the appearance of a scroll bar between an active and inactive window. In Macintosh, if the document window is inactive, the elements of the scroll bar are not shown at all.

Only the outline of the scroll bar as a whole appears. Figure 5.29 shows an active document window with an inactive scroll bar and an inactive window with an inactive scroll bar.

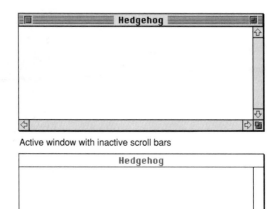

Active window with inactive scroll bars

**FIGURE 5.29  Macintosh
Active and Inactive
Scroll Bars**

Inactive window with inactive scroll bars

Scroll bars can be manipulated by dragging the scroll box, pointing and clicking on the scroll arrow, or pointing and clicking in the space between the arrow and the scroll box.

When the user drags the scroll box up or down the scroll bar shaft, a gray ghost or dotted outline of the scroll box appears and moves with the pointer until the user releases the mouse button. At the release of the mouse button, the gray ghost or dotted outline disappears. The scrolling is complete. The view of the contents of the window is displayed relative to the position of the scroll box. When the user clicks on a scroll arrow, the window scrolls in the direction in which the arrow points. The view of the contents of the display shifts in proportion to the relative distance the scroll bar handle moves. Clicking on the scroll bar above or below (in the case of a horizontal scroll bar), or to the right or left (in the case of a vertical scroll bar), of the scroll box causes the view of the contents of the display to shift in the direction of the closest scroll bar arrow.

When a window is split horizontally, each window pane has its own vertical scroll bar perpendicular to the split bar. However, there is only one horizontal scroll bar which is shared by both window panes. Similarly, when a window is split vertically, each window pane has its own horizontal scroll bar. However, there is only one vertical scroll bar which is shared by both window panes.

There are four scroll bars when the screen is divided into four panes. The upper two panes can be scrolled vertically using the upper-right scroll bar, and the lower two panes can be scrolled vertically using the lower-right scroll bar. The left two panes can be scrolled horizontally using the scroll bar at the lower left; similarly, the right two panes can be scrolled using the scroll bar at the lower right.

### Design Tips

Provide a scroll bar if the information is not fully visible within a particular window in a particular direction. Provide a scroll bar along the dimension in which more information is available. Continuous display of scroll bars should be supported. The application designer should consider a distinguishing appearance between active and inactive scroll bars. Sufficient contrast is important for ease of use. Allocating space for scroll bars at all times produces a visually consistent view within each window.

## 5.16 Size Control

*Size controls* are parts of the window that allow the user to change the size of the window. Resizing affects the width and height of a window. The window frame contains resize borders, one at each corner, and one at the midpoint of each side of the window. Figure 5.30 shows an example of a resize border.

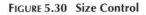

FIGURE 5.30 **Size Control**

To change the height of a window, the user drags the horizontal parts of the frame. To change the width of a window, the user drags the vertical parts of the frame. To change both the height and width of the window, the user selects and drags one of the corners of the window frame diagonally. The pointer changes in appearance (for example, to a bi-directional arrow or a hand pointer) when it is positioned over the window frame. The user drags the edge or corner of the window frame to a desired position. As the user drags, a gray ghost or dotted outline of the window frame appears and moves with the pointer until the user releases the mouse button. At the release of the mouse button, the window assumes the new size.

The GUIs in the comparison, except for Macintosh and NeXT-STEP, provide resize borders for changing the size of the window. Resizing in the Macintosh and NeXTSTEP is done through the *size box* and *resize bar*, respectively. OSF/Motif, Presentation Manager, and Microsoft Windows have similar interaction techniques for resizing a window using direct manipulation. These GUIs also provide similar menu options for resizing a window.

In Macintosh, the application determines the minimum and maximum size of the window. The size of the window is based on the physical size of the display. Unlike other GUIs in the comparison, the user can change the size of the window only by using the size box. "The size box is located in the lower-right corner of the window, if a window has one. When the user drags the size box, a dotted outline of the window moves with the pointer. The upper-left corner of the window remains in the same place. It acts like an anchor on the screen; the window shrinks or grows from that point. The outline of the lower-right corner of the window follows the pointer. When the user releases the mouse button, the window is drawn in the shape of the dotted outline" [MHIG, pp. 156–157].

In NeXTSTEP, the resize bar as shown in Figure 5.31 is used to change the size of the window. It is a narrow strip located at the bottom of a window. The resize bar is divided into three regions: a large middle region and two smaller end regions. To change the height of the window, the user drags vertically from the middle region of the bar. To change the width of the window, the user drags horizontally from either end region of the bar. To change both height and width of the window, the user drags diagonally from an end region. As the resize bar is dragged, an outline of the window follows the pointer. No special pointer appears to indicate the resize mode.

FIGURE 5.31   NeXTSTEP Resize Bar

In OSF/Motif, a digital readout appears outside the pointer as the window is being resized, showing the window size in pixels. The change in appearance of the pointer, as well as showing the window size in pixels, provides effective feedback to the user.

In Microsoft Windows, pressing the Escape (Esc) key while dragging one of the resize borders to a new location terminates the resize operation. Also, the user can decrease the size of the window to the point at which there is insufficient space to display all window components. In this case, a scroll bar appears and the menu bar wraps to display all selections.

### Design Tips

In resizing a window, the application designer should provide the following visual cues:

- Bi-directional arrow pointer or hand pointer to indicate that the resizing will take place

- Gray ghost or dotted outline window frame to show the new size of the window

- Digital readout outside the pointer showing the window size in pixels

Visual effects, such as animation, provide an effective feedback for resizing a window using direct manipulation. However, it should be used sparingly.

## 5.17 Slider

A *slider* is a dialog box control for displaying and changing a current value relative to the range of possible values. A slider consists of a *bar* or *shaft*, *handle* or *slider arm*, and *slider buttons* (as illustrated in Figure 5.32). The bar appears in a horizontal or vertical track that is represented as a scale to indicate the range of values. The handle is a visual indicator in the slider that the user can move to change the value. The slider buttons are used to move the slider arm one increment in a particular direction, as indicated by the directional arrow on the buttons. Optionally, a slider label may appear, often above or to the left of a horizontal slider, to identify its contents.

FIGURE 5.32  Sliders

Sliders share the same basic interaction techniques across GUIs. The user can move the handle by dragging it with the mouse. In some GUIs (e.g., Macintosh), the handle can be moved along the appropriate direction, even when the mouse pointer is not within the handle, after the mouse button is depressed. However, in other GUIs (e.g., Microsoft Windows), the handle will not respond to movements of the mouse (while the mouse button remains pressed), but it jumps to a new location when the pointer again enters the track of the slider. When the user releases the mouse button, the handle no longer responds to the mouse movement. Usually there is no visual cue signifying that the handle is in an "armed," or movable, state. If an editable text box appears near the slider, the user can enter a value into the text box, and the handle will jump to the appropriate location in the slider.

OSF/Motif calls this control a *scale*. A scale consists of a ". . . slider that moves within an element that indicates the size of the range, called the trough, and a Label that indicates the current value" [OSF/Motif, p. 9-111]. The relative position of the slider indicates the value of the variable in question.

The *IBM CUA Guide to User Interface Design* defines a slider "as an analog representation of a value" [IBM CUA, p. 54]. Figure 5.33 illustrates the different components of a slider—slider arm, slider shaft, and, optionally, detents, a scale, and slider buttons. The guide suggests that if a scale is displayed, the user should be allowed to change the units of measure that the scale represents.

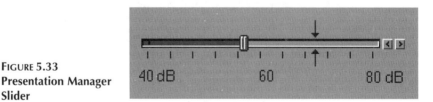

**FIGURE 5.33**
**Presentation Manager**
**Slider**

In NeXTSTEP, a slider consists of a horizontal or vertical *bar* and a *knob* that moves on the bar as illustrated in Figure 5.34. The position of the knob in the slider indicates its current value [NeXTSTEP, p. 145]. The user can change the position of the knob, and thus alter the value, by aligning a linear mark on the knob with marks or values shown along the side of the bar representing the range, or by changing the alphanumeric value in an accompanying display located near the bar.

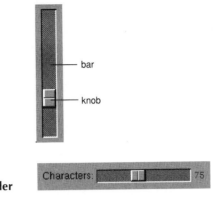

**FIGURE 5.34**
**NeXTSTEP Slider**

## 5.18 Spin Box

A *spin box* is a control that accepts only a limited set of discrete, ordered input values. A spin box consists of a text box with a pair of opposite arrows arranged vertically and attached to the right side of the text box. A spin box is based on the spin lock or tumbler lock metaphor. A spin box is also known as a *spin button* (Presentation Manager), *arrow* (OSF/Motif), or *little arrows* (Macintosh). Figure 5.35 shows an example of a spin box.

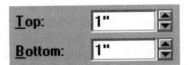

**FIGURE 5.35   Spin Box**

The user can change the displayed value by typing a new value into the text box, or by clicking the mouse while the pointer is positioned over the Up Arrow to increase the value, or over the Down Arrow to decrease the value. The value can be changed in increments of one. The arrows function like a scroll bar, except for the items being hidden. Usually, reverse-video highlighting is used to indicate that the control is in a selected state.

NeXTSTEP does not have a control specifically referred to as a spin box or button. However, it supports a miscellaneous action represented as adjacent arrows pointing in opposite directions.

### Design Tips

The term *discrete value selector* best describes the function of this control. This control should be used to display a list of choices that have a logical consecutive order such as months of the year. Otherwise, a drop-down list or combination box should be used. In designing applications using this control, the application designer should consider whether all possible values can be in the list. When all possible values are in the list of choices, the spin button field should be a read-only field. Otherwise, this control should be designed as an entry field as well.

## 5.19 Split Box

A *split box* is a solid box-shaped component located at the top of the vertical scroll bar and at the left end of the horizontal scroll bar beyond the tip of the scroll arrow. A split box enables a user to divide the screen into different viewing regions. Figure 5.36 shows a split window, with the split box located between the two vertical scroll bars. A split bar is a bar-shaped control that is used to determine where a window will be split by separating the window panes.

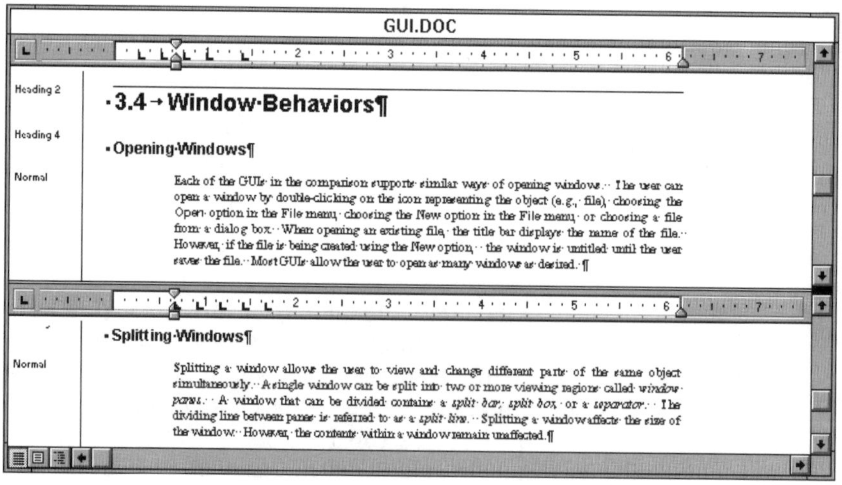

FIGURE 5.36  Microsoft Windows Split Box

Dragging or double-clicking on the split box separates a window into panes (as shown in Figure 5.36). The pointer changes to a split pointer when the pointer is positioned over the split box. The user can drag anywhere on the split box or split bar to adjust and split the window. When the mouse button is released, the window is split into window panes. After splitting the window, the split bar can be used to change the relative size of the window panes.

In OSF/Motif, primary windows can be divided into panes. The border between panes is called a *separator,* and there is a *sash* (handle) on each separator for adjusting the size of panes. Dragging a sash away from one pane toward the adjoining pane causes the former to enlarge while the latter contracts equally.

### Design Tips

The terms *split box* and *split bar* are more widely accepted than *separator* and *sash*, and, thus, should be used to describe these components. The appearance of the split box should convey a meaningful and recognizable metaphor. In designing applications, allow the user to split the window multiple times both vertically and horizontally. Distinguish and separate the window panes with horizontal and vertical split bars.

## 5.20 Text Box (Text Field)

A text box is a two-part control consisting of text and a rectangular box into which the user can type information. This control is sometimes called a *text field* or *text entry field*. OSF/Motif refers to it as simply *text*. Most of the GUIs call the text contained within a text box an *entry field*. In Macintosh, this field is referred to as an *editable text field*.

Generally, the text box limits the entry to one line. However, applications may also use multiple line text boxes, such as in the case of a comment box. The length of the text box is usually equal to the average amount of text that will be entered into the field. In the case of multiple entry-line text boxes, GUIs in the comparison provide scroll bars so the user can see any text that exceeds the size of the text box.

Figure 5.37 shows examples of single and multiple text boxes.

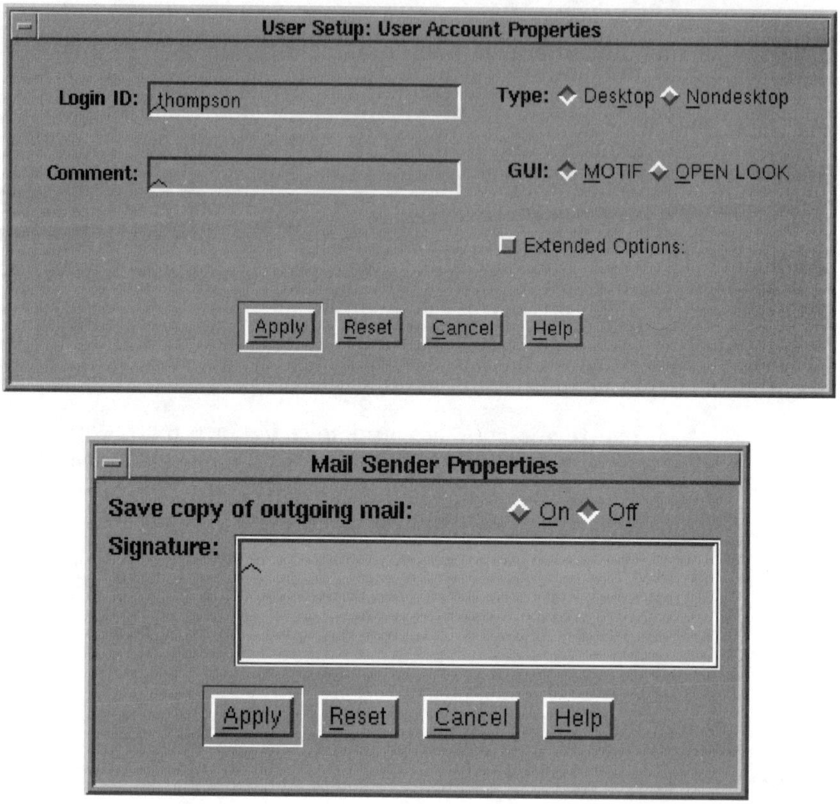

FIGURE 5.37   **OSF/Motif Single and Multiple Text Boxes**

When the text box is first displayed, it is either blank or contains an initial value. If an initial value is displayed, the entire content area is highlighted. The user can accept the current text, edit it, delete it, or replace it. The text in the text box is activated in the following ways:

- When the user clicks the mouse while the pointer is over the text box, the highlighting of the content area is removed. The insertion point is placed within the text box where the pointer was positioned when the mouse-click occurred.

- When the user types the first character, the initial value is automatically deleted. The user can type the information required.

- Pressing the Left and Right Arrow moves the insertion point within the text in a text box. The insertion point is placed at the beginning or end of the text by using an accelerator key, such as Control + Left Arrow. At this time, the user can edit the text.

- Pressing the Tab key activates the next control in a predetermined sequence, thus accepting the value in the text box.

Microsoft Windows suggests that "in multi-line text boxes, data that is too long for one line may either wrap to the next line or extend beyond the right boundary of the text box. Both single-line and multi-line text boxes should support automatic keyboard and mouse scrolling to allow hidden data to be brought into view" [MICROSOFT, p. 114]. Microsoft Windows further suggests that a text box should be dimmed if it is inactive.

NeXTSTEP recommends that "the text field (or text box) have a white background and be surrounded by a beveled border that makes it appear inset from the surface of the screen. When the text field is temporarily disabled, the text becomes gray (just like the label of a button), but the background color does not change" [NeXTSTEP, p. 143]. Like Microsoft Windows, NeXTSTEP supports distinguishing between active (editable or selectable) and inactive text fields by changing the background to gray with no beveled border.

### Design Tips

Although the term *text field* is most commonly used, the term *text box* more accurately describes this control. A text box should have distinguishing features to differentiate it readily from other types of controls. For single-line and multi-line text boxes, line wrapping or scroll bars should be supported so the user can see any text that exceeds the size of the text box. Lastly, active (editable or selectable) text boxes should be highly distinguishable from inactive text boxes. An approach similar to the one implemented by Microsoft Windows or NeXTSTEP should be followed.

## 5.21 Toolbar

A toolbar is a collection of buttons that provides quick and convenient access to many choices and commands that are frequently used within an application. They may occupy a fixed position within the application window, or may be placed in a supplemental window or dialog box.

Figure 5.38 shows an example of a toolbar for a word processing application. The icons represent the choices and commands available from the menu bar.

**FIGURE 5.38   Microsoft Word for Windows Toolbar**

Toolbars are usually movable and resizable. The user can move the toolbar to the left or right edge of the screen, or to the top or bottom of the screen. The user positions the mouse pointer in an empty area in the toolbar and drags the toolbar to the desired location. A dotted outline of the toolbar is displayed as the toolbar is being moved to another location to provide feedback to the user. Aside from the left or right edge of the screen or the top or bottom of the screen, the toolbar can be positioned anywhere on the screen. The toolbar is referred to as a *floating toolbar*. It looks and behaves like a window. It has its own control menu. It is movable and resizable.

## 5.22  Value Set

The *value set control* is a group of related buttons represented as graphics or text labels. Value sets are particularly appropriate for options that can be best represented by graphical labels. For example, using value sets for the color palette, fonts, and drawing tool allow the user to see all the available choices when he makes his selection. The items within a value set control may include bitmaps, icons, text strings, and colors. Figure 5.39 shows an example of a value set.

**FIGURE 5.39   Microsoft Word for Windows Value Set**

A value set is similar to the radio button control in function. Both value set and radio button controls allow the user to select an item from an existing set. However, unlike radio buttons, the value set provides a graphical set of selectable items. Although a value set control may be used to display textual or numeric data, radio buttons are recommended for this purpose.

# CHAPTER 6

# Dialog Boxes

Dialog refers to the communication between a user and the computer. It is an observable two-way exchange of symbols and actions. One way in which the user communicates with the computer is through dialog boxes. A dialog box is a type of window that presents choices to the user and provides a graphical means to input information to an application. Since a dialog box supplements the interaction in the primary (main) window, most GUIs consider a dialog box as a secondary (supplemental) window.

Like a window, a dialog box has a window border, title bar, and, at least, a control menu (close control). Some dialog boxes require the user to complete the dialog box before continuing to work in the application window from which the dialog box was displayed. Other dialog boxes allow the user to interact with the application window outside the dialog box. Depending on the type, the user can move and/or resize the dialog box.

A dialog box contains user interface components (controls) that allow the user to make choices and enter information. The user clicks one or more of the buttons in a dialog box to select, confirm, or cancel the choices. Some examples of dialog box controls are command buttons, check boxes, radio buttons, drop-down lists, and spin buttons.

This chapter presents an overview of dialog boxes—their components, the types of dialog boxes according to various characteristics or behaviors, and dialog boxes common to all applications. It also presents a summary of the various dialog box controls supported by the GUIs in the comparison. It presents some guidelines for designing dialog boxes.

## 6.1 Elements of a Dialog Box

Dialog boxes look like basic windows (document or secondary windows). Dialog boxes generally have a title bar with a close control (control menu) and a dialog title that describes the command that displayed the dialog box. Dialog boxes do not generally contain a content area, a menu bar, a message area, a status bar, and resizing buttons (maximize, minimize, and restore buttons). (For more information on these elements, refer to Chapter 3, "Windows.") A dialog box can be moved within the window, and/or resized (expanded to display additional options), depending on the type. Dialog boxes usually suspend the application until the user either provides the needed information or cancels the operation.

Figure 6.1 illustrates the different elements of a dialog box. In most cases, there is a HELP dialog box control.

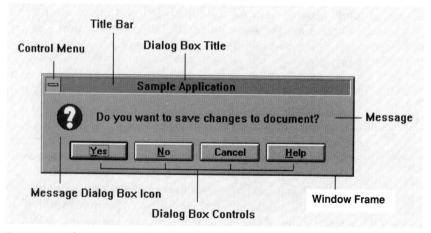

FIGURE 6.1   Elements of a Dialog Box

*Alert boxes* are a special case of dialog boxes in Macintosh. An alert box displays messages to inform the user of a situation (e.g., report an error). An alert box contains an icon, text, and buttons. There is no title bar or other controls, such as a close box. The user can switch to another application, only after clicking one of the buttons. Clicking one of the buttons closes the alert box. Figure 6.2 shows the essential elements of a Macintosh alert box.

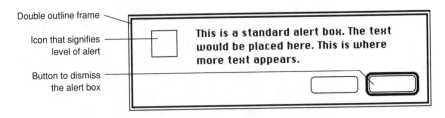

Double outline frame

Icon that signifies level of alert

Button to dismiss the alert box

This is a standard alert box. The text would be placed here. This is where more text appears.

**FIGURE 6.2   Elements of a Macintosh Alert Box**

OSF/Motif and IBM CUA style guides consider dialog boxes as secondary windows. Secondary windows look like primary windows. Both have a window border, title bar, and at least a control (system) menu symbol. They are generally movable and resizable. (For more information on secondary windows, refer to Chapter 3, "Windows.")

In NeXTSTEP, dialog boxes are referred to as *panels*. A panel is a rectangular area by which a user can give instructions to the application. It performs secondary functionality, supporting the functionality of the standard window. A panel has a title bar, although it usually does not have a miniaturize button. Panels can be *ordinary panels* or *attention panels*.

An *ordinary panel* looks and acts very much like a standard window. It is typically in the same tier as standard windows, and it competes for screen space. It has a title bar, but does not have a miniaturize button. Every ordinary panel has a close button so the user can dismiss the panel when it is not needed. Unlike standard windows, an ordinary panel can never be the main window [NeXTSTEP, p. 76].

An *attention panel* demands attention from the user. It is active until dismissed. An attention panel differs from an ordinary panel in that it has a blank title bar and no close box. The attention panel is dismissed by one or more buttons in the content area.

Figure 6.3 illustrates the features of an attention panel, which differentiates it from other windows.

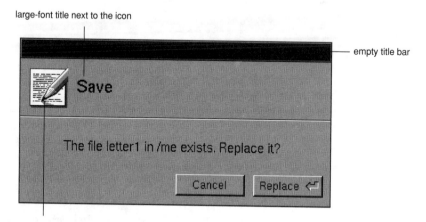

FIGURE 6.3   NeXTSTEP Attention Panel

In Microsoft Windows, the window border, title bar, and control menu constitute the basic elements of a dialog box. The appearance may vary depending on the type of dialog box.

## 6.2  Dialog Box Controls

Dialog box controls are user interface components that appear primarily in dialog boxes. However, these controls can appear in any window. Dialog box controls enable the user to make choices, display certain types of information, and inquire about a user-requested action. The controls in a dialog box are as follows:

- Check Box
- Combination (Combo) Box
- Command Button

- Container

- Drop-Down Combo Box

- Drop-Down List Box

- List Box (single-selection and multiple-selection)

- Notebook

- Radio Button

- Scroll Bar

- Slider

- Spin Box

- Text Box

- Value Set

In addition to the above controls, there are various controls specific to multimedia applications such as Back Step, Eject, Fast Forward, Forward Step, Pause, Play, Record, Rewind, and Stop. (For detailed information on dialog box controls, refer to Chapter 5, "Controls.") Figure 6.4 shows some examples of dialog box controls.

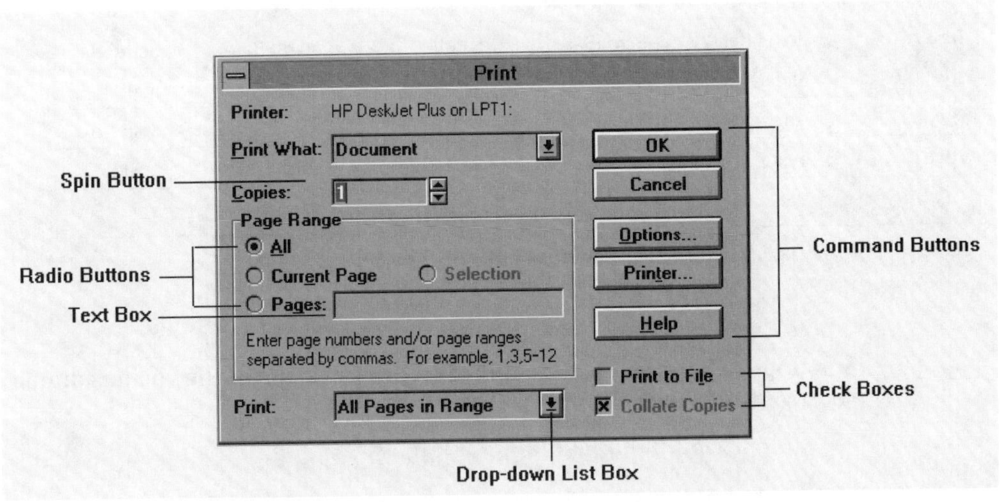

FIGURE 6.4 **Examples of Dialog Box Controls**

Table 6.1 compares the different dialog box controls used by the various GUIs.

**TABLE 6.1  Comparison of Dialog Box Controls**

|  | Macintosh | OSF/Motif | NeXTSTEP | Presentation Manager | Microsoft Windows |
|---|---|---|---|---|---|
| *Check Box* | Check Box | CheckButton | Button or Switch | Check Box | Check Box |
| *Combo Box* | Note 1 | — | — | Combo Box | Combo Box |
| *Command Button* | Button | PushButton | Button or Action Button | Pushbutton | Command Button |
| *Container* | — | — | — | Container | File Folder |
| *Drop-Down Combo Box* | Note 1 | — | — | Drop-Down Combo Box | Drop-Down Combo Box |
| *Drop-Down List Box* | Pop-up Menu[1] | OptionMenu | Pop-Up List or Pull-Down List | Drop-Down List Box | Drop-Down List Box |
| *List Box* | Scrolling List | List | Selection List or Multiple List | List Box | List Box |
| *Notebook* | — | — | — | Notebook | — |
| *Radio Button* | Button | RadioButton or ToggleButton | Button | Pushbutton | Command Button |
| *Scroll Bar* | Scroll Bar | ScrollBar | Scroller | Scroll Bar | Scroll Bar |
| *Slider* | Slider[1] | Scale | Slider | Slider | Slider |
| *Spin Box* | Arrow[1] | Arrow | — | Spin Button | Spin Box |
| *Text Box* | Text Entry Field | Text | Text Field | Entry Field | Text Box |
| *Value Set* | Value Set[1] |  |  | Value Set | Value Set |

[1]These controls are application-specific; they are not supported by the Macintosh Toolbox.

Figure 6.5 shows the graphical representation of the various dialog box controls for the GUIs in the comparison.

FIGURE 6.5 Comparison of Dialog Box Controls (Gallery)

| Control | Macintosh | OSF/Motif | NeXTSTEP | Presentation Manager | Microsoft Windows |
|---|---|---|---|---|---|

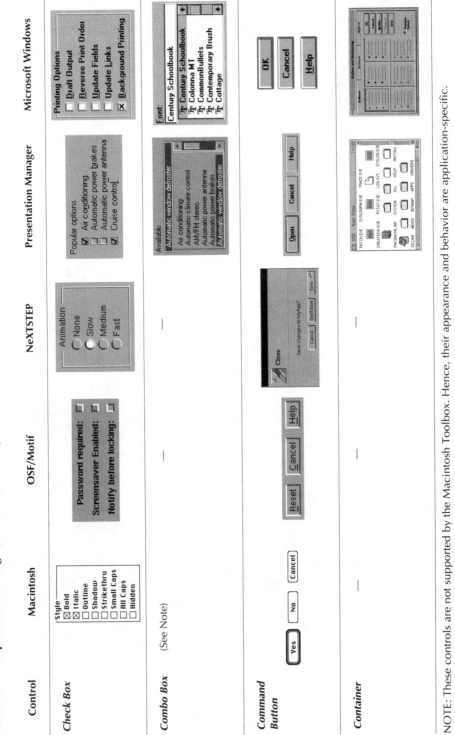

NOTE: These controls are not supported by the Macintosh Toolbox. Hence, their appearance and behavior are application-specific.

*(continued)*

**FIGURE 6.5** Comparison of Dialog Box Controls (Gallery), *Continued*

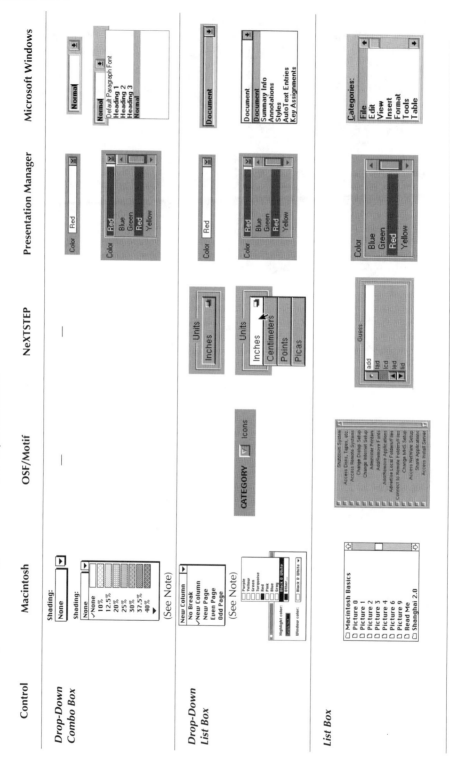

| Control | Macintosh | OSF/Motif | NeXTSTEP | Presentation Manager | Microsoft Windows |
|---|---|---|---|---|---|

NOTE: These controls are not supported by the Macintosh Toolbox. Hence, their appearance and behavior are application-specific.

*(continued)*

**FIGURE 6.5** Comparison of Dialog Box Controls (Gallery), *Continued*

| Control | Macintosh | OSF/Motif | NeXTSTEP | Presentation Manager | Microsoft Windows |
|---|---|---|---|---|---|
| *Notebook* | — | — | — | | — |
| *Radio Button* | | | | | |
| *Scroll Bar* | | | | | |
| *Slider* | (See Note) | | | | |

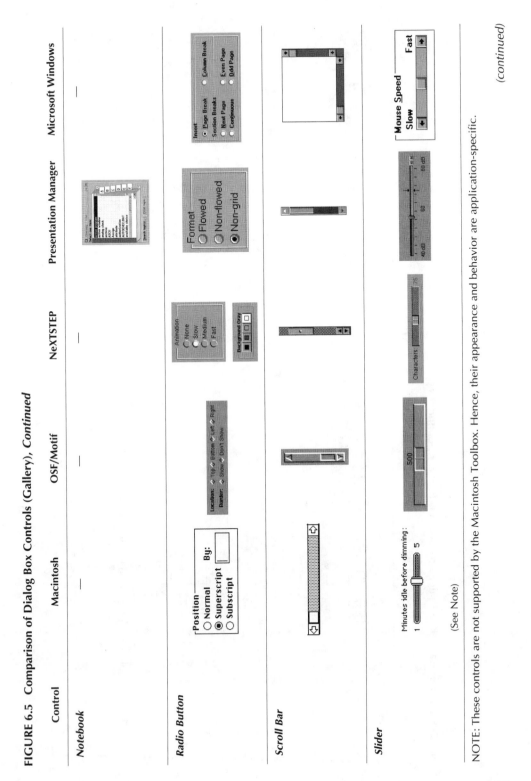

NOTE: These controls are not supported by the Macintosh Toolbox. Hence, their appearance and behavior are application-specific.

*(continued)*

**FIGURE 6.5  Comparison of Dialog Box Controls (Gallery), *Continued***

| Control | Macintosh | OSF/Motif | NeXTSTEP | Presentation Manager | Microsoft Windows |
|---|---|---|---|---|---|
| *Spin Box* | 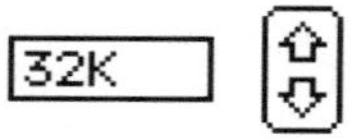 <br>(See Note) | 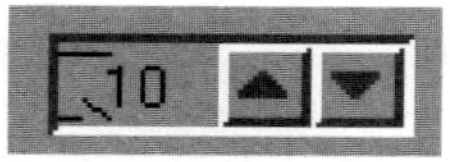 | — |  | 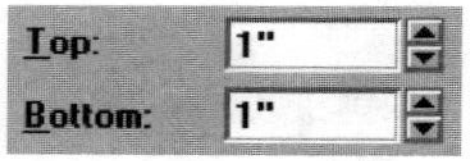 |
| *Text Box* | 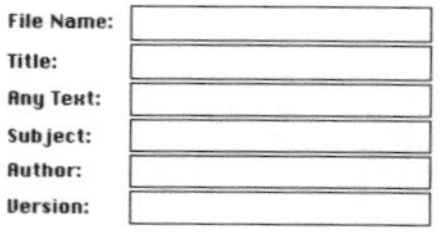 |  | 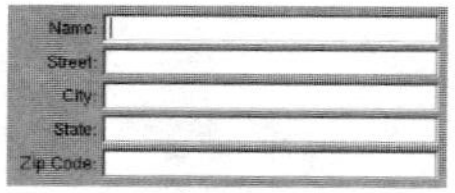 |  | 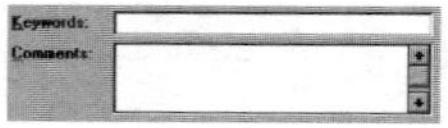 |
| *Value Set* |  <br>(See Note) | | | 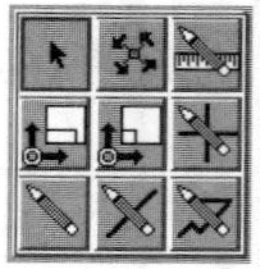 |  |

NOTE: These controls are not supported by the Macintosh Toolbox. Hence, their appearance and behavior are application-specific.

## 6.3  Dialog Box Behaviors

Dialog boxes can be classified according to their characteristics or behaviors:

- modal versus modeless
- movable versus fixed
- sizable versus nonsizable
- unfolding dialogs

### Modal versus Modeless

A *modal dialog box* prevents the user from engaging in any action until the user responds to the option displayed in the dialog box (Marcus, 1992, p. 148). The modal dialog box is often, but not always, fixed in size, but may be relocatable. A modal dialog box does not have a title bar. It usually has at least two command buttons; namely, OK and Cancel. OK initiates the action according to the information provided and closes the dialog box. Cancel terminates the action to be performed and closes the dialog box. In some cases, a modal dialog box may have no buttons. The purpose of such a modal dialog box is to inform the user of an ongoing operation. The user has no way to control or dismiss this type of modal dialog box.

A *modeless (nonmodal) dialog box* allows the user to perform operations without responding to the dialog box. A modeless dialog box may be fixed or changeable in its size or location. The modeless dialog box can be dismissed by pressing the Escape (Esc) key or clicking on the control menu and choosing the **Close** menu option. In the case of Macintosh or NeXTSTEP, the modeless dialog box can be dismissed by clicking on the close button (or close box).

Figure 6.6 shows examples of Microsoft Windows modal and modeless dialog boxes.

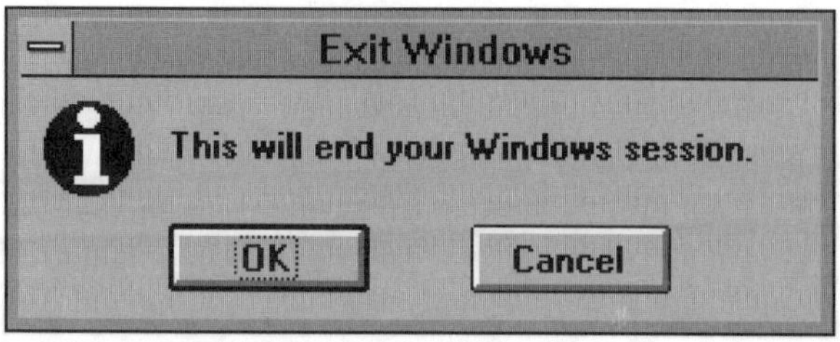

**FIGURE 6.6   Microsoft Windows Modal and Modeless Dialog Boxes**

Table 6.2 lists the different types of dialog boxes in OSF/Motif.

**TABLE 6.2   OSF/Motif Types of Dialog Box Behaviors**

| Type of Modal Dialog Box | Description |
|---|---|
| *Primary Modal* | Does not allow interaction with any ancestor of the window |
| *Application Modal* | Does not allow interaction with any window created by the same application even if the application has multiple primary windows |
| *System Modal* | Does not allow interaction with any window on the screen. This includes windows from all other applications and any icon box. To indicate a system modal secondary window, the pointer should change shape to a caution pointer whenever it leaves the system modal secondary window. |
| *Modeless* | Allows interaction with the secondary window and all other windows. |

Source: *OSF/Motif Style Guide,* p. 6-45.

Macintosh identifies the following four main types of dialog boxes:

- A *modeless dialog box* looks like a Macintosh document window except that it does not have a size box or scroll bars. "The user can move a modeless dialog box, make it inactive and active again, and close it like any document window. With modeless dialog boxes, people can change things in their documents, perform actions with the data in their documents, or get information about their documents or applications" [MHIG, p. 178].

- A *movable modal dialog box* is a modal dialog box with a title bar (but no close box) that allows the user to move the dialog box. It allows the user to switch to another application.

- A *modal dialog box* allows interaction within the dialog box. The user cannot move a modal dialog box. The user can dismiss the dialog box only by clicking one of its buttons.

- An *alert box* is a special case of modal dialog box. It warns or reports an error to the user. An alert box typically consists of text describing the situation and buttons to allow the user to acknowledge or rectify the problem. Its appearance is similar to a modal dialog box, except that a modal dialog box can contain editable text items and additional controls such as radio buttons and pop-up menus.

Figure 6.7 illustrates four types of Macintosh dialog boxes.

Modeless dialog box

Movable modal dialog box

Modal dialog box

Alert box

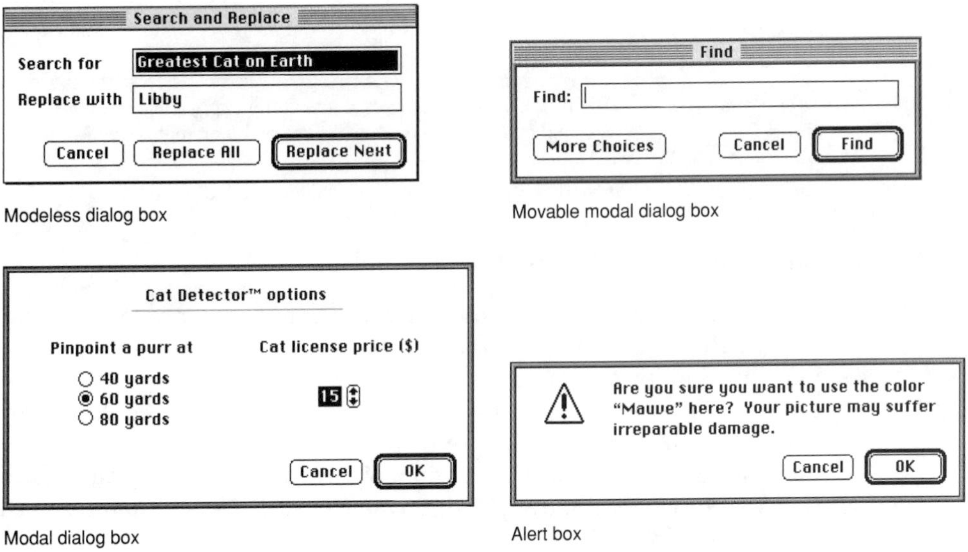

**FIGURE 6.7  Examples of Macintosh Dialog Boxes**

In NeXTSTEP, modal dialog boxes are referred to as *modal panels*. Most NeXTSTEP applications have a print command in the main menu, that brings up a modal *print panel*. When the modal print panel appears, the menu item remains highlighted. The user cannot do anything else with the application until he or she selects one of the action buttons in the print panel or press the Escape (Esc) key to cancel. NeXTSTEP also uses a special kind of modal panel, called an *attention panel*, to signal important decisions that the user has to make in order to proceed with the task. An attention panel has a blank title bar and no close box. The attention panel is dismissed by one or more buttons in the content area. The modal panels apply only to the active application. The user may switch to another application, and when he or she returns to the previous application, it will still be in the same mode.

In NeXTSTEP, modeless dialogs are referred to as *nonmodal panels*. Modal panels do not interfere with the operation of the application, and permit users to interact with other windows.

Table 6.3 describes the Windows classification of dialog boxes.

**TABLE 6.3   Microsoft Windows Types of Dialog Box Behaviors**

| Type of Dialog Box | Description |
| --- | --- |
| *Application Modal* | The user must respond to the dialog box before continuing work in the current application. The user can switch to, and work in, other applications without responding. |
| *System Modal* | The user must respond before any applications can continue. |
| *Application Semimodal* | The user can engage in a limited number of operations outside the dialog as a means of responding to the dialog. |
| *Application Modeless* | The user can continue work in the current application without responding to the dialog box; the dialog box remains on display. |

Source: *The Windows Interface: An Application Design Guide,* p. 127.

## Movable versus Fixed

A *movable dialog box* is a dialog box that the user can relocate to any area of the screen. It is similar in many ways to a tear-off menu. A movable dialog box is usually modeless (nonmodal) and may be fixed or changeable in size. It has a title bar containing a control menu (which usually includes the **Move** and **Close** commands). The user can move the dialog box within the window by dragging its title bar. All the GUIs in the comparison support movable dialog boxes (or panels in the case of NeXTSTEP).

Macintosh differentiates a modal dialog box from a movable modal dialog box. A movable modal dialog box includes a title bar with "racing stripes" similar to the title bar of an active document window. It does not have a close box or zoom box. The interaction sequence for moving a movable modal dialog box is the same as that for moving a document window. It allows limited user actions to occur outside the dialog box.

### Resizable versus Nonsizable

A *resizable dialog box* allows the user to change its height and width. A resizable dialog box may be modal or nonmodal, movable, or fixed in location. In most GUIs, a modeless dialog box may be changeable in size. In NeXTSTEP, ordinary panels may have a resize bar. The user can resize them in the same manner as standard windows are resized. Attention panels are typically not resizable.

### Unfolding Dialogs

Microsoft Windows defines two sizes for a dialog box: a small size containing the basic controls, and a large size including advanced or additional options. The dialog box illustrated in Figure 6.8 contains the basic controls for using the **Printers** command. The Add>> button is called the *unfold button*.

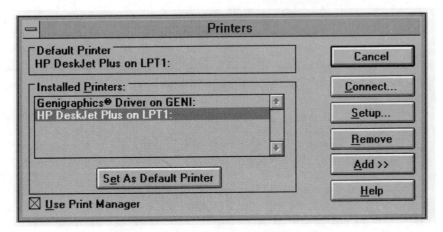

FIGURE 6.8  **Microsoft Windows Unfolding Dialog Box (Folded)**

The user clicks on the Add>> button to install an additional printer supported by Microsoft Windows. When the Add>> button is clicked, the Printer dialog box expands downward as shown in Figure 6.9. The dialog box now displays the basic controls as well as additional options for the installation of printer drivers. This dialog box is called the *unfolded dialog box*. Notice that the unfold button is dimmed after the dialog box is expanded, to indicate that the button is unavailable.

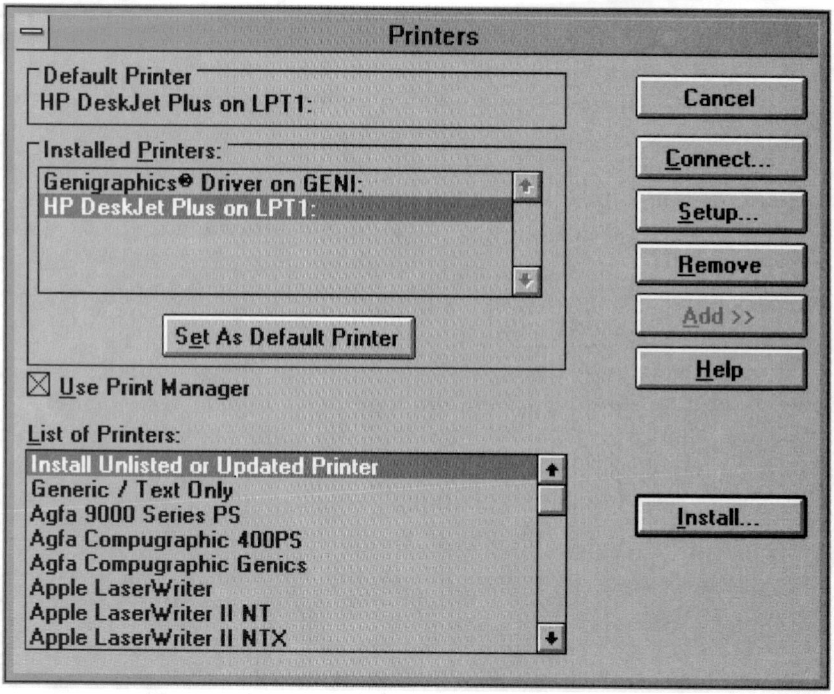

FIGURE 6.9   Microsoft Windows Unfolding Dialog Box

### Design Tips

Modal dialog boxes should be used when there is some unfavorable system state or action, or anticipated consequence of the user's behavior that warrants the user's confirmation before the interaction state can proceed any further. Modal dialog boxes should be used sparingly, if at all, in other interaction contexts, because dialog boxes tend to disrupt the task and annoy the user. Application semimodal dialog boxes (as defined in Microsoft Windows) are preferred over modal dialog boxes in all noncritical situations. When density of the contents of the dialog box is a concern, the unfolding dialog box as implemented in Microsoft Windows should be considered.

## 6.4  Common Dialog Boxes

Dialog boxes common to all applications are Message, About <application-name>, File Open, Page Setup, and Print.

### Message Dialog Boxes

A message dialog box supplies information, warnings, or critical messages (i.e., the system is about to enter a potentially dangerous or irrecoverable state) that are not requested by the user. The user's response options are typically limited to a simple yes-or-no decision, or in irreversible system states, simple acknowledgment of the message (Marcus, 1992, p. 149).

In Macintosh, message dialog boxes are referred to as *alert boxes.* An alert box is a special case of modal dialog box used for displaying messages. Table 6.4 identifies the three kinds of alert boxes. Each kind of alert box is identified by a standard icon.

TABLE 6.4  **Macintosh Types of Alert Boxes**

| Message Type | Message Icon | Description |
|---|---|---|
| *Note* | | Provides nonthreatening information to the user and usually contains only one button—the OK button. |
| *Caution* | | Contains information of a more severe nature than Note alert boxes. It warns the user in advance of a potentially dangerous action. It always contains two buttons, an OK (or Continue) button, and a Cancel button. |
| *Stop* | | Informs the user of the most severe level of error. It typically has only one button—the OK button. Stop alert boxes notify the user that an action cannot be completed. |

Source: *The Macintosh Human Interface Guidelines,* p. 195.

Figure 6.10 shows examples of the different kinds of alert boxes and their associated icons.

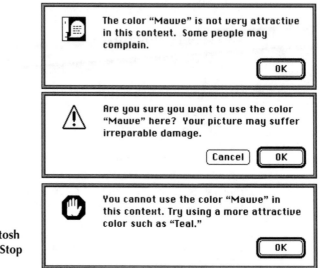

FIGURE 6.10 Macintosh Note, Caution, and Stop Alert Boxes

In OSF/Motif, message boxes are called *MessageDialogs*. Message-Dialogs are nonmodal. There are several types of MessageDialogs: ErrorDialog, InformationDialog, QuestionDialog, WorkingDialog, and WarningDialog.

In NeXTSTEP, the attention panels could be considered message dialog boxes. They do not categorize the types of messages or employ a symbol to communicate explicitly the nature of the messages.

In Presentation Manager, the message window displays information to report an unexpected or undesirable situation to the user. The IBM CUA style guide recommends messages to be as modeless as possible. Table 6.5 shows the various message types and their associated symbols.

In Microsoft Windows, message boxes are called *message dialogs*. They are modal dialog boxes used to present three kinds of messages; namely, information, warning, and critical. Table 6.6 illustrates the kinds of message dialogs and their associated symbols.

TABLE 6.5  **Presentation Manager Message Types**

| Symbol | Message Type |
|---|---|
| | Information Message |
| | Warning Message |
| | Action Message (when the user's immediate attention is not required, such as when the situation will not worsen with time) |
| | Action Message (when the user's immediate attention is required) |

Source: *IBM Common User Access Advanced Interface Design Reference,* p. 144.

TABLE 6.6  **Microsoft Windows Message Dialogs**

| Symbol | Message Type | Description |
|---|---|---|
| | Information | Provides information about results of commands. Offers no user choices; user acknowledges message by clicking OK button. |
| | Warning | Alerts the user to an error condition or situation that requires user decision and input before proceeding, such as an impending action with potentially destructive, irreversible consequences. |
| | Critical | Informs the user of a serious system-related or application-related problem that must be corrected before work can continue with the application. |

Source: *The Windows Interface: An Application Design Guide,* p. 129.

### Design Tips

In designing message dialog boxes, the name of the object and the action or situation that caused the message to appear should be included in the window title. Depending on the type of message involved, the dialog box should be as modeless as possible. An appropriate symbol that visually identifies the type of message conveyed should be used. A message dialog box should contain only command buttons. It should have at least two buttons—one that initiates the action and closes the dialog box (such as the OK button); the other closes the dialog box without initiating any action (such as the Cancel button). Lastly, the message that is usually located to the right of the message symbol should be clear and concise.

## About <application-name> Dialog Boxes

An About <application-name> dialog box displays basic information about the application (program). The information displayed usually includes the name of the application, application icon, copyright information, and release level (version) of the application. Some GUIs include the names of the authors, software license number, and system resource status. The dialog box is displayed when the user selects the About <application-name> menu item from the **Help** menu. There is usually at least one command button (OK button) present in this dialog box. The dialog box is dismissed when the user clicks on the OK button. If there is no OK button provided, the user can press the Escape (Esc) key or select the **Close** menu item in the control (system) menu to dismiss the dialog box.

In Macintosh, the About <application-name> is the first item in the Apple menu. In NeXTSTEP, the About <application-name> dialog box is called the *Info panel*. The main menu contains the **Info** menu. When selected, a submenu containing the Info Panel option is displayed. In Presentation Manager, it is called the *Product Information* dialog box. It is displayed when the user selects the Product Information item from the **Help** menu.

Figure 6.11 shows an example of an About <application-name> dialog box.

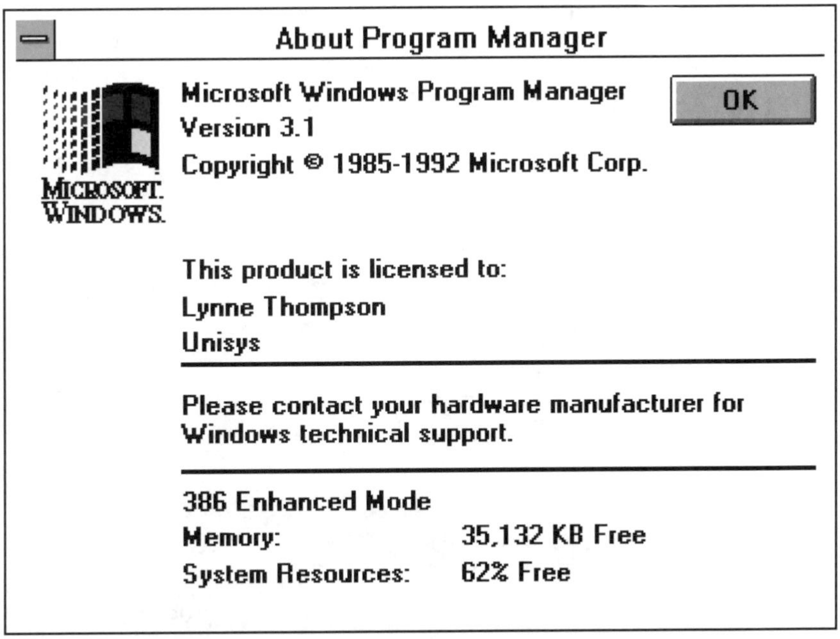

FIGURE 6.11    Microsoft Windows About <application-name> Dialog Box

### Design Tips

Every application must have an About <application-name> dialog box. The application designer should provide at least the basic product information. The application icon should appear to the left of the product information. The icon should be the same one that typically appears on the desktop. The dialog box should include the official name of the application in the title bar. Additional product information, if provided, should follow the basic product information.

## File Open Dialog Boxes

A File Open dialog box is displayed when the **File** menu is selected. The appearance of the File Open dialog box varies from GUI to GUI. The File Open dialog box allows the user to browse the file system and the network. It should contain at least a File Name text box with list boxes underneath for file type, file name, drive, and directory. The File Open dialog box should contain at least the OK, Cancel, and Help command buttons. Figure 6.12 shows an example of a Presentation Manager File Open dialog box. Note the icons used to indicate the status of the various directories.

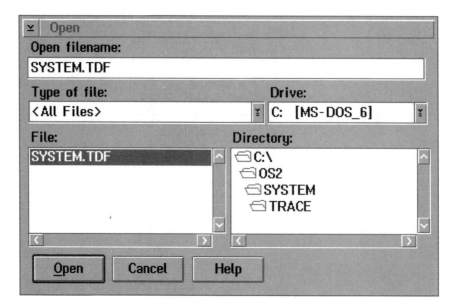

FIGURE 6.12   **Presentation Manager File Open Dialog Box**

## Page Setup Dialog Boxes

The Page Setup dialog box provides controls for specifying properties about the page elements and layout. A Page Setup dialog box is specific to the application. Hence, the layout varies from application to application. There is no common dialog layout for setting page margins and layout among the GUIs in the comparison. Figure 6.13 shows an example of a Microsoft Windows Page Setup dialog box. Note the use of the file folder container to group options for Margins, Paper Size, Paper Source, and Layout.

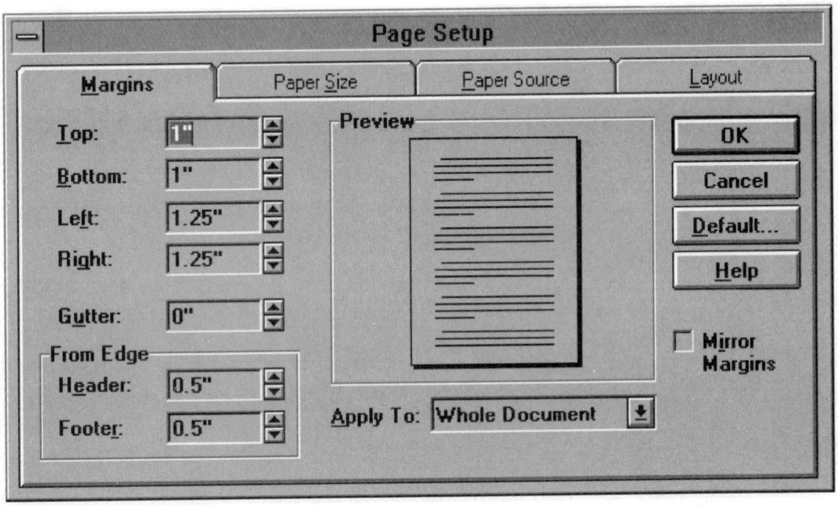

FIGURE 6.13 **Example of a Microsoft Windows Page Setup Dialog Box**

## Print Dialog Boxes

The Print dialog box allows the user to control the printing of a document—number of copies, specific pages, printer selection, and other printing properties. There is no common Print dialog box layout among the GUIs in the comparison. Figure 6.14 shows an example of a Print dialog box.

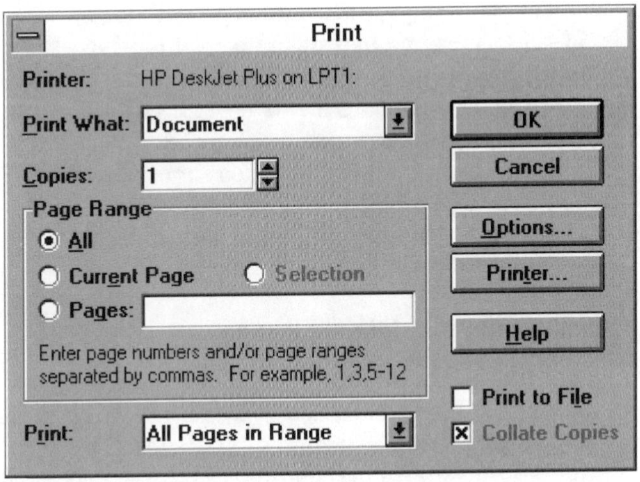

FIGURE 6.14 **Example of a Microsoft Windows Print Dialog Box**

*Design Tips*

The following are basic guidelines in designing a Print dialog box:

- The Print dialog box should be modal.

- The page range selections should be grouped. The Print dialog box should allow the user to enter the appropriate page numbers in the From and To text boxes.

- A drop-down list box should be used where appropriate to occupy less space.

- Additional printing options such as printer selection should be provided as a GoSub button to avoid cluttering the dialog box.

## 6.5 General Design Tips

The functional design and content of the dialog box should consider the following aspects:

- Selection of dialog box types
- Layout (placement, alignment, ordering, grouping)
- Selection of dialog box controls

### Selection of Dialog Box Types

In selecting the appropriate type of dialog box to use, an understanding of the different types of dialog boxes—how they look and behave—is very important. Dialog boxes should be as modeless as possible. Use movable dialog boxes if it is necessary for the user to view information that might be obscured by the dialog box. Whether dialog boxes are movable or not, all dialog boxes should have a resizable window frame. The type of dialog box closure (e.g., control menu with a **Close** option) should also be determined at this time.

### Placement of Dialog Boxes

All dialog boxes must fit completely on the screen for all supported screen resolutions. Dialog boxes should be centered vertically and horizontally within the window (application or document). However, if a more appropriate location for the dialog box is chosen, the placement should draw the user's attention.

When the user chooses a command that displays a modal or modeless dialog box, that dialog box appears on top of the active window. Modal dialog boxes, whose purpose is to prevent the user from engaging in any action until a response is provided, must be placed on top of all the other open application or document windows. They remain on top until the user responds to the dialog box request. Modeless dialog boxes may become partially or totally obscured, in the process of switching between windows, before being released.

## Size of Dialog Boxes

The following guidelines with respect to the size of the dialog box should be observed:

- Design dialog boxes that have two sizes: a small size containing the basic controls, and a larger size that includes additional options. For example, Microsoft Windows provides an unfolding dialog box that expands from the small size to the larger size in response to an unfold command button. The dialog box expands to the right, downward, or in both directions.

- The dialog box should not obscure other windows but should be kept small so as to effect its supplemental nature.

- Make sure that any list boxes are large enough to display six to eight choices at a time, or all choices if fewer than six. Make list boxes at least wide enough to display the choices of average width.

- Resizing the dialog box in which a list box is displayed can affect the display of choices in the list box. For example, if the user increases the size of the dialog box in which a list box is displayed, the number of choices in the list box should increase appropriately.

When the user reduces the size of the dialog box in which a list box is displayed, the number of choices displayed in the list box should be decreased to a minimum of six.

## Selection of Dialog Box Controls

For each of the GUIs in the comparison, there are a number of dialog box controls from which to choose. The controls used within an application should be evaluated carefully. Use the predefined controls supplied by the GUIs as much as possible before using custom controls.

Table 6.7 lists the different dialog box controls and guidelines for their appropriate usage.

**TABLE 6.7   Selection Guidelines for Dialog Box Controls**

| Control | When to Use |
|---|---|
| *Check Box* | On or off state, single or multiple choice, less than six fixed options |
| *Combo Box* | List of choices with user entry option, greater than six choices |
| *Command Button* | For frequently used fixed action or routing choices, less than six choices |
| *Container* | Used to group and to view any number of objects |
| *Drop-Down Combo Box* | Drop-down list of choices with user entry option, greater than six choices, conserves space |
| *Drop-Down List Boxes* | Drop-down list with no user option, greater than six fixed choices, conserves space |
| *List Box* | Selectable list of choices—text or graphics, greater than six choices |
| *Notebook* | Used to display large number of objects or setting choices (except another notebook) that can be arranged in a logical group (tabbed divider-pages) |
| *Radio Buttons* | Single choice, mutually exclusive, less than six fixed choices |
| *Scroll Bar* | Large list, not fully visible within a window |
| *Slider* | Analog representation, fixed setting in a range, less than sixty visible increments |
| *Spin Box* | Ordered input values, less than ten fixed choices |
| *Text Box* | Used for entering text |
| *Value Set* | Graphical choices that are mutually exclusive like color palettes |

## Organization of Dialog Box Controls

There can be as many types of controls in a dialog box as needed. Controls should be placed in locations that are functional and consistent within the application as well as across applications. Dialog box controls should be arranged for easy visual scanning.

### Arrangement of Buttons

Command buttons are often present in a dialog box. Every dialog box should have at least one command button that closes the dialog box; for example, a message dialog box containing one button labeled OK, requiring acknowledgment from the user. Other dialog boxes contain at least two buttons: one that initiates the action and closes the dialog box, and the other that closes the dialog box without initiating an action. For example, the OK or <action name> button initiates an action and closes the dialog box. The Cancel button closes the dialog box without initiating an action.

Command buttons can be arranged horizontally or vertically. If arranged horizontally, command buttons should be placed across the bottom of the dialog box. Macintosh recommends that the command buttons be placed in the lower-right corner, with the Cancel button to the left. If arranged vertically, the command buttons should be stacked along the right border of the dialog box, from top to bottom. The buttons should generally be the same width, accommodating the longest button text. Microsoft Windows recommends that the command buttons be grouped according to function. For example, the OK and Cancel buttons should be grouped together, separated from other command buttons.

Figure 6.15 shows the Macintosh recommended location for buttons and text in dialog boxes, alert icons, and a dialog box message.

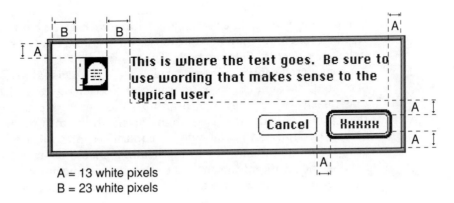

A = 13 white pixels
B = 23 white pixels

FIGURE 6.15  **Macintosh Recommended Dialog Box and Alert Box Layout**

There should always be a button designated as the default button. The visual appearance of the default button should be distinguishable from other buttons. For example, most GUIs emphasize the default button with a heavy border. The default button should be placed at the top if the arrangement is vertical, and at the right if the arrangement is horizontal.

The Help button should be placed after all other buttons so that it is visible to the user.

### Alignment of Controls

The following are guidelines pertaining to the position of the controls and contents of the dialog box, other than command buttons:

- Dialog box controls should be at the top, left justified.

- Group boxes should be positioned so that their title text aligns horizontally with other text elements.

- If a group heading is used instead of a group box, place the group heading above each group of fields. The fields in each group under their associated group heading should be indented. Align group headings vertically with the left edge of other group headings.

### Grouping of Components

The controls in a dialog box should be broken into logical groups. Group boxes, group headings or titles, and white spaces should be used for aesthetics, clarity, and distinctness of grouped components. A group box is a single-line rectangular frame with a title bar that groups related choices. A group heading or title identifies a related set of entry fields, or selection field, or both. Though group boxes are technically not considered controls, they provide an effective visual arrangement of related functional tasks or information. Setting the controls becomes much easier when they are in groups. Position group boxes so that their group heading (or title) aligns horizontally with other text elements. Group headings should be capitalized and placed above the group of related fields. The group heading should be explanatory, reflecting the nature of the choices contained within the group.

Figure 6.16 shows an example of a dialog box with grouped components.

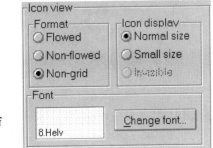

**FIGURE 6.16  Example of Grouping Dialog Box Controls**

### Placement of Text and Icons

In the case of message dialog boxes or alert boxes, messages should be simple, clear, and make sense to the user. They should be placed to the right of the dialog box icon, if present. Sufficient space must be allotted for the messages so that consecutive lines of text do not touch.

A dialog box icon can be used to communicate the message clearly. In choosing an appropriate and effective icon for the message dialog box, make the icon easy to recognize. The icon should convey the message being presented to the user through the dialog box. Take care to use depth effects consistently. Rendering objects requires care to maintain a credible illusion of depth. Color provides numerous advantages. However, the effect of color depends entirely on where and how it is used. Lastly, the dialog box icon, if present, should be placed to the left of the message.

## Density of Dialog Boxes

Designs should be neat, aligned, and uncluttered. Consider using drop-down combination boxes, list boxes, or unfolding dialog boxes to conserve space. The drop-down list box in most of the GUIs may display over the dialog window boundaries if the number of options is lengthy.

### Other Design Tips

Design all buttons so that they can be activated by a keyboard, mouse, or a pointing device. Avoid designing user interfaces that require the user to change interaction techniques frequently.

Dialog boxes are often used to change the visual attributes and properties of objects. It is helpful to provide a preview box within the dialog box to show the result of the options the user specifies before applying them.

## 6.6 Dialog Box Trends

As experts gain a better understanding of the relationship between humans and the computer, conventional dialog boxes will continue to be enhanced to reflect the results of their research and experimental studies. Hence, the appearance and behavior of conventional dialog boxes will undergo many changes.

### Dialog Box Metaphors

Conventional dialog boxes are being enhanced to better correlate to well-known metaphors such as the notebook and the office (file folder) metaphors. New controls such as the spiral bound notebook and file folder (containers) organize logically related dialog box information into sections with tabbed dividers. The user can switch from one section to another using the tabs. (Refer to Chapter 5, "Controls," for more information on the notebook and file folder (container) controls).

Figure 6.17 shows an example of a Presentation Manager dialog box using the notebook control.

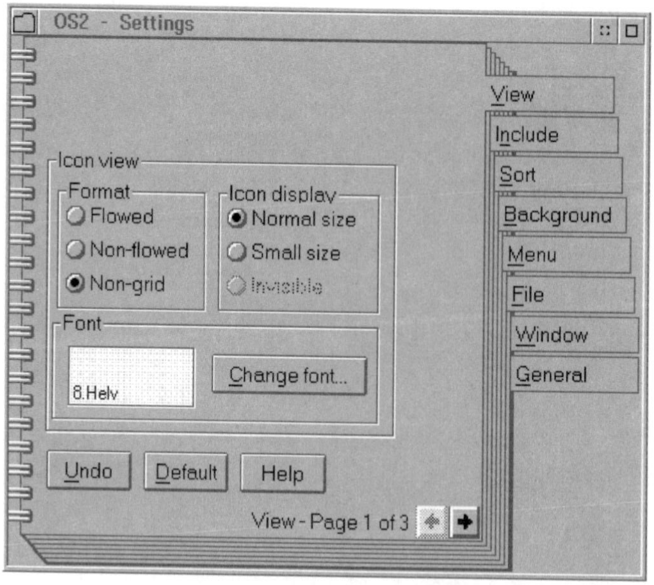

FIGURE 6.17   **Presentation Manager Dialog Box Using the Notebook Control**

Figure 6.18 shows an example of a Microsoft Windows file folder container.

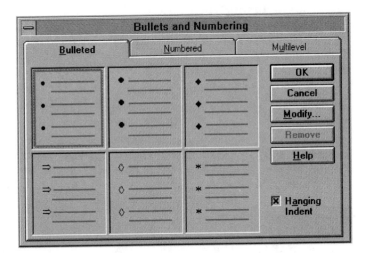

**FIGURE 6.18  Microsoft Windows Dialog Box Using the File Folder Container**

## Multimedia Considerations

Multimedia will play an important role in the next generation of user interfaces. Within the computing industry, the term *multimedia* refers to the integration of two or more interrelated media types to deliver a high-value information content. These data types include animation, graphics, full- or partial-screen motion video, still images, text, and voice. Today's graphical user interfaces will evolve beyond the *w*indows, *i*cons, *m*enus, and *p*ointing device (WIMP) paradigm to "involve elements such as virtual realities, sound and speech, pen and gesture recognition, animation, and highly portable computers in cellular or wireless communication capabilities" [Nielsen, 1993].

The use of multimedia information will enrich and improve communications between the user and the computer. Dialog boxes will use complex types of information such as synchronized audio, animation, speech, music, and video images. For example, sound adds richness to the dialog, and thus provides additional information about the user's action or system state. When the user navigates through a list of sound (e.g., .WAV) files in a scrollable list box, the computer can play back each wave file to help the user in the file selection. The process of opening and closing each of the files in the user's directory could be avoided.

Future dialog boxes will provide a *preview box* to display the contents of a multimedia file. For example, the user can view screen motion video clips through the preview box before incorporating the desired clip into a presentation.

Settings, or choices, will be increasingly iconic, thus reducing absolute dependence on text and addressing the needs of those with limited reading skills (for example, those who read English as a second language).

Designing dialog boxes using multimedia information is more challenging than designing conventional dialog boxes. The application designer must be knowledgeable about designing multimedia user interfaces. Multimedia designers should consider the use of new controls and icons for audio, still images, screen motion video, and voice. The application designer should consider the use of multimedia capabilities as a means of providing effective feedback. For example, the use of an auditory icon enriches the dialog and thus provides additional cues to the user without adding to the complexity of the primary interaction. In designing a help system, the application designer should take advantage of multimedia techniques. Lastly, animation serves the role of embedded help. Animated icons convey the meaning of a message better than a static image. Consider animating the icon only when it is being pointed at.

## Conclusion

The user interface interaction model described in Chapter 7, "Interaction and Feedback," defines the dialog between the user and the computer. The user conducts a dialog with the computer through a set of interactive controls, options, and messages as instructions to the application on how to proceed. The importance of designing a consistent dialog box can be neither overemphasized nor should it be overlooked. It is the key to effective communication between the user and the computer.

# CHAPTER 7

# Interaction and Feedback

Interaction is the collaboration between a user and the computer, via some medium, to perform a task. The study of human-computer interaction is a new and exciting field. The efforts devoted to this endeavor are geared toward a better understanding of how to make this interaction work effectively and efficiently. The interaction between a user and the computer involves both hardware and software, cognitive modeling, methodology, techniques, and tools. For example, the user interacts with an object on the screen by using a pointing device such as a mouse. The user identifies the desired object and indicates actions to apply to that object. A consistent technique must be defined by the application so that the user can apply the same technique in another situation.

Effective feedback is a part of the interaction that has a significant effect on the user. In performing a task or function, the user wants to know the result. For example, if the trash can icon expands as the user drops a folder icon into it (assuming that there are no items in the trash can prior to the user's action), the user knows that the folder was indeed put into the trash can. Through good feedback, the user can gauge the effects of his or her actions. Visual cues, either textual or graphical, are commonly used for feedback. The use of animation and audible cues, such as speech and music, are becoming increasingly popular. They enhance and improve communications between a user and the computer.

This chapter describes the interaction model that defines the communication between the user and the computer. The chapter provides an overview of the various interaction devices such as the keyboard, mouse, pen, touch screen, and speech recognition, along with the operations they employ. It describes the object-action model and focus, object types and classes, and manipulation principles. The chapter also discusses the selection concept, including selection highlighting, selection types, and various selection techniques for the various data objects. Lastly, the chapter discusses graphical, textual, and auditory feedback provided by the GUIs in the comparison as a result of an interaction.

## 7.1  Interaction Model

The user environment in which an interaction takes place between the user and the computer involves aspects such as presentation (display), input devices, device operations, interaction techniques, objects and applications, and feedback. The user must be able to use the computer effectively to perform actions and achieve results in the chosen workplace.

The user interacts with the computer using an input device such as a keyboard, mouse, pen, touch screen, or speech recognition. Associated with these input devices are defined operations on the devices such as pressing a key or key sequence on the keyboard, clicking the mouse, tapping the pen, and touching the screen. The device operations allow for the following:

- *Location or pointing* within the user's presentation workspace

- *Selection* of specific objects via pointing and selection techniques

- *Navigation* through the presented interface

- *Activation* (*execution*) of operations, commands, and objects

- *Transfer* of information to or from a selected object

This interaction supports a noun-verb paradigm, where the target objects are nouns, and the user operations are verbs.

The *object and application types* targeted by these actions are presented and communicated to the user through the user interface components such as windows and dialog boxes. The subject GUIs typically categorize these data types as textual, tabular, and graphical. All user environment objects may be organized into object relationship structures called containers and folders.

Interaction with the objects involves *manipulation techniques* such as *selecting* a desired object and *activating* the object to perform functions. Once a user-computer *dialog* has been established, a variety of visual (graphical) feedback is exhibited. Emerging interfaces are now exploiting new ways of providing feedback using multimedia devices. The collective techniques and graphical indicators that objects utilize to exhibit feedback to the user may also be considered their *behavior*.

The complete interaction-feedback loop now becomes the user-computer *dialog*. The visualization of objects and data, the presentation, display, and feedback to the user are usually called the *look*. The user device and object operations are known as the *feel*.

Figure 7.1 models the user and his or her surroundings in the human-computing dialog, including information visualization (visual models), the devices for interaction and feedback, the various interaction techniques for positioning/pointing and manipulation, the objects and applications servicing the user, and the behavioral techniques for providing specific feedback on the user's object working set.

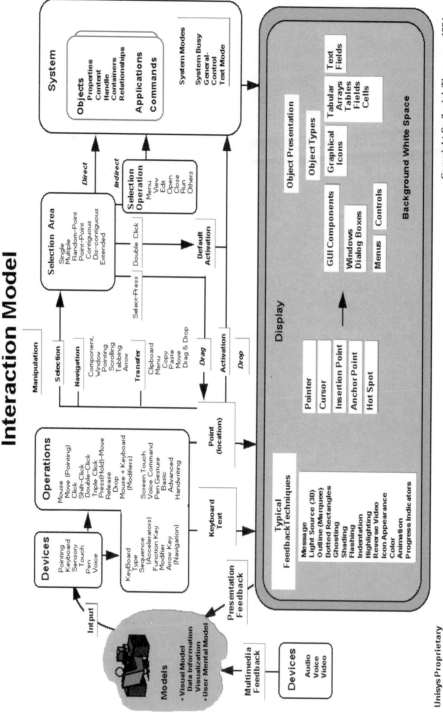

FIGURE 7.1  Interaction Model

Unisys Proprietary

Copyright Smilonich/Thompson 1994

## 7.2 Interaction Devices and Their Operations

The increased concern for human factors has drawn together experts from different fields to better understand the relationship between humans and the computer. A particular area of interest in the hundreds of ongoing academic and industrial studies on various aspects of human factors is interaction devices. This can be attributed to the significant advancement of hardware as well as input device technologies. New devices, as well as variants of the existing devices, continue to emerge. The keyboard remains the primary input device. In general, it is needed only to enter text. The use of pointing devices such as the mouse augment the human-computer interaction. The pointing devices can be used for all other operations, such as using controls and making selections. The increasing popularity of pointing devices has led to stimulating innovations such as the stylus, the trackball, eyetrackers, and the DataGlove. Future computing will likely include input devices for direct specification of 3D/4D positioning and orientation, hybrid gesture-direct manipulation interaction, and effective continuous-speech recognition.

Associated with each interaction device are device operations. Operations differ from one device to another. For example, pointing, clicking, and dragging are device operations for the mouse; tapping is for the pen device; and keys such as Insert (Ins), Delete (Del), and Enter (Return) are keyboard input.

## Keyboard

In some computers, the keyboard is the primary input device. It serves two major functions: to send text to the application currently in execution, and to issue commands to the application. The keyboards used by the GUIs in the comparison vary slightly. Figure 7.2 shows an example of a keyboard used in NeXTSTEP, including the Command, Help, and system control keys.

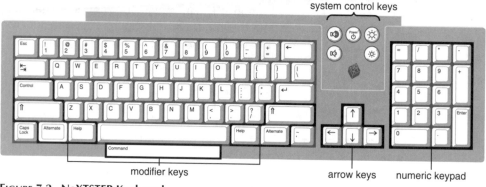

**FIGURE 7.2** NeXTSTEP Keyboard

Table 7.1 shows the types of keys found in a keyboard, and the functions they perform.

Table 7.2 lists the common functions of the modifier keys. The modifier keys are usually pressed at the beginning of the operation and held down during the operation. Combinations of the modifier keys provide additional application-defined functions.

TABLE 7.1  **Keyboard Input**

| Type of Key | Description |
|---|---|
| **Text Key** | Alphanumeric (a–z, 0–9), punctuation, symbol, Tab, Enter, and Spacebar keys |
| **Editing Key** | Keys used for editing, such as Insert (Ins), Delete (Del), and Backspace |
| **Mode Key** | Changes the action of other keys. There are two types of mode keys—toggle and modifier keys. |
| *Toggle Key* | Turns a particular mode on or off each time the key is pressed and released. The principal toggle keys are Insert, Caps Lock, Num Lock, and Scroll Lock. |
| *Modifier Key* | Changes the effect of a keyboard or a mouse. The mode established by these keys remains in effect while the key is pressed down. The most common modifier keys are Shift, Control (Ctrl), and Alternate (Alt). |
| **Navigation Key** | Involves keys dedicated to keyboard navigation of data items, windows, and controls. These keys can also be used singly or in combination with various modifier keys. They include the arrow keys, Home, and End. |
| **Shortcut Key (keyboard alternative)** | Provides more rapid access to frequently performed operations. There are two types of shortcut keys—function keys and control (accelerator) keys. |
| *Function Key* | Keys with assigned functions, for example, F1 for Help. |
| *Control Key (Accelerator Key)* | A combination of keys that invokes an application-defined function without accessing the menu bar. They are usually designated by a symbol and a letter. For example, instead of using the Edit menu command in Windows, the user can send the same command by holding down the command key , in this case, the Control key and typing the letter E. The control keys are often used for menu commands and, in the case of NeXTSTEP, panel buttons. |

TABLE 7.2  **Modifier Keys**

| Modifier Key | Function |
|---|---|
| **Shift** | *Alphanumeric keys:* Uppercase character or the character inscribed on the top half of the key. With Caps Lock on, it yields lowercase characters. *Mouse click or navigation keys:* Extends or shrinks the contiguous selection range *Functions Keys:* Alters the meaning of action; for example, F1 brings up the Help application, pressing Shift+F1 enters Help mode |
| **Control (Ctrl)** | *Alphabetic keys:* Yields shortcuts. *Mouse click:* Selects or deselects an item without affecting previous selections. *Navigation keys:* Moves cursor by a larger unit than the unmodified key. |
| **Alternate (Alt)** | *Alphabetic keys:* Navigates to the menu or control marked with that key as a mnemonic. |

Table 7.3 lists common control or accelerator keys used by most GUIs in the comparison.

TABLE 7.3   **Typical Accelerator (Control) Keys**

| Control Key Shortcut | Function |
|---|---|
| *Control+Z* | Undo |
| *Control+X* | Cut |
| *Control+C* | Copy |
| *Control+V* | Paste |

## Pointing Devices

A pointing device allows the user to interact with the objects on the desktop. Rather than entering a keyboard command for an action, the user simply points to an object and indicates what is to be done with it using the pointing device. There are a plethora of pointing devices—the mouse, the stylus pen, the trackball, and the joystick. However, the mouse is the standard pointing device for most computers.

### Mouse

The mouse is a hand-operated device, usually (but not necessarily) connected by a long, flexible cable to the computer. It generally has one, two, or three buttons. The user grasps the mouse and moves it on a flat, smooth surface. The most important mouse operations are pointing, clicking, double-clicking, pressing, and dragging. These operations may be combined with modifier keys such as Shift, Control (Ctrl), and Alternate (Alt). In general, moving the mouse changes the location, and possibly the shape, of the pointer. A mouse action is proposed when the mouse button is pressed down and confirmed when the mouse button is released.

Table 7.4 lists the mouse operations common to most GUIs in the comparison.

Table 7.5 shows a comparison of mouse operations for the GUIs in the comparison. Macintosh and NeXTSTEP define an additional mouse operation—multiple-clicking. NeXTSTEP multiple-clicking can be a *double-click* or *triple-click*. Triple-click is used for selecting text objects such as a paragraph (i.e., all the text between return characters).

TABLE 7.4   **Common Mouse Operations**

| Mouse Operations | Description |
|---|---|
| *Pointing* | Placing the mouse pointer over an object. |
| *Clicking* | Pushing down on the mouse button and quickly releasing it while the mouse remains in a fixed position. |
| *Double-clicking* | Clicking a second time immediately following the first click. It is commonly used as a shortcut to other actions. For example, clicking on a file icon twice opens the file immediately, without having to select the file icon and then choose the **Open** option from the **File** menu. |
| *Pressing* | Holding down the mouse button for a time while the mouse remains stationary. |
| *Dragging* | Pressing the mouse button, moving the mouse to a new position, and then releasing the mouse button. Dragging is used for window or component selection, such as a block of text, a range of objects, or a menu item. It can be used to move an icon or object from one location to another, or to resize an object or window. |

TABLE 7.5   **Comparison of Mouse Operations**

| Macintosh | OSF/Motif | NeXTSTEP | Presentation Manager | Microsoft Windows |
|---|---|---|---|---|
| Pointing | Pointing | Pointing | Pointing | Pointing |
| Clicking Double-clicking Multiple-clicking | Click MultiClick | Clicking Multiple-clicking (Double-click Triple-click) | Clicking Double-clicking | Clicking Double-clicking |
| Pressing | Press MultiPress | Pressing | Pressing | Pressing |
| Dragging | Motion MultiMotion | Dragging | Dragging | Dragging |
| Release | Release | | Release | |

OSF/Motif defines the following various mouse operations [OSF/ Motif, pp. 2-6 to 2-7]:

- *MultiPress* indicates a number of clicks in quick succession without a final release. As in MultiClick, MultiPress are often referred to by the actual number of presses.

- *MultiMotion* indicates a MultiPress action followed by moving the position of the pointer. The action of a MultiMotion operation ends with a release action. As in MultiClick, MultiMotion is often referred to by the actual number of presses.

- *Motion* indicates pressing a mouse button without releasing it and then moving the position of the pointer. The action of a drag operation tracks the position of the mouse pointer. The drag ends when the mouse button is released.

Most GUIs assume that the mouse has two buttons. The left button is the default button and is used primarily for selection. The right button is used to initiate context-specific actions and options. However, OSF/Motif assumes that the mouse has three buttons. Table 7.6 defines the functions of the three buttons.

TABLE 7.6    **OSF/Motif Three-Button Mouse Definition**

| Mouse Button | Description |
|---|---|
| *BSelect* | Used for selection, activation, and setting the location cursor. This button must be the leftmost button, except for left-handed users where it can be the rightmost button. |
| *BTransfer* | Used for moving and copying elements. This button must be the middle mouse button, unless dragging is integrated with selection. |
| *BMenu* | Used for popping up menus. This button must be the rightmost button, except for left-handed users, where it can be the leftmost button. |

Source: *OSF/Motif Style Guide,* pp. 2-4 to 2-5.

In NeXTSTEP, the left and right buttons normally behave identically. However, the **Preferences** application allows the user to assign a special function to one of the buttons. For example, the user can make either one of the buttons a menu button. When the button is pressed, a copy of the main menu of the current application appears underneath the cursor.

"The pointing device used most often in a CUA environment is a two-button mouse. One of the two buttons is called the *selection button*.

The other mouse button is called the *manipulation button*, and is used for direct manipulation. The user can choose either the left or right mouse button for either function, selection, or manipulation. If a three-button mouse is used, the third button is called the *menu button*" [IBM CUA Guide to User Interface Design, p. 30].

### Pen

A pen is a direct input device that provides a natural and intuitive way of interacting with the computer. It is more than a mouse. The user is able to input commands and data directly onto the display screen or by "writing" on a flat surface. The pen selects data and manipulates objects with greater accuracy. It requires less coordination than manipulating objects with a mouse. A pen can specify a selection as well as an action directly through a gesture. For example, a simple curl gesture can be interpreted as a command and applied to the data directly under the gesture.

A pen serves two purposes—pointing and writing. The mode of the pen depends on where the pen is placed. When used as a pointing device to perform mouse-like operations such as selecting a menu command, the basic pen operation used is *tapping*. To tap, the user presses the pen tip on the screen and releases it without moving the pen. Tapping the pen once on the screen is equivalent to clicking the left button of the mouse once. A double-tap is equivalent to a double-click. Table 7.7 summarizes the principal pen techniques.

**TABLE 7.7   Microsoft Windows Pen Computing Techniques**

| Pen Technique | Examples of Use |
|---|---|
| *Tap* | Select object or menu command; set insertion point in text; push command button. |
| *Double-tap* | Open object; select word. |
| *Drag* | Move object (e.g., to move a window, drag its title bar); resize object (e.g., to resize a window, drag its border; to resize a graphical object, drag its resize handles). |
| *Press/hold/drag* | Select text from pen-down location to pen-up location; perform drag operations (e.g., object movement or marquee selection) in contexts where the pen normally functions as a writing or drawing tool. |
| *Write/draw* | Enter text or graphics; execute gestural commands (see Table 7.8). |

Source: *The Windows Interface: An Application Design Guide,* pp. 196.

When the pen is used for writing, the "ink" patterns appear on the display as the user writes. Certain patterns are interpreted as *gestures*. Gestures are special symbols used to issue a command. Gestures eliminate the "select an object, then select an operation from a menu" interface enforced by the mouse or the keyboard. With the pen, the user makes a single gesture at an object. For example, the ^ symbol is used for pasting text. After a gesture is interpreted, its ink is removed from the display [MICROSOFT, p. 196].

Most gestures act positionally. They contain a "hot spot" that can be used to determine where the gesture should act. For example, the hot spot for the pasting text gesture is at the top of the ^ symbol. When the user draws the paste gesture, the pasted data is inserted at the location of the hot spot [MICROSOFT, p. 198].

The pen retains the capability of the mouse. The pen can be used for drag selection of text, outline selection of graphical objects, moving or copying of objects, or any mouse-like operations. To drag an object with a pen, the user presses and holds the pen tip onto the screen over the object, and moves the pen along the surface of the screen without lifting it.

Microsoft Windows support for pen computing provides several predefined gestures including:

- Selection gestures (e.g., to extend a selection)

- Operation gestures (Copy, Paste, and Undo)

- Gestures for noncharacter keys (Backspace, Spacebar, Tab, and Enter)

Refer to Table 7.8 for a list of standard pen gestures.

Microsoft Windows for pen computing also allows the user to define his or her own gestures by circling letters. For example, the circled-C means copy, and the circled-B means bold to a word processing application. The user can implement application-specific *recognizers* for more graphical gestures. Recognizers are dynamic-link libraries (DLL) that collect characters from the display driver and interpret those characters as one or more alphabetic characters.

**TABLE 7.8  Microsoft Windows Pen Gestures**

| Name | Glyph | Hot Spot | Acts Where? | Granularity | Effect | Equivalent |
|------|-------|----------|-------------|-------------|--------|------------|
| *Space* | | | | | Insert space where drawn | Space character |
| *New Line* | | First Point | | | Insert new line where drawn | New line character |
| *Tab* | | | | Insertion point | Insert tab where drawn | Tab character |
| *Paste* | | Top | Positional | | Paste where drawn | Shift + Insert |
| *Extend Selection* | | Center | | | Extend selection from anchor point to gesture | Shift + Click |
| *Backspace* | | Lowest Point | | Character | Delete character under gesture | Backspace |
| *Delete words* | | Left, right | | Word | Delete words under gesture | Double-click + Delete |

Source: *The Windows Interface: An Application Design Guide*, p. 197.

*(continued)*

TABLE 7.8    **Pen Gestures,** *Continued*

| Name | Glyph | Hot Spot | Acts Where? | Granularity | Effect | Equivalent |
|------|-------|----------|-------------|-------------|--------|------------|
| *Edit Text* | | Inside center of lower "v" | | | Put selection (if any) or word into Edit Text dialog | — |
| *Cut* | | First point | Act on selection if one exists; otherwise positional (always positional in boxed edit controls). | Selection or word | Cut selection, if any, otherwise cut word under gesture | Shift + Delete |
| *Copy* | | Center of bounding box | | | Copy selection, if any, otherwise copy word under gesture | Control + Insert |
| *Delete* | | Lowest point | | Section or character | Delete selection, if any, otherwise delete character under gesture | Delete |
| *Undo* | | None | Nonpositional | Operation | Undo last operation | Alternate + Backspace |

Source: *The Windows Interface: An Application Design Guide,* p. 197.

### Touch Screen

Touch screens are visual devices that the user can touch to provide input to the system. The touch screen employs a natural metaphor for selection—touching the screen with the fingers, the most natural pointing device. The use of touch screen is effective when the primary inputs from the user to the system are selection decisions. Typically, the application displays an object on the screen and the user indicates a selection by directly touching the object on the screen. Touch screens are appropriate for simple tasks where entering a large amount of data is not required. The fatigue effect of reaching toward a screen is not a factor.

### Speech Recognition

Sound serves as a channel for communication between the user and the computer. The human voice is used as input to the computer. It is normally restricted to commands with precisely defined meanings to the system. The use of natural language is an unperfected discipline. Speech recognition offers the promise of rapid data capture. It is likely to play an increasing role in user interfaces as the technology improves.

## Pointers and Cursors

A visible cue associated with the keyboard and pointing devices is provided to show where the interaction will take place. The visible cue for the pointing devices is the *pointer;* the visible cue for the keyboard is the *cursor.*

### Pointers

The pointer is attached, logically, to the mouse or pointing device. On the screen, the pointer follows the movement of the pointing device. The user positions the pointer over the object he or she wants to work with. Each pointer has a "hot spot." Macintosh defines it as the "portion of the pointer that must be positioned over a screen object before the mouse clicks can have an effect on that object" [MHIG, p. 270]. The hot spot is the precise position of the mouse where the mouse action occurs. Similarly, screen objects have a "hot zone." Macintosh defines it as "the area that the pointer's hot spot must be within in order for the mouse clicks to have an effect" [MHIG, p. 270].

The shape of the pointer changes as the pointer moves about the screen. Table 7.9 shows the shapes of the pointer and their usage and hot spots, common to most of the GUIs in the comparison.

TABLE 7.9   **Common Pointer Shapes**

| Pointer | Name | Usage |
|---------|------|-------|
| | Upper-left Arrow | General-purpose pointer; used in window areas for selecting and activating single objects. The hot spot should be in the tip of the arrow. |
| | Upper-right Arrow | Used for selecting lines, rows, and cells. It is usually located at the left margin of a document or cell. The hot spot should be in the tip of the arrow. |
| | I-beam | Used for selecting and inserting text. The hot spot of the I-beam should be on the vertical bar of the I-beam about one-third from the bottom. |
| | Crosshair (Sighting) | Usually used by graphics (drawing) applications to indicate a pixel to fill or the connecting points of lines. The hot spot should be at the spot where the lines intersect. |
| | 4-Directional Arrow | Indicates that a move operation is in progress, or a resize operation before the resize direction has been determined. The hot spot should be the spot where the arrow intersects. During a move operation, the object, or an outline of the object, should move to track the location of the pointer. During a resize operation, the pointer is used to indicate a direction for resizing. The 4-directional arrow should change to an appropriate resize arrow when the resize direction is determined. |
| | Hourglass | Indicates that a lengthy operation is in progress |
| | Watchpointer | Indicates that a lengthy operation is in progress. The hot spot is located at the top of the watchpointer, although it should not be used for activation. |
| | Resize arrows | Used for changing the size of the window vertically, horizontally, and diagonally. |

### Cursors

A cursor is a symbol cue that shows the current position of the keyboard-input focus. The keyboard cursor can be a text cursor or selection cursor. Most GUIs represent the text cursor as a vertical bar or pipe ( | ) when the user is in insert mode. It is displayed in text that can be edited or selected and currently has the input focus as shown in Table 7.10. OSF/Motif defines the different text cursor shapes depending on whether the text has the keyboard focus or not:

TABLE 7.10   **OSF/Motif Text Cursor Shapes**

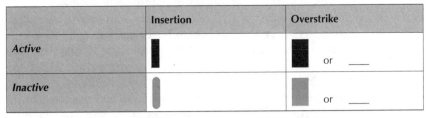

|  | Insertion | Overstrike |
|---|---|---|
| *Active* | | or ___ |
| *Inactive* | | or ___ |

A selection cursor, which is not really a cursor, is a visual component that indicates the location where the keyboard events are sent. It is depicted in a number of ways, depending on the type of component with the keyboard focus. The representations for a selection cursor common to the GUIs in the comparison are the box style cursor drawn around the object, and the dotted outline highlight cursor drawn around the object. The dotted outline highlight cursor style is used within menus to show the menu item with the selection cursor. Figure 7.3 shows an example of an OSF/Motif selection cursor. The rectangular box style cursor drawn around the command button indicates the selection made.

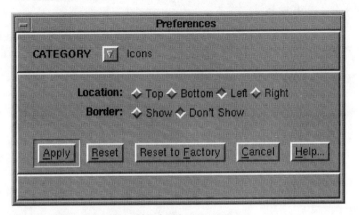

FIGURE 7.3   **Example of OSF/Motif Selection Cursor**

## 7.3 Object-Action Model

People create a model by putting together sets of perceived rules and patterns in a way that explains the situation. A model facilitates learning and reduces the amount of system-specific knowledge required to perform work tasks. Models also enhance consistency. The user can apply the same set of rules and patterns in another situation, which gives the user a sense of control.

The interaction between the user and the computer employs a model; that is, an *object-action model*. The object-action model allows the user to select an object and then select an action to apply to that object. This model provides a direct and intuitive way to accomplish work tasks. The objects include recognizable objects such as windows and controls, as well as "component elements that are not always recognized as discrete objects like individual letter of a text file" [OSF/Motif, p. 4-1].

The following sections discuss in detail the aspects involved in the interaction between the user and the computer. They include direct manipulation, selection, activation, navigation, and data transfer.

## 7.4 Object Types and Classes

Objects are the focus of the user's attention. Interaction between the user and the computer usually involves a *source object* and a *target object*. The source object is usually the object the user is working with, and a target object is usually the object that the user is transferring information to. Each GUI in the comparison classifies objects differently.

OSF/Motif defines groups of elements into the following types of collections:

- List-like collection (i.e., the pointer or cursor location is considered to be on an element)

- Text-like collection (i.e., the pointer or location cursor is considered to be between two elements)

- Graphics-like collection (i.e., the pointer or location cursor is considered to be on or between elements)

The IBM CUA guidelines defines three types of objects: data (e.g., text, graphics, audio, video), container (e.g., folders, delete folders, workareas, and workplaces), and device (e.g., printer).

(Refer to Chapter 2, "Desktop," for more information on the different types of objects.)

Macintosh classifies objects as array, field, graphics, and control. An array is an arrangement of a field containing information such as text and graphics through which the user navigates using the Tab key. A field is a data item separated from other data by blanks, tabs, or other specific delimiters. A graphic object is information presented in the form of a picture or an image. A control is an object on the window.

In general, objects can be text, field, and graphic data.

## Text Data

Text data are strings of alphanumeric symbols. In most applications, the user edits text at some point. Some applications are designed only for text editing, so they may have no other kinds of data objects. Other applications may display text-data objects within controls (e.g., within text boxes within dialog boxes). Regardless of where text appears within an application, the user generally selects and edits text data in a consistent manner across applications, and across GUI platforms.

A block of text is a string of characters. A text selection is a substring of this string, containing any number of characters ranging from zero to a whole block.

## Field Data

The term *field data* refers to data objects in an *array*. An array is a tabular arrangement of fields. One-dimensional arrays are called *lists;* two-dimensional arrays are called *forms,* or *tables.* A form is something that the user fills outs. An array can be identified by its rows and columns of fields (referred to as cells). Applications or dialog boxes that contain many editable-text fields are considered forms.

An array commonly appears in spreadsheet documents, occasionally as tables in word processing documents, as lists in dialog box controls such as list boxes. Note, however, that lists in dialog box controls may not always conform to selection and highlighting standards for field data in documents.

## Graphic Data

The term *graphic data* refers to the basic selectable elements and groups of elements that comprise editable pictures in electronic documents. Graphic data may be object-based or pixel-based (i.e., bitmap).

In object-based graphics, the picture is composed of selectable elements called *graphic primitives*. These elements are fundamental geometric entities such as points, lines, segments, circles, triangles, and squares. The user generally can assign primitives to discretely selectable groups and can assign groups to other discretely selectable groups and supergroups. Some GUIs and applications may also provide predetermined object-group (e.g., any closed polygon, or all objects on a conceptual layer). These groups usually are selectable via special techniques such as option-click or, if by layers, via menu commands.

Although the user defines and manipulates object-based graphics in terms of graphic primitives, unless object-based output devices (e.g., vector displays and plotters) are used, all object-based graphics must be converted to raster images (bitmaps) for on-screen display and printing. This conversion process is mostly automatic, and usually is not of much concern to the user.

In pixel-based graphics, the picture is composed of individual pixels. The user can select individual pixels and ranges of pixels.

Graphic-data objects behave like other types of data objects; that is, when the user selects an object using a mouse, as opposed to the keyboard, the object becomes highlighted when the mouse button is pressed, and becomes selected when the mouse button is released.

## 7.5 Manipulation Principles

The user can manipulate objects on the screen *directly* or *indirectly*. The user interface design principles such as empowering the user, directness, and providing visible and immediate feedback are some of the essential factors to consider in choosing a manipulation technique.

The IBM CUA style guide describes the manipulation techniques for the object-action paradigm (see Figure 7.4), with direct manipulation at one end, and indirect manipulation at the other end. Drag-and-drop, pop-up menus, and menu bars are other manipulation techniques that fall between direct and indirect manipulation.

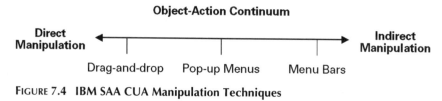

**FIGURE 7.4  IBM SAA CUA Manipulation Techniques**

Source: *IBM SAA Common User Access Guide to User Interface Design*, p. 42.

## Direct Manipulation

Direct manipulation is a technique that puts the user in control by performing actions on the objects directly. With this interaction technique, the object and action are bound together closely. Direct manipulation usually is accomplished with the use of a pointing device such as a mouse. For example, the user can size a window immediately by selecting a window border with a mouse and moving the border to the desired size. A size action is implied by and associated with the window border. As the operation is being performed, visual feedback is provided to indicate the progress and result of the direct manipulation.

Figure 7.5 shows resizing a Macintosh window using direct manipulation. The inset window is the initial size of the user's window. The window is resized by selecting the lower-right corner of that window with the mouse pointer and moving the pointer diagonally toward the lower-right corner of the screen. To indicate to the user that the resizing is taking place, the mouse pointer changes its appearance to a double-pointed arrow. A dotted outline of the window moves with the pointer. The inset window remains in the same place. When the user releases the mouse button, the window is drawn in the shape of the dotted outline.

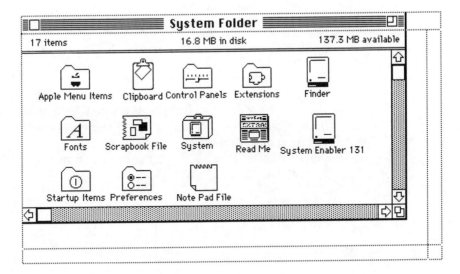

FIGURE 7.5 **Resizing a Window Using Direct Manipulation in Macintosh**

Direct manipulation is particularly useful in pen-based systems. The pen points directly to the object on the screen, which requires less coordination than dragging objects with a mouse. A unique virtue of the pen is its ability to specify a selection and an action directly through a gesture. To drag an object with a pen, the user presses the pen tip onto the screen over the object and moves the pen along the surface of the screen without lifting it. The application then determines which data to change and which operation to perform.

## Indirect Manipulation

Indirect manipulation is an interaction with objects through choices and controls using a keyboard or a mouse. This interaction technique is employed when a keyboard is used exclusively to interact with the computer. With this interaction technique, the object and action are separated from each other. The principle of indirect manipulation requires the user to select an object first, then make a choice that performs the actual manipulation.

## Other Manipulation Techniques

Other manipulation techniques fall between direct and indirect manipulations, such as drag-and-drop, pop-up menus, and menu bars. Pop-up menus allow the user to interact with an object more directly than using menu bars and pull-down menus. For example, a pop-up menu for an application object provides a quick and easy way to access commands. The user does not have to navigate the menu bar or control bar to browse through the menu items. However, pop-up menus are less direct than drag-and-drop.

For more information on pop-up menus and menu bars, refer to Chapter 4, "Menus."

## 7.6 Selection

A user interacts with an object by identifying one or more desired objects to which subsequent actions will be performed. *Selection* is a fundamental characteristic of a user interface by which the user designates one or more objects to be operated on, making them distinguishable from other objects.

## Selection Types

Microsoft Windows classifies selection as *single* (involving only one item) or *multiple* (involving more than one item). "A multiple selection can be either *contiguous* or *disjoint*. Contiguous selection allows the user to select one or more data objects that are proximal within a collection of data objects. Multiple selection can be further classed as homogeneous or heterogeneous, depending on the properties selected" [MICROSOFT, pp. 22–23]. The selection types are illustrated in Figures 7.6 to 7.9.

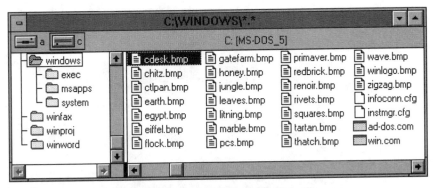

**FIGURE 7.6** **Example of a Microsoft Windows Single Selection**

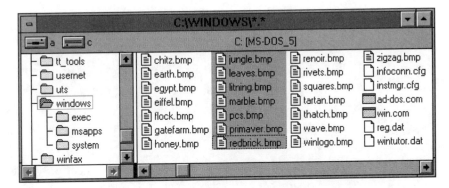

**FIGURE 7.7** **Example of a Microsoft Windows Contiguous Multiple Selection**

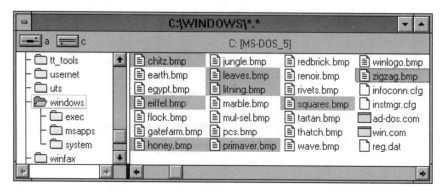

**FIGURE 7.8   Example of a Microsoft Windows Disjoint Multiple Selection**

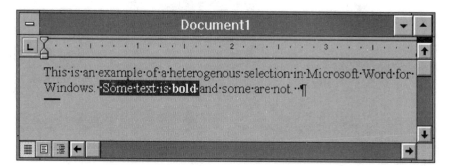

**FIGURE 7.9   Example of a Microsoft Windows Heterogeneous Selection**

IBM CUA guidelines define three types of selection based on the number of objects that can be selected [IBM CUA, p. 20]:

- *Single selection* allows at most one object to be selected at any time in a scope.

- *Multiple selection* allows the user to select one or more at any time in a scope.

- *Extended selection* allows the user to select only one object at a time or to extend the selection to more than one object.

## Selection Highlighting

In most GUIs, the appearance of the data object changes when it is selected. The data object appears highlighted. The highlighting of a selected data object is dependent upon the display hardware. On black-and-white screen displays, highlighting is shown by reverse video (black pixels turn white and white pixels turn black). On color screen displays, the user has the option of choosing the color of the background of highlighted areas, and the foreground color (the color of the data object) does not change when highlighted.

The *Macintosh Human Interface Guidelines* recommends that the highlighting of a selection should begin immediately after the user presses down the mouse button, as opposed to when the user releases the mouse button.

## Selection Techniques

Selection techniques are the interaction mechanisms used for selecting data objects. Most GUIs in the comparison define techniques for both the keyboard and the mouse. The IBM CUA style guide and Microsoft Windows define interaction techniques for additional input devices such as the pen.

The selection techniques supported by the GUIs in the comparison can be summarized as *point selection*, *point-to-endpoint selection*, and *random-point selection*. Point selection allows the user to select only one object at a time. Point-to-endpoint selection allows the user to select all objects between two or more specified points. Random-point selection allows a user to select objects as the pointer passes over them, in whatever order the user chooses.

### Text Data

The user selects an insertion point by clicking the mouse when the pointer is positioned over the desired data-object. In most GUIs, a single click in text selects an insertion point. Immediately after the mouse button is pressed, a vertical bar or pipe ( | ) appears between two characters at the point of insertion that is nearest to the hot spot of the I-beam pointer. When the mouse button is released, the vertical bar, or cursor, begins flashing. In some GUIs, the pointer may disappear after the insertion point has been selected, and does not reappear until the user moves the mouse.

*Text Data Selection Techniques Using a Mouse.* Figure 7.10 illustrates the selection techniques for text data objects.

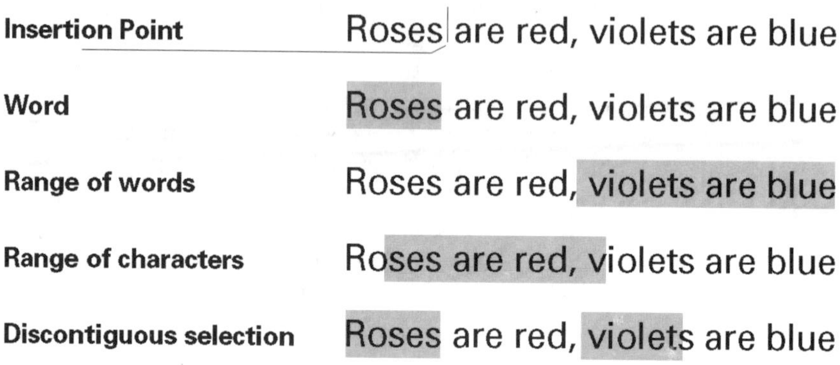

**Insertion Point**          Roses are red, violets are blue

**Word**          Roses are red, violets are blue

**Range of words**          Roses are red, violets are blue

**Range of characters**          Roses are red, violets are blue

**Discontiguous selection**          Roses are red, violets are blue

FIGURE 7.10   Text Data Selection

Selection techniques for a range of characters, words, lines, or paragraphs are very similar to that of the insertion point. The user selects a whole word by double-clicking somewhere within that word. The user can select various groups of characters by multiple-clicking. In most GUIs, double-clicking selects an entire word, and triple-clicking selects an entire line or sentence. Some GUIs and applications even provide support of quadruple-clicking and quintuple-clicking for selection of paragraphs, pages, and so on. The feedback for these multiple techniques is basically the same as for single-clicking, except that when the mouse button is held down on the second click an entire word is highlighted, on the third click an entire line is highlighted, and so on. Immediately after the mouse button is released, the highlighted text becomes selected.

The user selects characters (as opposed to an insertion point, words, and so on), either individually or in a range, by dragging the mouse. The position of the pointer when the mouse button is first pressed acts as an anchor point. Immediately after the user presses the mouse button, all the characters between the anchor point and the current pointer position become highlighted. Immediately after the mouse button is released, all the characters between the anchor point and the mouse pointer when the mouse button is released become selected.

*Text Data Selection Techniques Using a Keyboard.* In most GUIs, the user can press the arrow or the cursor keys to move the insertion point cursor in text. To select characters using the arrow keys, the user holds down the Shift key while pressing any of the arrow keys. The Right and Left Arrow keys move the cursor one character to the right or left, respectively, with each press. If the user holds down the Shift key and presses either the Left or Right Arrow key, the first character to the left or right, respectively, of the current insertion point is highlighted and selected. If the user continues to press the Left or Right Arrow key while pressing the Shift key, the cursor moves, one character at a time, in the direction of the key that is being pressed. Each character traversed by the cursor in this manner while the Shift key is down becomes highlighted and selected.

The Up Arrow and Down Arrow keys move the cursor one line up or down, respectively, with each press. If the user presses either the Up Arrow or Down Arrow key while pressing the Shift key, all the characters between the original insertion point and the new insertion point, which would be either one line up or down, become highlighted and selected. If the user continues to press the Up Arrow or Down Arrow key while pressing the Shift key, all the lines that are traversed by the cursor become highlighted and selected.

*Text Data Selection Techniques Using a Keyboard-Modified Mouse.* Extending a text selection is usually not possible without using the keyboard. Generally, with the appropriate modifier key held down, the user may extend an existing text selection using any of the preceding techniques. However, selection of discontiguous text characters is rarely supported, because of the ambiguity it would create for such actions as typing new characters. For some other actions (for example, assigning fonts and styles) selection of discontiguous text characters is a potentially useful feature.

Several different selection models exist to determine which characters will be selected or de-selected when various techniques are used in different situations. However, it is usually not beneficial for GUIs to mandate, beyond a certain level of simplicity, which models are supported in given scenarios, because the need for powerful editing techniques outweighs the need for consistency among situations that a majority of users encounter only infrequently.

In most text-editing situations, when the user *clicks* the mouse while the Shift key is down, all characters between the location of the pointer and the current insertion point, or any currently selected characters, are added to the current selection.

If the user *drags* the mouse while the Shift key is down, the results may differ depending on whether a selection problem exists. If no selection exists, then this technique works the same as when no key is held down, except that the current insertion point acts as the anchor point. If characters are currently selected when the user begins a drag and the Shift key is down, one selection model uses the end of the current selection furthest from the current pointer location as the anchor point. In this model, if the user drags the mouse so that the pointer location is on the other side of the current selection than it was when the drag began, the anchor point switches from one end of the current selection to the opposite end.

Another text-selection model prescribes that all the characters between the current selection and the initial location of the pointer become highlighted, and, if the user drags the pointer beyond the other side of the current selection, those characters become highlighted as well. This model provides the ability to extend an existing selection in both directions via a single mouse action.

Those GUIs and applications that allow discontiguous selections use another model. This model works similarly to the previous one, except that if the user drags the mouse so that the pointer moves within the current selection, all the characters within the current selection that are also within the range of the current drag action become de-highlighted, and all the characters outside the current selection and inside the current drag action become highlighted.

In all of the preceding models, when the user releases the mouse button, the highlighted characters become selected.

If discontiguous selections are allowed, a modifier key other than the Shift key is commonly designated so the system can identify whether the user intends to make a discontiguous selection or a contiguous one. This key is usually either the Command key (in Macintosh) or the Control key. When the Command or Control key is held down, as opposed to the Shift key or no key, the selection that would otherwise have been made is simply added to the existing selection. In other words, if the Command or Control key is held down and characters are currently selected, a range selection that begins at least one character away from either end of the current selection and continues in a direction away from the current selection, results in a discontiguous extension of the current selection. If the Command or Control key is held down and the newly selected text is completely within the current selection, the newly selected text becomes de-highlighted.

*Comparison of Text Data Selection Techniques.* Text data selections in the Macintosh are indicated by a change in appearance of the selected text. On black-and-white screen displays, text highlighting is shown by reverse video (black pixels turn white, and white pixels turn black). On color screen displays, the user has the option of choosing the color of the background of highlighted areas, and the foreground color (the color of the text) does not change when highlighted. According to the *Macintosh User Interface Guidelines*, the highlighting of a selection should begin immediately after the user presses down the mouse button, as opposed to when the user releases the mouse button.

The *NeXTSTEP User Interface Guidelines* describes three mouse-based techniques to select contiguous elements. NeXTSTEP calls these techniques *dragging to select, clicking to select,* and *multiple-clicking to select.*

The user can apply the *dragging to select* technique by executing the following consecutive steps:

- Set an anchor point by pressing the mouse button at the cursor location;

- Drag the mouse to the end point of the selection range; and

- Release the mouse button at the end point of the selection range.

The user can apply the *clicking to select* technique by executing the following consecutive steps:

- Set an anchor point by clicking the mouse button at the cursor location;

- Move the mouse to the end point of the selection range; and

- Click the mouse button at the end point of the selection range while holding down the Alternate (Alt) key.

The *multiple-clicking to select* technique applies only to text objects, and a "multiple-click always selects a linguistically significant unit," [NeXTSTEP, p. 28]:

- A double-click on a text object selects a word.

- A triple-click on a text object selects a paragraph (i.e., all the text between return characters).

The *NeXTSTEP User Interface Guidelines* refers to multiple individual selection as *extending a selection*. More specifically, NeXTSTEP considers this type of selection a form of *discontinuous extension*. The user can accomplish the *discontinuous extension* technique by pressing the Shift key while clicking on the desired items.

This selection technique is common for editable graphics, icons, and items in a list, but not for normal text.

### Field Data

*Field Data Selection Techniques Using a Mouse.* Figure 7.11 illustrates the various field data selection techniques.

| Color | Font |
|-------|------|
| Blue | Arial |
| Green | Gothic |
| Orange | MS Serif |
| Red | Roman |
| Yellow | System |

**Single Field Selection**

| Color | Font |
|-------|------|
| Blue | Arial |
| Green | Gothic |
| Orange | MS Serif |
| Red | Roman |
| Yellow | System |

**Column Selection**

| Color | Font |
|-------|------|
| Blue | Arial |
| Green | Gothic |
| Orange | MS Serif |
| Red | Roman |
| Yellow | System |

**Range Selection**

| Color | Font |
|-------|------|
| Blue | Arial |
| Green | Gothic |
| Orange | MS Serif |
| Red | Roman |
| Yellow | System |

**Discontiguous Selection**

FIGURE 7.11   **Field Data Selection**

The user can select one or more fields or part of the contents of a field. To select a single field or cell, the user clicks in the field while the mouse pointer is over the field. On mouse-down, the field becomes highlighted, and on mouse-up, the field becomes selected.

Columns and rows are similar to words and paragraphs in that they are groups of elements that are selectable as a whole via a single mouse action. A table can support selection of rows and columns. To select a column, the user clicks the mouse while the pointer is within the field that contains the column header. Similarly, the user may select a row by clicking the mouse while the pointer is within the field that contains the row header.

Generally, the user may select a range of columns or rows by dragging the pointer through the header fields of the desired selection.

The user may select a range of individual fields by dragging as well. If the user clicks and drags the pointer through a range of fields that are all in the same column or row, all the fields between the beginning point of the drag and the ending point of the drag become highlighted, and, upon release of the mouse button, the highlighted fields become selected. If the user drags the pointer diagonally across both columns and rows, all the fields between the beginning point of the drag and the ending point of the drag, in both horizontal and vertical directions, become highlighted, and, upon release of the mouse button, the high-lighted fields become selected.

*Field Data Selection Techniques Using a Keyboard-Modified Mouse.* Generally, the user can only accomplish extensions to existing selections in collections of contiguous field-data objects via a keyboard-modified mouse interaction. In most GUIs and applications, when a single field is currently selected, a Shift-click highlights all the fields, in both horizontal and vertical directions, between the current selection and the point of the click. When a range of fields is currently selected, a Shift-click highlights all the fields, in both horizontal and vertical directions, between the point of the click and the corner of the current selection that is farthest from the point of the click. In either case, the highlighted fields become selected upon release of the mouse button.

A Shift-drag is very similar to a Shift-click except that, as the user drags the mouse, the current selection acts as the anchor point for the drag if only a single field is currently selected. If a range of fields is currently selected, the field at the corner of the current selection that is farthest from the pointer location acts as the anchor point for the drag action. As with other selections, on mouse-down, all the fields included in the selection become highlighted as they fall within the range of the selection, and all highlighted fields become selected immediately upon release of the mouse button.

The user can either Shift-click or Shift-drag to make contiguous extensions to existing selections. However, discontiguous selections are also common in a field-data context. This necessitates designation of a modifier key other than Shift so the system can identify whether the user intends to make a discontiguous selection or a contiguous one. This key is usually either the Command key or the Control key. When the user holds down this key, as opposed to the Shift key or no key, the selection that would otherwise have been made is simply added to the existing selection.

*Field Data Selection Techniques Using a Keyboard.* Selection of fields using the keyboard is similar to selection of text characters from the keyboard except that, in fields, there is no equivalent to an insertion point between fields as there is between characters, and the selection order of fields is based on spatial adjacency rather than on a linear sequence as in text. Generally, if no field is selected, the current selection is usually a text insertion point inside a field. In either case, pressing any of the arrow keys while holding down the Shift key results in a selection consisting of the currently selected field, or the field that the insertion point is currently within, and the next field in the direction of the arrow key that was pressed. If the user presses the arrow key and the Shift key continuously, each successive field in the direction of the arrow key that is being pressed is added to the current selection. When the last field in a row or column is selected in this way and the user is still pressing the arrow and Shift keys, the selection continues with the next field in an order that is predetermined by the GUI or the application. In some GUIs and some applications, when the user reaches the edge of a table while extending a selection in this manner, the currently selected fields are extended as a whole in a direction perpendicular to the direction represented by the arrow key the user is pressing.

If more than one field is currently selected, the result of pressing an arrow key and the Shift key depends on two conditions: (1) the depth and width of the current selection and (2) which of the arrow keys is pressed. A few examples follow:

- If the current selection is two fields *wide* and the user presses the Shift and Up Arrow keys, the selection is extended *upward* one row at a time in two-field groups.

- If the current selection is two fields *deep*, and the user presses the Shift and Right Arrow keys, the current selection is extended to the *right* one column at a time in two-field groups.

- If the current selection is two fields wide and three fields deep, and the user presses the Shift and Right Arrow keys once, the current selection is extended to the *right*. The resulting selection measures *three* fields wide by three fields deep. Then, if the user presses the Shift and Down Arrow keys once, the current selection is extended *downward* and the resulting selection is three fields wide and *four* fields deep.

*The Macintosh Human Interface Guidelines* refers to field-data objects as arrays: "An array is a one- or two-dimensional arrangement of fields. The user can select one or more fields or part of the contents of a field. . . . To select a single field, the user clicks in the field. The user can also select a field by moving to it with the Tab or Return key. . . . To select part of the contents of a field, the user must first select the field. The user then clicks again to select the desired part of the field. Because the contents of the field are either text or graphics, selections within a field follow the appropriate rules for either text or graphics. A table can support selection of rows and columns. The most convenient way for the user to select a column is to click in the column header. To select more than one column, the user drags through several column headers. The same behavior applies to selecting rows. . . . Pressing the Tab key cycles the insertion point through the fields in an order determined by your application. From each field, the Tab key selects the 'next' field. Typically, the sequence of fields is from left to right, and then from top to bottom. When the last field in a form is selected, pressing the Tab key selects the first field in the form. The user can press Shift-Tab to navigate in the opposite direction. . . . The Return key selects the first field in the next row. The user can use Shift-Return to navigate up to the previous row in an array. If the idea of rows doesn't make sense in a particular context, then the Return key should have the same effect as the Tab key" [MHIG, p. 299].

The visual feedback for selection of field objects is similar to that for text. On a black-and-white screen display, when the user selects a field, the area contained by the field is shown in reverse video. On color screen displays, the background of a selected field is shown in the highlight color that the user has set in the Colors control panel, and the foreground color remains unchanged.

### Graphic Data

Graphic data objects behave like other types of data objects. When the user selects an object using a mouse, the object becomes highlighted when the mouse button is pressed, and becomes selected when the mouse button is released.

*Object-based Graphic Selection Techniques Using a Mouse.* Because working with object-based graphics is conceptually similar to drawing on paper (there is no set starting point, end point, or sequence in which parts of the picture must be drawn), there is no inherent spatial or conceptual order among object-based graphics. Therefore, the concepts of contiguous and discontiguous selection generally do not apply in object-based graphics, and all objects or groups of objects must be discretely selected either by dragging or clicking.

The most basic element of an object-based graphic image is a point. If the point has not been assigned by the user to a multipoint group, an individual point is usually selectable via a single mouse-click. An unselected point generally appears as a very small (approximately three pixels by three pixels), black-outlined, empty square. Selected points usually have the same appearance as unselected points, except a selected point appears as a filled, black square.

In applications used to create object-based graphics, all other selectable elements usually are expressed in terms of points; for example, any closed polygon in a picture typically has one point at the end of each side segment. If all the points that describe a higher-level element, such as a line segment or polygon, have been grouped, the group is selectable as a whole via a single mouse-click on any part of the group. When the user clicks on a group, all its associated points become highlighted by appearing as filled-in squares. Points that describe higher-level forms are often referred to as *handles*. Figure 7.12 shows a selection handle around a graphic object.

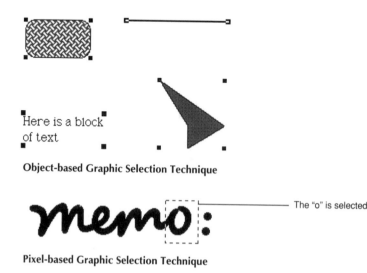

**Object-based Graphic Selection Technique**

**Pixel-based Graphic Selection Technique**

The "o" is selected

FIGURE 7.12   Graphic Selection Techniques

Some kinds of applications, such as page-layout applications, are designed for importing graphics, but not creating them. Object-based graphics that have been imported into these applications usually are not editable at a component level. In other words, object-based graphics in these applications are selectable only as a whole. When the user selects a graphic in this context, it usually appears with one filled handle at each corner, and at the midpoint of each side of the rectangle it occupies.

Because most display devices are raster-based, as opposed to object-based, dragging to select object-based graphics is much the same as dragging to select other kinds of data-objects, even though the selectable elements of object-based graphics have no inherent order. In other words, when dragging in an object-based graphics context, just as in dragging through pixel-based graphics or fields in a table, the system still *highlights a rectangular area* based on the rows and columns of pixels that comprise the area through which the pointer is dragged. The beginning point of the drag action marks one corner of the rectangle and the current pointer location marks the opposite corner.

Highlighting begins immediately after the mouse button is pressed and generally has the appearance of a dashed outline enclosing the rectangular area. The active corner of the rectangle continues to follow the pointer as the drag action occurs.

When the mouse button is released, the drag action ceases, and any graphics objects that lie within the rectangular area become selected. Some GUIs and applications support the convention that all objects that fall *completely* within the drag-rectangle become selected. Other GUIs and applications support the convention that all objects that fall completely, *or partially,* within the drag-rectangle become selected.

*Object-based Graphic Selection Techniques Using A Keyboard.* There are no widely supported keyboard-only selection techniques for object-based graphics.

*Object-based Graphic Selection Techniques Using a Keyboard-Modified Mouse.* Because the concept of contiguous and discontiguous selections does not apply in object-based graphics contexts, the Shift key is generally the only key required to make any kind of extended selection. If a current selection exists, the user can extend the selection by Shift-clicking or Shift-dragging to select other elements. Feedback for these techniques is generally identical to that for unmodified clicking or dragging.

If the user has not explicitly grouped all the points comprising a higher-level element, all the element's points often may be selected as a whole by clicking any part of the element while also pressing the Option key. In those GUIs and applications that support the convention that any grouped object falling partially within a drag-area becomes selected, the Option-drag technique usually may be used to select *ungrouped* objects that fall completely, *or partially,* within the drag-area.

If previous selections exist, the user usually may employ Shift-Option-drag to extend the current selection to include ungrouped objects that fall completely, *or partially,* within the drag-area.

*Pixel-based Graphic Selection Techniques Using a Mouse.* Most GUIs and applications do not support selection of elements in pixel-based graphics contexts via a mouse-click. Some applications provide special tools that can be used to select, via a mouse-click, groups of pixels that have certain similarities; for example, a *magic wand tool* in some applications selects all spatially adjacent pixels whose color values fall within given parameters.

Generally, any selection in a pixel-based graphics context must be done by dragging. Dragging to select pixel-based graphics is very similar to dragging to select field-data-objects in tables. In other words, when the user drags in a pixel-based graphics context, just as in dragging through fields in a table, the pointer still *highlights a rectangular area* based on the rows and columns of pixels that comprise the area through which the pointer was dragged. The beginning point of the drag action marks one corner of the rectangle and the current pointer location marks the opposite corner. This highlighting begins immediately after the mouse button is pressed, and generally has the appearance of a dashed outline enclosing the rectangular area. The active corner of the rectangle continues to follow the pointer as the drag action occurs. When the mouse button is released, the drag action ceases, and all pixels that lie within the rectangular area become selected. Figure 7.12 shows a pixel-based graphic selection and feedback.

*Pixel-based Graphic Selection Techniques Using a Keyboard-Modified Mouse.* Although pixels on a raster display device are arranged identically to fields in a table, selections of pixel-based graphics in some GUIs and applications cannot be extended. In other GUIs and applications, extensions are supported but the concept of contiguous and discontiguous selection is not. That is, any selection may be extended by Shift-dragging, but pixels lying between the current selection and the new selection are *not* automatically added to the current selection, as they are in field-data-objects in tables when the same technique is used.

*Pixel-based Graphic Selection Techniques Using a Keyboard.* There are no widely supported keyboard-only selection techniques for object-based graphics.

## 7.7 Drag and Drop

Drag-and-drop is a form of direct manipulation using a pointing device such as a mouse. No pull-down or pop-up menus are required to perform actions on an object when drag-and-drop manipulation is used. The principle of direct manipulation prescribes *dragging* an object with the mouse and *dropping* it on another object. Dragging consists of positioning the pointer on an object, pressing and holding the mouse button (usually the left button), moving the mouse, and releasing the mouse button. The object remains visible while the user performs physical actions. The result of those operations on the object is immediately visible with this kind of operation on an object. Drag-and-drop is frequently used for moving an object from one location to another. However, other actions, such as copying, deleting, printing, and saving, can be accomplished using this direct manipulation technique.

Drag-and-drop usually involves a *source object* and a *target object*. The source object is usually the object the user is working with, and a target object is usually the object that the user is transferring information to. The result of a drag-and-drop depends on the source object and target object. For example, the user drags a document object and drops it onto a folder to move the document to the target folder. However, dragging the same document object and dropping it onto a printer object prints the document. The document object remains in its original location.

Figure 7.13 shows a document object being moved to another directory as an example of direct manipulation using the mouse as a pointing device. The drag was performed by placing the pointer on the document (object), and pressing and holding the left button of the mouse while the mouse pointer was moved to a different location on the screen. The document object was then dropped in the new location (in this case, to another directory). The direct manipulation is complete when the mouse button is released.

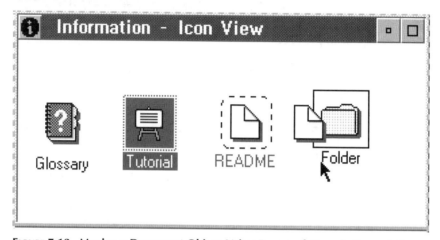

**FIGURE 7.13   Moving a Document Object Using Drag-and-Drop in Presentation Manager**

With the advent of multimedia, the use of animation is the best way to show the user that a requested action is being carried out. For example, dragging a data icon (document) onto a printer object initiates the printing of that document. The use of an animated printer reassures the user during the printing of a large document that the task is in progress without any problems.

## 7.8 Activation

Activation is the invocation of basic components or controls such as windows, command buttons, tear-off menus, and **Help** menus, resulting in an action associated with that component or control. The basic activation model imitates the real-life button activation in that pressing a button activates it. When the user selects a command button, clicking the left button of the mouse activates the operation associated with that command button. The appearance of the button changes to indicate that it has been selected and activated. The command button can be activated by pressing the Enter (or Return) key on the keyboard when the location cursor is on the button. Figure 7.14 illustrates the appearance of the button changes.

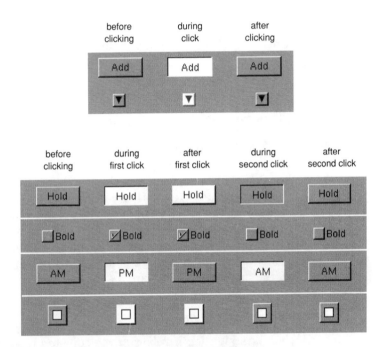

FIGURE 7.14  Appearance of Buttons in NeXTSTEP

A TearOff Button is composed of a button with a graphic that indicates the tear-off action. It tears off a menu in place when activated, or it is dragged to tear off and move in one action.

A window is activated by clicking anywhere within that window. The window appears in the foreground. All other windows are inactive. An active window is distinguishable from other windows by the emphasis displayed on its title bar and border. In Macintosh, the title bar of an active window displays racing stripes, and controls in the window frame are visible. The user can deactivate a window by closing (using the close box or control menu), minimizing (using the minimize button), hiding (using the **Hide** command as in the case of NeXTSTEP), and terminating (using the **Quit** or **Exit** command) the window. When the window that belongs to an application becomes inactive, the visual characteristics of the active state reverse.

## 7.9 Navigation (Transversal)

The user needs to navigate around the screen (that is, change the location of the cursor to a new position) regardless of whether the input device is a keyboard, mouse, or both. "Navigation is an action that causes the focus to move to another component" [OSF/Motif, p. GL-9]. The navigation model varies depending on the input device. For example, the navigation model for the keyboard is more complicated because several keys are reserved for keyboard navigation. The navigation model for the mouse is simple. By moving the mouse, the user can move the mouse pointer to any new location on the screen.

### Keyboard Navigation

Keyboard navigation involves keys dedicated to keyboard navigation of data items, windows, and controls. Table 7.11 lists the different navigation keys and their associated functions as single keys. These navigation keys can also be used in combination with various modifier keys. When the Control+key combination is used, the function of the navigation key changes. For example, a Control+Home moves the cursor to the top left position in the current field or document. If there is no left dimension, the key combination may also be used to move to the top position.

TABLE 7.11    **Navigation Keys**

| Navigation Key | Function (Cursor Movement) |
| --- | --- |
| *Home* | Beginning of line (leftmost position in current line) |
| *End* | End of line (rightmost position occupied by data in current line) |
| *Page Up* | Screen up (previous screen, same horizontal position) |
| *Page Down* | Screen down (next screen, same horizontal position) |
| *Left Arrow* | Left one unit; for text, the unit is one character |
| *Right Arrow* | Right one unit; for text, the unit is one character |
| *Up Arrow* | Up one unit; generally maintaining the same horizontal position |
| *Down Arrow* | Down one unit; generally maintaining the same horizontal position |
| *Tab* | For dialogs, next field; may move left or right, top to bottom, at designer's discretion. After last field, wraps to first. (Shift+Tab moves in the reverse order) |

### Mouse Navigation

The mouse is used to move the focus among controls. Simply moving the mouse pointer (without pressing the mouse button) moves the pointer. Most actions take place when the user positions the pointer over an object on the screen, then presses and releases the mouse button.

## 7.10  Data Transfer

A data transfer operation allows the user to move data, copy data, or create a new object. The most common techniques used by most GUIs to transfer data within an object, or from one object to another, are drag (drag-and-drop) and clipboard transfers. OSF/Motif defines additional techniques such as primary transfer, and quick transfer. Microsoft Windows relies on a combination of techniques including direct manipulation and the **Edit** menu commands (Cut, Copy, Paste, Paste Link).

These techniques are described as follows:

- *Drag Transfer (drag-and-drop)* is a form of direct manipulation using a pointing device such as a mouse. Refer to section 7.7, "Drag-and-Drop," for more detailed information.

- *Clipboard Transfer* is a transfer of data within an object, or from one object to another. Clipboard transfer consists of operations such as Cut, Copy, and Paste. Some GUIs provide other operations such as Paste Link or Paste Special. These operations paste, or embed, the contents of the clipboard into another application in a specified format, or create a link to information in another application that can be updated.

The clipboard is a window, and looks and acts like a window. The contents are visible, but usually uneditable. The clipboard holds whatever data is cut or copied from a document. It stores data in multiple formats so that the user can transfer data between applications that use different formats. Not all formats are displayable on the screen. Those formats that cannot be displayed are dimmed to distinguish them from the other formats.

Data is stored in the clipboard until the user replaces it with a new cut or copy operation. The contents of the clipboard are available to other applications. The user can switch from one application to another without affecting the contents of the clipboard.

*Primary Transfer* transfers the primary selection directly to its destination. In OSF/Motif, primary transfer is invoked by clicking the BTransfer or through the standard keyboard bindings. The three primary transfer operations are move, copy, and link.

*Quick Transfer* is a mechanism where a range of elements is immediately transferred to the destination. OSF/Motif implements the quick transfer by using <Alt> BTransfer Motion, with the standard modifiers used to force the various transfer operations.

## 7.11  Providing Feedback

When a user is performing a task or function, it is important to keep him or her informed about the state or progress of the task or function by providing feedback. In nearly all human efforts, feedback is the key to the learning process. Providing immediate and tangible feedback keeps the user informed about the status of a request or action. The common manifestations of feedback are visual (either graphical or textual). However, the use of multimedia data types such as sound and digital video enhance and supplement today's techniques of providing immediate and tangible feedback. Feedback incorporating these multimedia elements can enrich and improve communication between the user and the application.

## Visual Feedback

Visual feedback can consist of animation, graphics, text, and video. In most cases, graphical feedback is provided. Feedback is provided by changing the shape of the pointer, displaying a status indicator or progress indicator, using flashing techniques, and providing audible cues to get the user's attention.

### Pointers

The pointing device is associated with a pointer on the screen. The user manipulates the pointer to direct the application as to what to do and where to do it. By positioning the pointer over a screen object and clicking a button on the mouse, the user can select data, windows, controls, commands, and icons to initiate and complete actions. The pointer changes its shape according to the current action or current pointer position on the screen. For example, the pointer changes to an I-beam shape while it is over text to indicate the location of the insertion point when the mouse button is pressed. The use of modifier keys can supplement these pointers. Animated pointers prove to be an effective technique for drawing the user's attention. However, they should be used sparingly.

Different pointer shapes are available for selection, resizing, and movement. Figure 7.15 shows the different pointer shapes and their uses for the GUIs in the comparison.

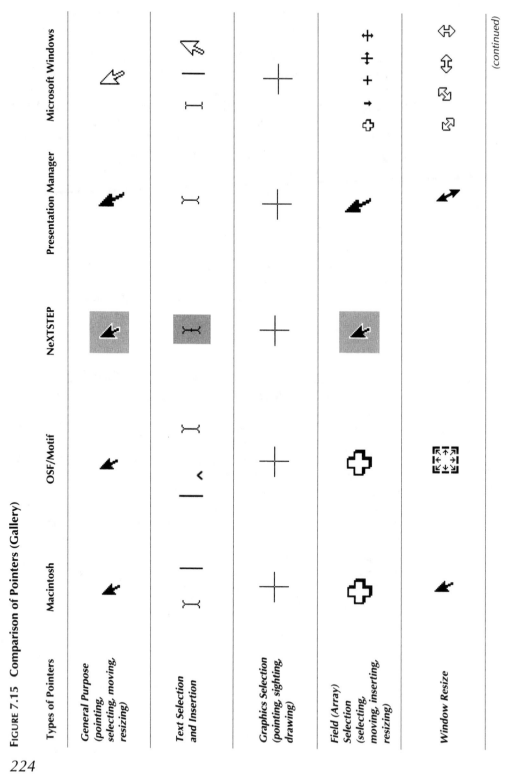

FIGURE 7.15 Comparison of Pointers (Gallery)

| Types of Pointers | Macintosh | OSF/Motif | NeXTSTEP | Presentation Manager | Microsoft Windows |
|---|---|---|---|---|---|
| *General Purpose* (pointing, selecting, moving, resizing) | | | | | |
| *Text Selection and Insertion* | | | | | |
| *Graphics Selection* (pointing, sighting, drawing) | | | | | |
| *Field (Array) Selection* (selecting, moving, inserting, resizing) | | | | | |
| *Window Resize* | | | | | |

*(continued)*

224

FIGURE 7.15 Comparison of Pointers (Gallery), *Continued*

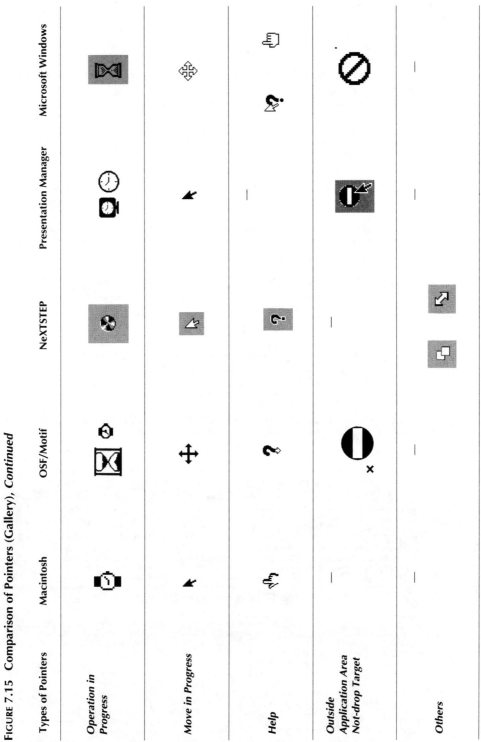

| Types of Pointers | Macintosh | OSF/Motif | NeXTSTEP | Presentation Manager | Microsoft Windows |
|---|---|---|---|---|---|
| *Operation in Progress* | ⌚ | ⧗ | ◉ | 🕐 | ⌛ |
| *Move in Progress* | ↖ | ✛ | ↖ | ↖ | ✛ |
| *Help* | 👆 | ❓ | ?• | — | ?◦ 👆 |
| *Outside Application Area Not-drop Target* | — | ⦸ ✕ | — | ⦸ | ⦸ |
| *Others* | — | — | ↗ ◰ | — | — |

### Feedback for Drag-and-Drop Operations

Visual cues should be used to keep the user well informed of the progress and result of a drag-and-drop manipulation. The following are common manifestations of feedback for a drag-and drop operation:

- The object, an outline, a dotted line, or some representation of the object should move along with the pointer.

- As the user drags the object to its target destination, the shape of the pointer should change to a do-not pointer to indicate that the current location is not valid as a drag-and-drop target.

- A visual cue that indicates the source object of a drag-and-drop operation should be displayed. For example, the contrast of the object being manipulated can be changed so that it appears dim.

- Feedback should be provided, if possible, for the target object of a drag-and-drop operation. For example, possible destination locations could be highlighted or otherwise emphasized as the object is dragged over them.

- During the drag-and-drop operation, feedback should be provided to reflect the operation (i.e., move, copy, or link) that will result if the object is dropped in the current location.

Figure 7.16 illustrates the visual cues used for providing feedback for a drag-and-drop operation [IBM CUA, p. 78].

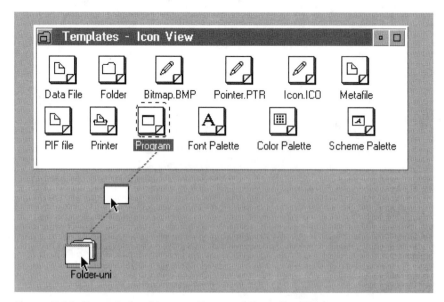

FIGURE 7.16   **Presentation Manager Drag-and-Drop Feedback**

### *Progress Indicators*

When an operation takes more than a few seconds, and the user cannot continue working in that application until the task is completed, feedback on the progress of the operation should be provided. The pointer may change its shape to inform the user that the system is busy. The hourglass, clock, and wristwatch are common pointers for this case. NeXTSTEP provides a system busy pointer, which looks like a spinning disk.

However, during a particularly lengthy operation when the user cannot proceed with other tasks or switch to another application until the operation in progress is completed, the application should display a *status indicator* or *progress indicator*. A progress indicator reassures the user that the operation is still underway. It should be dynamic; that is, it should indicate to the user the estimated total time of the operation. A progress indicator should also provide continuous feedback on the progress of the operation. Progress indicators are graphical. Most GUIs provide feedback on the progress of an operation in the form of a thermometer-type graphic device contained in a dedicated window (dialog box), or within a window's status area, if one exists. A progress indicator may appear as a rectangular bar that is initially empty. It is gradually filled with color from left to right as the operation proceeds, and is noninteractive. Percentage complete or elapsed-time messages can be used as a supplement or replacement for progress indicators.

An application displaying a progress indicator should provide a way of temporarily interrupting and resuming lengthy operations. The progress indicator should contain command buttons with labels, such as Pause and Resume. If the operation is uninterruptable, but does allow an irreversible interruption of the operation, the progress indicator should contain command buttons with labels, such as Cancel and Stop. Cancel interrupts the operations without affecting the application and data. Stop terminates the operation without reversing any changes that the operation has already caused.

Figure 7.17 shows a progress indicator that appears in the same window (in this case, a dialog box) from which the process was requested. The percentage completion of the task is displayed under the progress indicator. The Cancel button is provided to close the progress indicator window without applying any changes in that window. The progress indicator is filled as the copy operation progresses as shown in Figure 7.18.

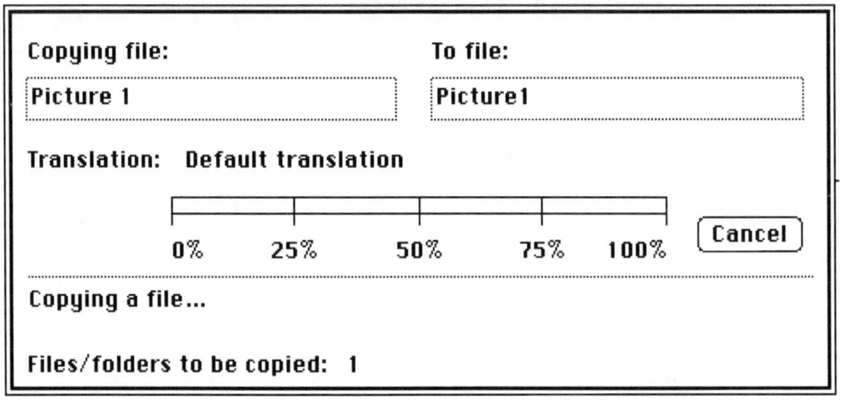

FIGURE 7.17   Macintosh Progress Indicator (Empty)

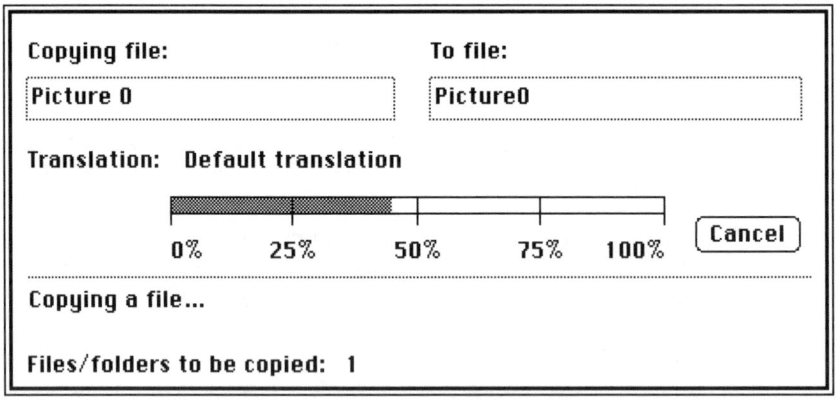

FIGURE 7.18   Macintosh Progress Indicator (Partially Filled)

The status bar (status area), which is a part of a window typically located at the bottom, can be used to indicate the progress of an operation or process. In Figure 7.19 the status area reflects the accurate status of the file open process.

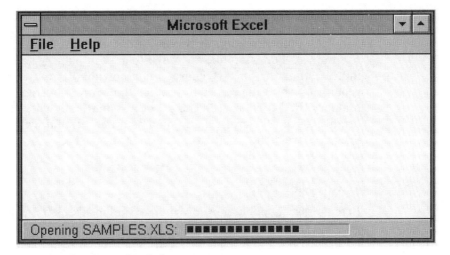

**FIGURE 7.19    Microsoft Windows Status Bar**

Multimedia applications playing waveform audio files (.WAV), Musical Instrument Digital Interface (MIDI) files, and audio CD tracks, can display a *media player track bar* as illustrated in Figure 7.20. The multimedia track bar is another form of progress indicator. It represents the open media sequence. The slider indicates the current playing position of the media sequence. The user can change the current playing position by dragging the slider to another location along the track bar, or by using the scroll arrows on the right.

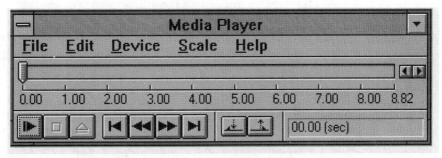

**FIGURE 7.20    Microsoft Windows Multimedia Track Bar**

### Flashing for Attention

The application can draw the user's attention by using flashing techniques. For example, in Macintosh, the battery icon flashes to indicate that the battery charge for a portable computer is low. It is prompting the user to act to protect the contents of Random Access Memory (RAM) before the computer automatically goes to sleep. The brightness of the screen is dimmed as an additional warning or feedback to attract the user's attention.

## Textual Feedback

In most cases, applications provide textual feedback in the form of brief messages. In general, most GUIs in the comparison provide these messages in the message bar, status bar, or in message dialog boxes. Textual feedback is used if graphical feedback cannot precisely convey detailed information.

## Auditory Feedback

Sound serves as an additional channel for communication between the computer and the user. The addition of sound to system events is an effective means to alert and inform the user about the state or progress of the task or function. Most GUIs in the comparison provide auditory feedback for system startup, system shutdown, error messages, warning messages, information messages, and printer error messages. The most common auditory feedback is the system beep, which draws the user's attention to minor and obvious errors. For example, if the user presses the End key on the keyboard while the text insertion cursor is at the end of the line, the system beeps instead of displaying a message.

## 7.12   System Modes

A system mode is a state of the system in which only certain actions are accessible to the user. Modes can restrict the user's option. However, they are useful in directing the user's interaction with the system.

There are three kinds of system modes; namely, system-busy, general control, and text modes.

## System-Busy Mode

A *system-busy mode* is the state of the system when the computer is unable to respond and process another input from the user in a timely manner due to ongoing operations. The system notifies the user of the progress of a task by changing the appearance of the pointer. System-busy pointers usually adopt a timepiece metaphor. Most GUIs in the comparison provide a system-busy pointer such as an hourglass, clock, wristwatch, and in the case of NeXTSTEP, a spinning disk. These pointers may or may not be animated.

While an operation is in progress, moving the mouse changes the position of the pointer relative to mouse movement. The pointer can change shape when it is located within a particular zone of the display. In other applications that use a modal-tool paradigm, the user can explicitly select the desired pointer type.

## General-Control Mode

The system is in general-control mode when there are no other modes in effect. The pointer assumes its normal shape. The general-control pointer is often referred to simply as the *pointer, arrow,* or *arrow pointer.* It is usually represented as an upper-left pointing arrow. The general-control mode pointer is usually not animated.

Moving the mouse changes the position of the pointer relative to mouse movement. The pointer can change shape when it is located within a particular zone of the display. In other applications that use a modal-tool paradigm, the user can explicitly select the desired pointer type.

Typically, when the pointer is positioned over a menu item or control such as the menu bar, the pointer shape is an upper-left pointing arrow pointer. It is used for single object selection and activation of most window areas. The pointer assumes an upper-right pointing arrow pointer shape when it is located at the left margin of a document or cell. It can be used for selecting lines, rows, and cells.

## Text-Editing Mode

When the pointer is positioned over an editable text block, the shape of the pointer changes to show that the system is in a text-editing mode. The text-editing mode pointer is referred to as the *I-beam* pointer. The GUIs in the comparison support a text-editing pointer that appears as a one-pixel vertical line with short cross bars at each end.

In some applications that provide capabilities for creating and editing data types other than text, the user must explicitly select a text-editing tool for the text-editing pointer to appear.

Moving the mouse changes the position of the pointer relative to mouse movement. The pointer can change shape when it is located within a particular zone of the display. In other applications that use a modal-tool paradigm, the user can explicitly select the desired pointer type.

Usually, the pointer only assumes the I-beam shape when it is positioned over editable text or within a zone that contains editable text. Some applications require explicit selection of text-editing mode because of a modal-tool paradigm. In these applications, the I-beam pointer usually remains in effect until the user selects some tool other than the text tool, or moves the pointer outside the data-editing area or over a control. The hot spot is usually located on the vertical stroke of the I-beam, about one-third or one-half the distance from the bottom to the top.

The text-editing pointer is used to determine the insertion point in editable text fields. The pointer is also used to select characters, words, lines, sentences, etc., within text blocks. In some applications, it is used to create and determine the location of new text fields.

The *NeXTSTEP User Interface Guidelines* does not distinguish between a pointer and cursor, and uses the term cursor to refer to both. Unlike some GUIs, NeXTSTEP hides the pointer when the user starts entering text, because ". . . it can get in the way when the user is concentrating on using the keyboard. A hidden cursor returns to the screen as soon as the user moves the mouse, signaling a shift in attention away from the keyboard back to the mouse" [NeXTSTEP, pp. 46–47].

## Conclusion

Because technology continually evolves, the user interface designer should exploit ways to enhance user feedback. For example, the application designer should consider the use of multimedia data types such as graphics, images, sound, speech, and video to supplement today's techniques of providing immediate and tangible feedback. Feedback incorporating these multimedia elements enriches and improves communication between the user and the application.

# Appendix A—Comparison of Windowing System Component Terminology

## Desktop and Desktop Managers

| Desktop | Macintosh | OSF/Motif | NeXTSTEP | Presentation Manager | Microsoft Windows |
|---|---|---|---|---|---|
| **Desktop** | Desktop | workspace (root window) | Workspace | Workplace | Desktop |
| **Desktop Manager** | Finder | window manager | Workspace Manager | Presentation Manager | Program Manager |

# Appendix A—Comparison of Windowing System Component Terminology

## Window Elements

| Element | Macintosh | OSF/Motif | NeXTSTEP | Presentation Manager | Microsoft Windows |
|---------|-----------|-----------|----------|---------------------|-------------------|
| Close Control | Close Box | window menu | Close Button | System Menu | Control Menu |
| Content Area | Content Area | Client Area | Content Area | Client Area | Content Area |
| Message Area | Status Bar | Message Area | — | Information Area | Message Bar |
| Menu Bar | Menu Bar | Menu Bar | (Main Menu) (Application Menu) | Menu Bar | Menu Bar |
| Status Bar | Status Bar | Status Bar | — | Status Bar | Status Bar |
| Scroll Bar | Scroll Bar | Scroll Bar | Scroller | Scroll Bar | Scroll Bar |
| Title Bar | Title Bar | Title Bar | Title Bar | Title Bar | Title Bar |
| Window Frame | Window Frame | Window Border | Window Border | Window Border | Window Frame |

# Appendix A—Comparison of Windowing System Component Terminology

## Controls

| Control | Macintosh | OSF/Motif | NeXTSTEP | Presentation Manager | Microsoft Windows |
|---|---|---|---|---|---|
| *Check Box* | Check Box | CheckButton | Button or Switch | Check Box | Check Box |
| *Close Control* | Close Box | window menu | Close Button | System Menu | Control Menu |
| *Combo Box* | [1] | — | — | Combo Box | Combo Box |
| *Command Button* | Button | PushButton | Button or Action Button | Pushbutton | Command Button |
| *Container* | — | — | — | Container | File Folder |
| *Drop-Down Combo Box* | [1] | — | — | Drop-Down Combo Box | Drop-Down Combo Box |
| *Drop-Down List Box* | Pop-up Menu[1] | OptionMenu | Pop-Up List or Pull-Down List | Drop-Down List Box | Drop-Down List Box |
| *List Box* | Scrolling List | List | Selection List or Multiple List | List Box | List Box |
| *Maximize Button* | (Zoom Box) | Maximize Button | — | Maximize Button | Maximize Button |
| *Minimize Button* | — | Minimize Button | Miniaturize Button | Minimize Button | Minimize Button |
| *Notebook* | — | — | — | Notebook | — |
| *Radio Button* | Button | RadioButton or ToggleButton | Action Button | PushButton | Radio Button |
| *Restore Button* | (Zoom Box) | Maximize Button | — | — | Restore Button |

[1]These controls are application-specific; they are not supported by the Macintosh Toolbox.

# Appendix A—Comparison of Windowing System Component Terminology

**Controls,** *Continued*

| Control | Macintosh | OSF/Motif | NeXTSTEP | Presentation Manager | Microsoft Windows |
|---|---|---|---|---|---|
| **Scroll Bar Control** | Scroll Bar | ScrollBar | Scroller | Scroll Bar | Scroll Bar |
| *Scroll Arrows* | Scroll Arrows | ArrowButtons | Scroll Buttons | Scroll Buttons | Scroll Arrows |
| *Scroll Bar Shaft* | Gray Area | — | Scroll Bar | Scroll Bar Shaft | Scroll Bar Shaft |
| *Scroll Box* | Scroll Box | Slider | Scroll Knob | Scroll Box | Scroll Box |
| **Size Control** | Size Box | Window Frame or Resize Borders | Resize Bar | Window Borders or Resize Borders | Window Frame or Resize Borders |
| **Slider** | Slider[1] | Scale | Slider | Slider | Slider |
| **Spin Box** | Arrow[1] | Arrow | — | Spin Button | Spin Box |
| **Split Box** | Split Bar[1] | — | — | Split Box | Split Box |
| *Split Bar* | Split Line | Separator and Sash | — | Split Bar | Split Bar |
| *Split Windows* | Window Panes | PanedWindows | — | Window Panes | Window Panes |
| **Text Box** | Text Entry Field | Text | Text Field | Entry Field | Text Box |
| **Value Set** | Value Set[1] | | | Value Set | Value Set |

[1]These controls are application-specific; they are not supported by the Macintosh Toolbox.

# Appendix A—Comparison of Windowing System Component Terminology

## Types of Windows

| Window Type | Macintosh | OSF/Motif | NeXTSTEP | Presentation Manager | Microsoft Windows |
|---|---|---|---|---|---|
| **Application** | (Virtual Window) | Primary Window or main application | (Virtual Window) | Primary Window | Application Window |
| **Document** | Document | Secondary Window Dialog Box | Standard Window or Main Window | Secondary Window | Document Window |
| **Others** | Dialog Box Alert Box | Menu Window | Panel Menu | Dialog Box | Dialog Box |

## Types of Menus

| Menu Type | Macintosh | OSF/Motif | NeXTSTEP | Presentation Manager | Microsoft Windows |
|---|---|---|---|---|---|
| **Pull-Down** | Pull-Down | Pulldown | — | Pull-Down or Action Bar Pull Down | Drop-Down |
| **Cascading** | Hierarchical or Submenu | Pulldown | Submenu | Cascaded or Cascading Pull-Down | Cascading or Submenu |
| **Pop-Up Menu** | Pop-Up | Pop-Up | — | Pop-Up | Pop-Up |
| **Tear-Off Menu** | Tear-Off | Tear-Off | Submenu | — | — |
| **Others** | Scrolling | Option | — | — | — |

# Appendix A—Comparison of Windowing System Component Terminology

**Standard Application Menus**

| Macintosh | OSF/Motif | NeXTSTEP | Presentation Manager | Microsoft Windows |
|---|---|---|---|---|
| Apple Menu Icon | window menu Icon | — | System Menu Icon | Control Menu Icon |
| File | File | Document | File (Application Windows) <object name> (Object Windows) | File |
| Edit | Edit | Edit | Edit | Edit |
|  | View | — | View | View |
| Application-specific | Application-specific | — | Application-specific (e.g., Option, Windows) | Application-specific |
| Help Icon | Help | Info | Help | Help |
| Keyboard Icon | — | — | — | — |
| Application Icon | — | — | — | — |

# Appendix A—Comparison of Windowing System Component Terminology

## Dialog Box Behavior

| Dialog Box Behavior | Macintosh | OSF/Motif | NeXTSTEP | Presentation Manager | Microsoft Windows |
|---|---|---|---|---|---|
| *Modal* | Modal<br>Movable Modal | Primary Modal<br>Application Modal<br>System Modal | Modal Panel | Modal | Application Modal<br>System Modal<br>Application Semimodal |
| *Modeless* | Modeless | Modeless | Nonmodal Panel | — | Application Modeless |
| *Others* | Alert Box | | Attention Panel | Unfolding Dialog | Unfolding Dialog |

## Types of Message Dialog Boxes

| Message Dialog Box | Macintosh | OSF/Motif | NeXTSTEP | Presentation Manager | Microsoft Windows |
|---|---|---|---|---|---|
| *Information* | Note | InformationDialog | N/A | Information | Information |
| *Warning* | Caution | WarningDialog | N/A | Warning | Warning |
| *Critical* | Stop | ErrorDialog | N/A | Action | Critical |
| *Others* | — | QuestionDialog<br>WorkingDialog | — | — | — |

# Appendix A—Comparison of Windowing System Component Terminology

## Mouse Operations

| Macintosh | OSF/Motif | NeXTSTEP | Presentation Manager | Microsoft Windows |
|---|---|---|---|---|
| Pointing | Pointing | Pointing | Pointing | Pointing |
| Clicking<br>Double-clicking<br>Multiple-clicking | Click<br>Multiclick | Clicking<br>Multiple-clicking<br>(Double-clicking,<br>triple-clicking) | Clicking<br>Double-Clicking | Clicking<br>Double-Clicking |
| Pressing | Press<br>MultiPress | Pressing | Pressing | Pressing |
| Dragging | Motion<br>MultiMotion | Dragging | Dragging | Dragging |
| Release | Release | — | Release | — |

## Types of Selection

| Macintosh | OSF/Motif | NeXTSTEP | Presentation Manager | Microsoft Windows |
|---|---|---|---|---|
| Selection by clicking<br>(single selection)<br>Selection by dragging<br>(anchor point to active end)<br>Selection with Shift-click<br>(Extended) | Single Selection<br>Browse Selection<br>Multiple Selection<br>Range Selection<br>Discontiguous Selection<br>Type Selection | Dragging to select<br>Clicking to select<br>Multiple-clicking to select<br>Selection Range anchor to<br>Endpoint | Single Selection<br>Multiple Selection<br>Extended Selection | Single Selection<br>Disjoint Multiple Selection<br>Contiguous Multiple Selection<br>Heterogeneous<br>Homogeneous |

# Appendix A—Comparison of Windowing System Component Terminology

## Pointers

| Types of Pointers | Macintosh | OSF/Motif | NeXTSTEP | Presentation Manager | Microsoft Windows |
|---|---|---|---|---|---|
| **General Purpose** *(pointing, selecting, moving, resizing)* | Arrow (Upper-left) | Upper-left pointing Arrow | Arrow (Upper-left) | Arrow Pointer Pencil Pointer | Upper-left Pointing Arrow |
| **Text Selection and Insertion** | Vertical bar (pipe) I-Beam | I-Beam Vertical bar (pipe) Caret | I-Bar | I-Beam | I-Beam Vertical bar or Pipe Upper-right Pointing Arrow |
| **Graphics Selection** *(pointing, sighting, drawing)* | Crosshair | Sighting Pointer | Crosshair Pencil | Crosshair | Crosshair Downward-pointing Arrow |
| **Field (Array) Selection** *(selecting, moving, inserting, resizing)* | Plus Sign | Plus Sign | Arrow (upper-left) | | Plus Sign Downward-pointing arrow Column-width Pointer Row-height Pointer |
| **Window Resize** | Arrow (Upper-left) | Resizing Pointer (8-Directional Arrow) | — | Double-headed Diagonal Pointer | Double-headed Diagonal Pointer |
| **Operation in Progress** | Wristwatch | Hourglass Watch Pointer | Spinning Disk | Wall Clock Alarm Clock | Hourglass |
| **Move in Progress** | Arrow (Upper-left) | 4-Directional Arrow Digital readout | Arrow (Upper-left) | Arrow Pointer | Upper-left Pointing Arrow 4-Directional Arrow |
| **HELP** | Pointing finger | Question Arrow Pointer | — | Pencil | Question Arrow Pointer Pointing Finger |
| **Outside application area Not-drop target** | | X Pointer Caution Pointer | | Do-not Pointer | Do-not Pointer |
| **Others** | | | Link Two-pages | | |

# Appendix B—Comparison of Windowing System Components—Graphical Representations

## Desktop Environments

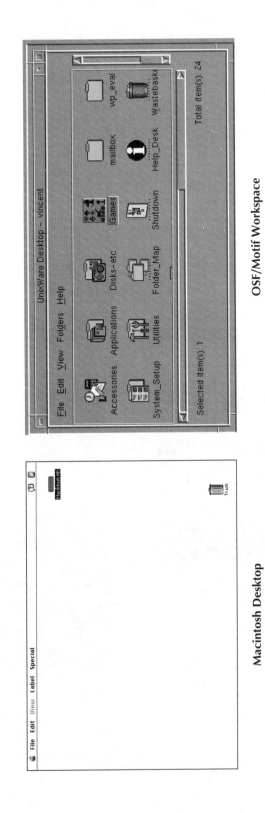

Macintosh Desktop

OSF/Motif Workspace

# Appendix B—Comparison of Windowing System Components—Graphical Representations

**Desktop Environments, Continued**

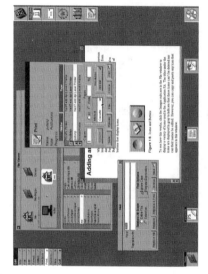

**NeXTSTEP Workspace**

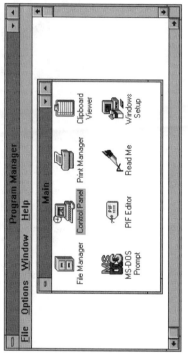

**Microsoft Windows Desktop**

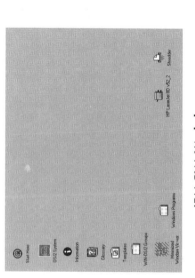

**IBM CUA Workplace**

# Appendix B—Comparison of Windowing System Components—Graphical Representations

## Window Elements

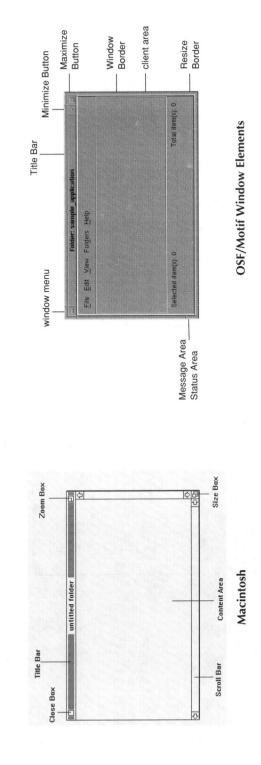

**Macintosh**

- Zoom Box
- Size Box
- Title Bar
- Close Box
- Content Area
- Scroll Bar
- untitled folder

**OSF/Motif Window Elements**

- Minimize Button
- Maximize Button
- Window Border
- client area
- Resize Border
- Title Bar
- window menu
- Message Area
- Status Area

Folder: sample application

File  Edit  View  Folders  Help

Selected Item(s): 0        Total Item(s): 0

# Appendix B—Comparison of Windowing System Components—Graphical Representations

## Window Elements, *Continued*

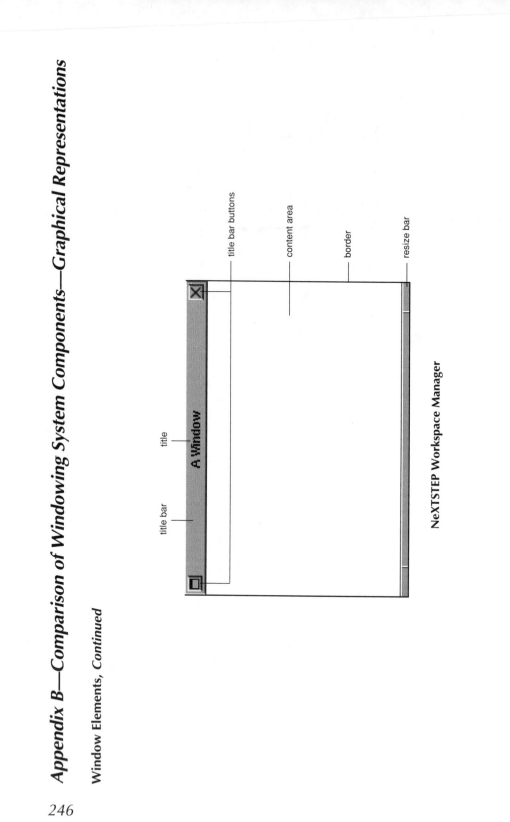

NeXTSTEP Workspace Manager

title bar

title

A Window

title bar buttons

content area

border

resize bar

# Appendix B—Comparison of Windowing System Components—Graphical Representations

## Window Elements, Continued

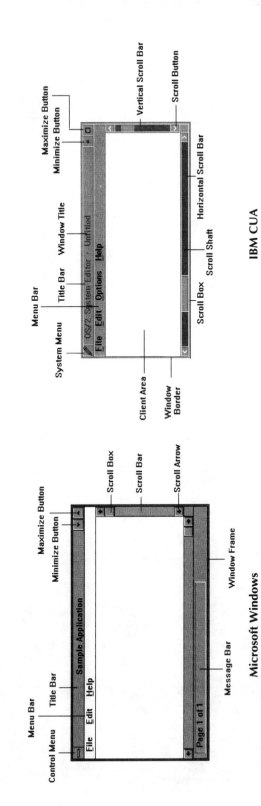

**IBM CUA**

Labels (IBM CUA diagram): Menu Bar, Title Bar, Window Title, Maximize Button, Minimize Button, System Menu, Client Area, Window Border, Scroll Box, Scroll Shaft, Horizontal Scroll Bar, Vertical Scroll Bar, Scroll Button

OS/2 System Editor - Untitled
File  Edit  Options  Help

**Microsoft Windows**

Labels (Microsoft Windows diagram): Menu Bar, Title Bar, Maximize Button, Minimize Button, Control Menu, Scroll Box, Scroll Bar, Scroll Arrow, Window Frame, Message Bar

Sample Application
File  Edit  Help
Page 1 of 1

# Appendix B—Comparison of Windowing System Components—Graphical Representations

Types of Message Dialog Box Icons

| Message Dialog Box | Macintosh | OSF/Motif | NeXTSTEP | Presentation Manager | Microsoft Windows |
|---|---|---|---|---|---|
| Information | | | — | | |
| Warning | | | — | | |
| Critical | | | — | | |
| Others | — | | — | | — |

# Appendix B—Comparison of Windowing System Components—Graphical Representations

**Pointers**

| Types of Pointers | Macintosh | OSF/Motif | NeXTSTEP | Presentation Manager | Microsoft Windows |
|---|---|---|---|---|---|
| *General Purpose (pointing, selecting, moving, resizing)* | | | | | |
| *Text Selection and Insertion* | | | | | |
| *Graphics Selection (pointing, sighting, drawing)* | | | | | |
| *Field (Array) Selection (selecting, moving, inserting, resizing)* | | | | | |
| *Window Resize* | | | | | |

(continued)

# Appendix B—Comparison of Windowing System Components—Graphical Representations

*Pointers, Continued*

| Types of Pointers | Macintosh | OSF/Motif | NeXTSTEP | Presentation Manager | Microsoft Windows |
|---|---|---|---|---|---|
| *Operation in Progress* | | | | | |
| *Move in Progress* | | | | | |
| *Help* | | | | — | |
| *Outside Application Area Not-drop Target* | — | | — | | |
| *Others* | — | — | | — | — |

# Appendix B—Comparison of Windowing System Components—Graphical Representations

## Controls

| Control | Macintosh | OSF/Motif | NeXTSTEP | Presentation Manager | Microsoft Windows |
|---|---|---|---|---|---|
| *Check Box* | Style: ☒ Bold, ☒ Italic, ☐ Outline, ☐ Shadow, ☐ Strikethru, ☐ Small Caps, ☐ All Caps, ☐ Hidden | Password required: ☐, Screensaver Enabled: ☐, Notify before locking: ☐ | Animation: ○ None, ◉ Slow, ○ Medium, ○ Fast | Popular options: ☑ Air conditioning, ☐ Automatic power brakes, ☐ Automatic power antenna, ☑ Cruise control | Printing Options: ☐ Draft Output, ☐ Reverse Print Order, ☐ Update Fields, ☐ Update Links, ☒ Background Printing |
| *Close Box* | | | | | |
| *Command Button* | Yes / No / Cancel | Reset / Cancel / Help | Save changes to MyApp? Cancel / Don't Save / Save (Close) | Open / Cancel / Help | OK / Cancel / Help |

*(continued)*

NOTE: These controls are not supported by the Macintosh Toolbox. Hence, their appearance and behavior are application-specific.

# *Appendix B—Comparison of Windowing System Components—Graphical Representations*

Controls, *Continued*

| Control | Macintosh | OSF/Motif | NeXTSTEP | Presentation Manager | Microsoft Windows |
|---------|-----------|-----------|----------|---------------------|-------------------|
| *Combo Box* | (See Note) | — | — | | |
| *Container* | — | — | — | | |
| *Drop-Down Combo Box* |  (See Note) | — | — | | |

NOTE: These controls are not supported by the Macintosh Toolbox. Hence, their appearance and behavior are application-specific.

252

*(continued)*

# Appendix B—Comparison of Windowing System Components—Graphical Representations

**Controls, Continued**

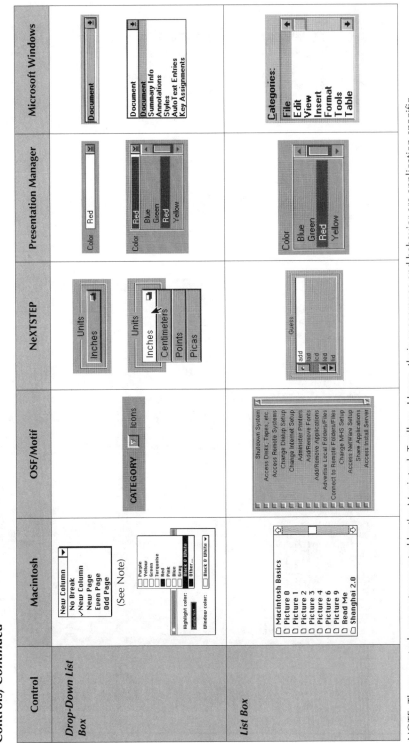

| Control | Macintosh | OSF/Motif | NeXTSTEP | Presentation Manager | Microsoft Windows |
|---|---|---|---|---|---|
| *Drop-Down List Box* | | | | | |
| *List Box* | | | | | |

NOTE: These controls are not supported by the Macintosh Toolbox. Hence, their appearance and behavior are application-specific.

*(continued)*

# Appendix B—Comparison of Windowing System Components—Graphical Representations

## Controls, Continued

| Control | Macintosh | OSF/Motif | NeXTSTEP | Presentation Manager | Microsoft Windows |
|---------|-----------|-----------|----------|----------------------|-------------------|
| Maximize Control | | | — | | |
| Minimize Control | — | | | | |
| Notebook | — | — | — | | — |

NOTE: These controls are not supported by the Macintosh Toolbox. Hence, their appearance and behavior are application-specific.

*(continued)*

254

# Appendix B—Comparison of Windowing System Components—Graphical Representations

**Controls,** *Continued*

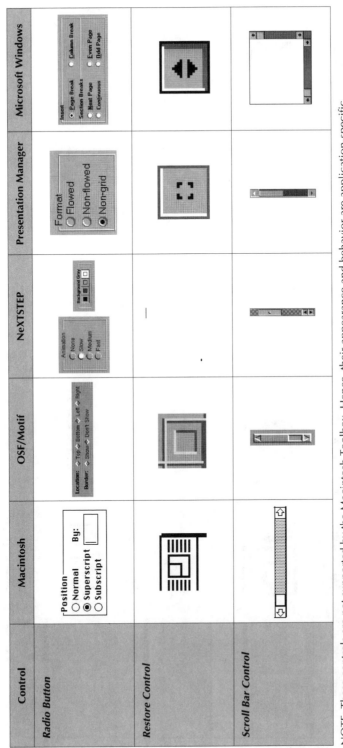

| Control | Macintosh | OSF/Motif | NeXTSTEP | Presentation Manager | Microsoft Windows |
|---|---|---|---|---|---|
| *Radio Button* | | | | | |
| *Restore Control* | | | | | |
| *Scroll Bar Control* | | | | | |

NOTE: These controls are not supported by the Macintosh Toolbox. Hence, their appearance and behavior are application-specific.

*(continued)*

# Appendix B—Comparison of Windowing System Components—Graphical Representations

## Controls, Continued

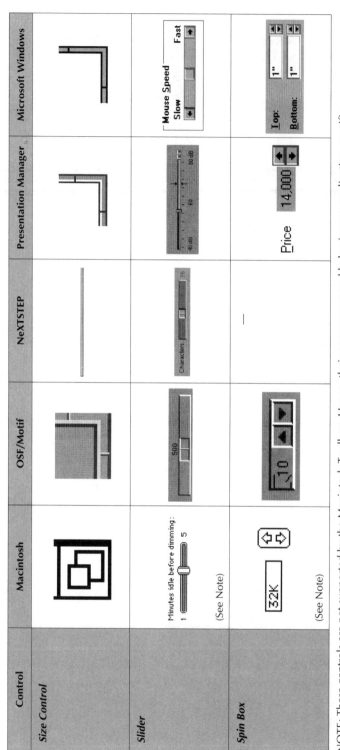

| Control | Macintosh | OSF/Motif | NeXTSTEP | Presentation Manager | Microsoft Windows |
|---------|-----------|-----------|----------|---------------------|-------------------|
| **Size Control** | | | | | |
| **Slider** | Minutes idle before dimming: 1 — 5<br><br>(See Note) | 500 | Characters 75 | 40 dB 60 80 dB | Mouse Speed<br>Slow — Fast |
| **Spin Box** | 32K<br><br>(See Note) | 10 | | Price 14,000 | Top: 1"<br>Bottom: 1" |

NOTE: These controls are not supported by the Macintosh Toolbox. Hence, their appearance and behavior are application-specific.

*(continued)*

# Appendix B—Comparison of Windowing System Components—Graphical Representations

## Controls, *Continued*

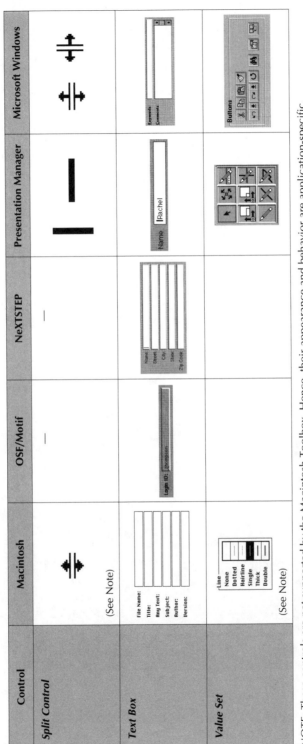

| Control | Macintosh | OSF/Motif | NeXTSTEP | Presentation Manager | Microsoft Windows |
|---------|-----------|-----------|----------|----------------------|-------------------|
| *Split Control* | | | | | |
| *Text Box* | (See Note) | | | | |
| *Value Set* | (See Note) | | | | |

NOTE: These controls are not supported by the Macintosh Toolbox. Hence, their appearance and behavior are application-specific.

257

# Selected Bibliography

Apple Computer, Inc. *Bento Specification*. Revision 1.0d5 by Jed Harris and Ira Reuben. August 1993.

Apple Computer, Inc. *Inside Macintosh: Macintosh Toolbox Essentials.* Reading, MA: Addison-Wesley Publishing Co., 1992.

Apple Computer, Inc. *Macintosh Human Interface Guidelines*. Reading, MA: Addison-Wesley Publishing Co., 1992. [MHIG]

Aziz, Atif. "Simplify and Enhance Your Application's User Interface with Dynamic Dialog Box." *Microsoft Systems Journal*. San Mateo, CA. Miller Freeman, Inc., March, 1994: 39–68.

Bly, S. A., and J. K. Rosenberg. "A Comparison of Tiled and Overlapping Windows." *Proceedings of CHI Conference on Human Factors in Computing Systems,* New York: ACM (1986): 101–106.

Brown, J. R., and S. Cunningham. *Programming the User Interface.* New York: John Wiley & Sons, 1989.

Capucciati, M. "Putting Your Best Face Forward: Effective User Interface." *Microsoft Systems Journal*. San Mateo, CA: Miller Freeman, Inc. (February 1993): 55–63.

Garfinkel, Simson L., and Michael K. Mahoney. *NeXTSTEP Programming. Step One: Object-Oriented Applications.* New York: The Electronic Library of Science (TELOS), 1993.

Hardman, L., Dick C.A. Butlerman, and Guido van Rossum. "The Amsterdam Hypermedia Model: Adding Time and Context to the Dexter Model." *Communications of the ACM* (February 1994): 50–62.

Hearst, M. *Microsoft Windows 3.0 by Example*. Redwood City, CA: M&T Books, 1990.

Hix, Deborah, and Rex Hartson. *Developing User Interfaces. Ensuring Usability Through Product and Process.* New York: John Wiley & Sons, 1993.

Horton, W. *The Icon Book: Visual Symbols for Computer Systems and Documentation.* New York: John Wiley & Sons, 1994.

IBM Corporation. *Common User Access: Advanced Interface Design Guide.* Boca Raton, FL: IBM, 1989.

IBM Corporation. *Common User Access: Advanced Interface Design Reference.* Cary, NC: IBM, 1991.

IBM Corporation. *Common User Access: Guide to User Interface Design.* Cary, NC: IBM, 1991.

Jacobson, I. *Object-Oriented Software Engineering: A Use Case Driven Approach.* Reading, MA: Addison-Wesley Publishing Co., 1992.

Jennings, R. *Discover Windows 3.1 Multimedia.* Carmel, IN: Que Corporation, 1992.

Khoshafian, S., and R. Abnous. *Object Orientation Concepts, Languages, Databases, User Interfaces.* New York: John Wiley & Sons, 1990.

Kobara, S. *Visual Design with OSF/Motif.* Hewlett Packard Company, 1991.

Koved, L., and Shneiderman, B. "Embedded Menus: Menu Selection in Context." *Communications of the ACM* 29 (1986): 312–318.

Marcus, A. *Graphic Design for Electronic Documents and User Interfaces.* Reading, MA: Addison-Wesley Publishing Co., 1992.

Microsoft Corporation. *The Windows Interface: An Application Design Guide.* Redmond, WA: Microsoft Press, 1992. [MICROSOFT]

Microsoft Corporation. *Microsoft Windows Multimedia: Authoring and Tools Guide.* Redmond, WA: Microsoft Press, 1991.

Microsoft Corporation. *Microsoft Windows Multimedia: Programmer's Workbook.* Redmond, WA: Microsoft Press, 1991.

Morse, A., and George Reynolds. "Overcoming Current Growth Limits in UI Development." *Communications of the ACM* (April 1993): 73–81.

NeXT Computer. Inc. *NeXTSTEP User Interface Guidelines.* Reading, MA: Addison-Wesley Publishing Co., 1992. [NeXTSTEP]

NeXT Computer. Inc. *NeXTSTEP Object-Oriented Software: User's Guide.* Redwood City, CA: NeXT Computer. Inc., 1992–1993.

Nielsen, J. "NonCommand User Interfaces." *Communications of the ACM* (April 1993): 83–99.

Norman, Kent. *The Psychology of Menu Selection: Designing Cognitive Control at the Human/Computer Interface.* Norwood, NJ: Ablex, 1991.

Open Systems Foundation. *OSF/Motif Style Guide:* Englewood Cliffs, NJ: P T R Prentice Hall, 1993. [OSF/Motif]

Peddie, J. *Graphical User Interfaces and Graphic Standards.* McGraw-Hill, Inc., 1992.

Poole, L. *MACWORLD Guide To System 7.1.* San Mateo, CA: IDG Books, 1993.

Shneiderman, B. *Designing the User Interface.* Reading, MA: Addison-Wesley Publishing Co., 1992.

Webster, B. *The NeXT Book.* Reading, MA: Addison-Wesley Publishing Co., 1989.

X/Open Company Limited. *Common Desktop Environment: Functional Specification.* Berkshire, UK: X/Open Company Limited, 1993.

# Index

# About the Authors

## Aaron Marcus

Aaron Marcus is the president of Aaron Marcus and Associates, a graphic design and consulting firm in Emeryville, California. Aaron Marcus received a BA in Physics from Princeton University (1965) and a BFA and MFA in Graphic Design from Yale University Art School (1966). He is an internationally recognized authority on the design of user interfaces, interactive multimedia, and printing/publishing documents, including charts, forms, icons, and screens. Aaron has given tutorials at SIGGRAPH, NCGA, and SIGCHI conferences in addition to seminars at businesses and academic institutions around the world. He co-authored *Human Factors and Typography for More Readable Programs* (1990) and *Graphic Design for Electronic Documents and User Interfaces* (1992), both published by Addison-Wesley.

Mr. Marcus has worked on and written about user interface design for 25 years. Mr. Marcus' current research interests include metaphors, semiotics, and visible languages for user interfaces, multimedia documents, and knowledge visualization.

## Nick Smilonich

Nick Smilonich is a chief Application Services Architect and technologist at Unisys Corporation. He is responsible for service definitions, new technology assessment, and standardized product architectures. He has held numerous engineering, management, and technical positions and has been involved with strategic areas such as user interfaces, desktop environments, 4GL/CASE, object, and multimedia. Mr. Smilonich has been a leading driver of GUI integration into product programs and has built associated cross-platform GUI human-computer design and implementation guidelines. Mr. Smilonich has authored papers and presented at technical forums such as FedUnix/Motif Developers conference. Mr. Smilonich's current research interests include multimedia data types as graphical presentation objects.

## Lynne Thompson

Lynne Thompson is a senior technical staff engineer at Unisys Corporation. She has designed and developed various user interface products. She has been involved in various strategic development areas such as 4GL/CASE, computer architecture, multimedia, object, programming languages, and user interfaces. Ms. Thompson specializes in graphical user interface design principles and guidelines, interaction paradigms, and implementation techniques across open platforms. Ms. Thompson has authored numerous technical articles on mathematical algorithms, comparison of industry user interfaces, object-oriented user interfaces, and object-oriented building blocks. She has presented her works at industry user interface conferences such as FedUnix/Motif Developers' Seminar. Ms. Thompson's current research interests include user interface icon design, and effective design and presentation of time-dependent multimedia information.